John Steinbeck's
The Grapes of Wrath

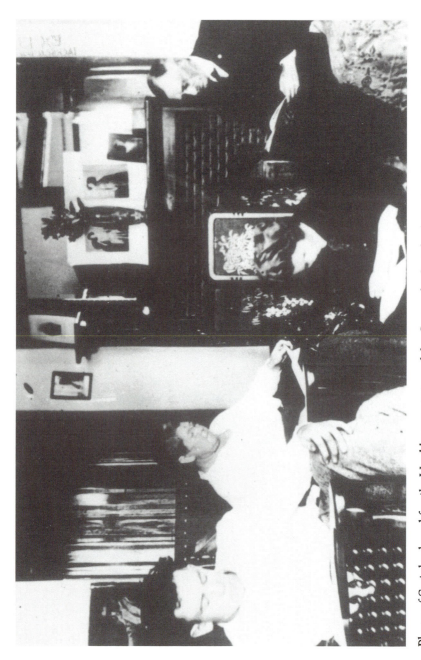

Photo of Steinbeck and family. Used by permission of the Center for Steinbeck Studies, San Jose State University.

John Steinbeck's
The Grapes of Wrath

A Reference Guide

BARBARA A. HEAVILIN

Greenwood Guides to Fiction

GREENWOOD PRESS
Westport, Connecticut • London

Library of Congress Cataloging-in-Publication Data

Heavilin, Barbara A., 1945–
   John Steinbeck's The grapes of wrath : a reference guide / Barbara A. Heavilin.
      p.   cm.—(Greenwood guides to fiction, ISSN 1535–8577)
   Includes bibliographical references and index.
   ISBN 0–313–31837–9 (alk. paper)
   1. Steinbeck, John, 1902–1968. Grapes of wrath.   2. Migrant agricultural laborers in
literature.   3. Rural families in literature.   4. California—In literature.   5. Labor camps in
literature.   6. Depressions in literature.   I. Title.   II. Series.
PS3537.T3234G853   2002
813′.52—dc21   2002016079

British Library Cataloguing in Publication Data is available.

Library of Congress Catalog Card Number: 2002016079
ISBN: 0–313–31837–9

First published in 2002

Greenwood Press, 88 Post Road West, Westport, CT 06881
An imprint of Greenwood Publishing Group, Inc.
www.greenwood.com

Printed in the United States of America

The paper used in this book complies with the
Permanent Paper Standard issued by the National
Information Standards Organization (Z39.48–1984).

10 9 8 7 6 5 4 3 2 1

Contents

Preface

Stephen K. George

Much has been written on John Steinbeck's epic novel, *The Grapes of Wrath*, since its appearance in 1939 near the end of the Great Depression. In particular, several comprehensive studies addressing such elements as explication, plot, context, and criticism have been published, including Warren French's 1963 *A Companion to "The Grapes of Wrath,"* Agnes McNeill Donohue's 1968 *A Casebook on "The Grapes of Wrath,"* and Louis Owens's 1989 *"The Grapes of Wrath": Trouble in the Promised Land.* Of all of Steinbeck's novels, *The Grapes of Wrath* remains, even at the start of a new millennium, his most esteemed and critically appraised work.

Yet Barbara Heavilin's *John Steinbeck's* The Grapes of Wrath: *A Reference Guide* fills a need that these other studies lack. Keeping in the foreground its intended purpose as a reference book for struggling undergraduate readers, *A Reference Guide* provides an updated examination of the novel's textual features (plot, structure, theme, characters) as well as its complex historical, cultural, and critical background. Moreover, by exploring the connections among the novel, the social context, the reader, and the author's professed intentions upon said reader, Heavilin's work opens new vistas of appreciation and reveals how, despite some critics' misreadings, *The Grapes of Wrath* moves beyond mere propaganda to become a work of lasting artistic merit. In short, *A Reference Guide* provides a sustained rebuttal to critics (such as Harold Bloom) who make sweeping literary pronouncements without performing the harder task of scholarly activity and analysis. Heavilin's *A Reference Guide* takes just the opposite tack—by placing the novel against the backdrop of the novelist's life, reading, intentions, and influences, as well as the book's broader literary context, we, the readers, are convinced as to why *The Grapes of Wrath* remains near the pinnacle of twentieth-century American literature.

However, as Heavilin also makes clear, the novel (for all its seeming simplicity) is not easily understood on its deepest levels and makes participatory demands of its readers that have served to alienate some critics. For these reasons, *A Reference Guide* provides a spectrum of perspectives by which the ordinary undergraduate may better understand Steinbeck's multilayered artistry. It begins with an introductory chapter that places the author against the backdrop of his early family life, reading, and personal experiences that bears on his writing of *The Grapes of Wrath*. Of particular interest is Heavilin's discussion of Steinbeck's letters and journals, which serve to fit *Grapes* within its broader context of world literature, including such works as the Bible, *Don Quixote*, and *Tom Jones*.

Chapter 2 explores the content of the novel with a chapter by chapter plot summary and an overview of the interchapters that reveals how the author established a dialogic relationship between the particular Joad narrative and the broader story of the dust bowl migration. Chapter 3, "Texts," examines the novel's genesis, including its beginnings in Steinbeck's early journalist efforts at reporting the migrant conditions in California and in his scathing warm-up draft of the novel, "L'Affaire Lettuceberg," which he wisely destroyed. Chapter 4, "Contexts," then moves from the novel itself to examine the immediate cultural, social, and historical conditions surrounding the work, including the dust bowl, the Okie migration, and the Great Depression. It is also in this chapter that Heavilin explains how *The Grapes of Wrath* taps into the more universal story of a dispossessed people searching for a promised land, a story that transcends any particular social era and finds resonance within all cultures.

From this exploration of contexts comes a close look at the novel's major themes in chapter 5, "Ideas." Steinbeck himself said the book could be read on at least five levels; the richness of such readings is evident as this section explores the major ideas of the book, including several paired sets of opposites: good versus evil, hospitality versus apathy, a faltering patriarchy against an emerging matriarchy, the desecration of both land and people versus seeing all things as part of a greater whole—Jim Casey's "one big soul." The next chapter, "Narrative Art," offers a revealing analysis of Steinbeck's literary craftsmanship, beginning with the juxtaposition of the author's careful intercalary organization (general, wide-lens, philosophical chapters alternated with close-ups of the Joads) with the chaos of the characters' lives within the novel. Further, it also closely examines the imagery, language, and stylistic devices of the novel, all of which reveal Steinbeck's deliberate desire to pull readers inside the text and never let them go—a design on readers made explicit in a letter to his editor, Pascal Covici. *A Reference Guide* concludes with a chapter surveying the critical reception of the novel over a period of some sixty years as well as a comparative bibliographical essay assessing critics on opposing sides of the issue of the aesthetic merit of *The Grapes of Wrath*. What is fascinating here is both the evolution and the stasis of these critics' views. As Heavilin notes, early critics who castigated both novel and author largely wrote from a purely subjective or "gut" response—Steinbeck's novel is sentimental, propaganda, dishonest, manipulative, poorly crafted, and the like—without providing a close reading (in the era of new criticism) to support their judgments. Regrettably, the same critical myopia occurs today, even in such recent offerings as Bloom's two critical anthologies. Yet Heavilin also makes clear that critical evolution, which has moved *The Grapes of Wrath* to the upper echelon of American literature and art, with an extended assessment of some of the finest efforts in Steinbeck scholarship. As this concluding chapter shows, a book that was once condescendingly labeled a "thirties" or "Depression Era" novel still provokes a variety of fresh critical approaches, including cultural, sociological, feminist, and postmodern perspectives.

All in all, *John Steinbeck's* The Grapes of Wrath: *A Reference Guide* leaves the typical Steinbeck reader with a richer understanding both of the novel's literary merit and of the creative and contextual means by which it was produced. This guide enables readers to appreciate how the various components of *The Grapes of Wrath*—characters, writing styles, symbols, structure, narrative voice—all fit together to pull them in and make them fellow travelers with the Joads on U.S. Route 66. Furthermore, this guide also explains, perhaps better than any other study of the novel, how John Steinbeck purposefully intended to do this by engaging his readers on all levels of their being: emotional, intellectual, ethical, spiritual. Critics and readers who approach this novel will only receive what they are able to bring to it. But Barbara Heavilin's *A Reference Guide* does enlighten us as to the banquet that awaits if we take Steinbeck's hand and come along for the ride.

Introduction

STEINBECK'S RELATIONSHIP TO HIS READER AND CRITIC

In a family photograph taken about 1918 when John Steinbeck was sixteen years old, John, his mother, a sister, and his father are sitting in their living room, each engrossed in reading a book. On the fireplace mantel in the right-hand side of the photograph are family pictures, a vase of flowers, and a candlestick. The corner of a lace-covered table may be seen on the right, and John, in a wooden chair with six turned spindles on the sides, is on the left. To the left of center, his mother sits in what appears to be a leather chair with brass upholstery tacks around the sides and back. To the right of center, lower than the rest, his sister is sitting on a stool or hassock. Dressed in his business suit, the father sits to the right by the mantel. The family does not appear to be posing, and it is speculated that Steinbeck's father may have used a time-release camera to take this photograph that captures a shared moment in time and endorses a family's values.

This photograph contrasts sharply with the usual family photograph today in which people smile cheesily for the camera, gathering close to one another. Or a photograph, more in line with what many families might be doing together today, would show members sitting together in a family room, eyes fixed on a common object, the television set. This family photograph of the Steinbecks, then, gives us a glimpse of another time when family pursuits required little more than energy for the light, some intellectual curiosity, an interest in the world of books, and the luxury of a quiet evening at home for reading.

This photograph makes a very important statement about Steinbeck as a person, as a reader, and as a writer. For family and books were to be mainstays throughout his life—with the word "family" expanded first to include neighbors and then to all humankind. Ma Joad, for example, moves to count those who are needy as family members who must be cared for responsibly. Written for his two sons, *East of Eden* memorializes his forebears and maintains at the same time a sense of a broadened family of humanity. A sense of family and love for those whom the Scriptures call "the least of these" prevails in Steinbeck's writing but never more prominently than in *The Grapes of Wrath*,[1] where the misfortunes of the Joads run parallel with but in the opposite direction of their awareness of the family of humankind. When they themselves are most destitute, they are conversely most keenly aware of the needs around them. As Ma Joad maintains, "There was a time when family was first. Now it's everybody."

The concept of family, then, has a major impact on Steinbeck as a writer, but so also does his lifelong devotion to reading. Although he often provides a hauntingly strong sense of place in his writings, Steinbeck is also very much aware of the inner spaces and places to which reading—like music or a well-wrought painting—takes people. For reading creates an inner reality in which the reader meets characters, visits places, and takes part in the story. Himself an actively involved, intensely focused reader, at the age of nine, Steinbeck was so taken with Sir Thomas Malory's *Morte d'Arthur* that he declared this book his own to use as a guide, pattern, and inspiration as others had used the Bible or *Pilgrim's Progress*. As a writer he wanted above all to create for his readers an experience as vital and real as the authors whom he admired had created for him. Therefore, he has designs on his readers, addressing them directly on occasion either in the text itself, or, as in *The Winter of Our Discontent*, in an opening epigraph: "Readers seeking to identify the fictional people and places here described would do better to inspect their own communities and search their own hearts, for this book is about a large part of America today." Here he describes a relationship between himself and readers, speaking as one with the moral authority to prescribe a course of action, advising them to take on the responsibility of inspecting their own communities and searching their own hearts. This admonition is Steinbeck's version of the Gospel that he is compelled to preach, and it is difficult to read his works without being troubled about the world and one's place in it. Like Viktor E. Frankl, Steinbeck strongly suggests that Americans need a Statue of Responsibility on the

West Coast to balance the Statue of Liberty on the East.[2] Taking on this cloak of moral authority, Steinbeck's role is rather like that of William Blake's all-seeing, all-knowing "Bard" in *Songs of Experience* whose voice the reader is admonished to "hear." Steinbeck's bardic persona, readers, and text thus intertwine, with the result that readers risk a heightened awareness that may call for change.

In *Grapes* particularly this change calls for greater compassion, and nowhere is this compassion more sharply and starkly drawn than in the novel's final tableau in which Rose of Sharon—her baby dead, placed in an apple box by Uncle John, and sent downstream as a mute testimony to the tragic story of dispossession—nurses a starving old man in a deserted barn (*Grapes* 446–53). But this scene has given readers pause from the very beginning. Even Steinbeck's editor, Pascal Covici, objected to it as being too sudden. In a letter written to Covici on January 16, 1939, published in Elaine Steinbeck and Robert Wallsten's 1989 *Steinbeck: A Life in Letters*, Steinbeck defends its artistic merit, stating that this ending has been in the design of the novel from the beginning and that everything in the Joad story leads inevitably to their destitution and this noble and compassionate response to another's need. He had no intention of satisfying his readers with a romantic ending; he had every intention of affecting them profoundly and leaving this human problem squarely in their hands. If readers do not comprehend the story, he implied, it is because they are too narrow-minded, small-hearted, and shallow. Steinbeck maintained, too, that those who do comprehend the story will see beneath its surface to discover layer upon layer of meaning. Stating that there are five of these layers, he insists that the depth of readers themselves will determine the depth of their comprehension. By implication, this letter thus delineates and prescribes the relationships among writer, reader, critic, text, and their literary and social contexts.

In this letter Steinbeck portrays the writer not only as the creator of a fictional world but also as a person of integrity who must be true to his vision so that this world reflects the reality of human exploitation, suffering, and transcendence that he has witnessed firsthand. As in the Greek drama *Oedipus Rex* in which Oedipus finds self-knowledge at the point of his downfall, so Steinbeck's *Grapes* reflects the "sweetness" to be found in adversity—to coin a Shakespearean phrase. He assures Covici, then, that the final tableau is not sudden, that the starving stranger and his son cannot be integrated into the story, and that the Joads' meeting with them must be accidental. Because such kindness and consideration for strangers has been a central, interwoven theme of this novel, it is here essential to its meaning (*SLL* 178–79).

Like Aristotle, Steinbeck demonstrates a belief that poetry and fiction reflect the human condition more truly than history because they portray values that people hold in common whereas history primarily presents facts. Therefore, he must be true to his artistic vision, holding the mirror for readers to see themselves and their society as they actually are, with all of their faults, in the hope that they will become more compassionate. Steinbeck's relationship to his readers, then, is that of a bard, a humane and moral figure of authority, guiding their responses to assure their participation in the experience of the migrants. He wants them to know what it is like to be dispossessed—a stranger in your own homeland, seeking in vain for respite from hunger, sickness, and homelessness in a land of plenty.

In a sense, therefore, Steinbeck is himself a participant in *Grapes*, held by the evocative power of his own story. Compelled to tell it, in turn he compels readers to hear and understand with their hearts as well as with their minds. Perhaps it is the intimate closeness of this novel that has led some to dismiss it on the basis of sentimentality—a most damaging, though undeserving, assessment. Wishing to remain coolly detached, some American critics are uncomfortable, not wanting to be drawn into such an emotionally compelling story.

A more detailed perusal of the January 16, 1939, letter to Covici, discussed above, reveals that Steinbeck sensed such a response from the beginning and outlined how *Grapes* should be read, guiding the reader's expectations. His discussion of the novel's final tableau is a central and key component to these guidelines, for he stresses that it is essential to structure and meaning and that the Joad family's chance encounter with the stranger and his son and the quick resolution are necessary because everything in the novel has led up to this moment. Reinforcing this point, Steinbeck maintains that the structure of the novel would be warped if these strangers were introduced sooner and that the whole focus must be on a relationship between strangers who have no previous acquaintance and no ties to one another. Structure and meaning are so carefully designed and balanced against one another that every part is integral and interdependent. He states further that any symbolism in this scene has to do with survival, not with heterosexual love. Drawing on a larger social context than that of the dispossessed "Okies" in the California of 1939, the story is a universal portrayal, patterned after people's lives.

He not only tells readers what to expect in the novel, he also outlines how he expects them to respond. He wants readers to be so involved with the story that they are left dissatisfied, discovering and exploring its implications for themselves.[3] They will only discover as much in *Grapes*, he asserts, as they themselves have the depth to comprehend. The climax in particular depends on the reader's participation and interpretation.

Steinbeck underscores and reinforces these guidelines by stating them negatively:

The novel has *no* flashy climax.

Its climax is *no* more prominent than the rest of the novel.

The stranger *cannot* be built into the book's structure.

Rose of Sharon's breast feeding the stranger is *no* more sentimental than providing bread.

This story is as old as humanity. All of our stories are old—we have *no* new ones.

The story is *not* intended to satisfy the reader emotionally.

Grapes is designed after human lives, *not* after the way books are made.

It does *not* have the usual emphasis on climax.

The text does *not* stand by itself in creating meaning but depends on the reader.[4]

Steinbeck thus clearly tells readers what they may expect to find in *Grapes*—a carefully integrated and balanced structure, with content and meaning derived from people's lives. With equal clarity he sets forth what he expects from his readers—an involvement of the heart—as well as the mind.

ASSESSING *GRAPES* IN LIGHT OF STEINBECK'S INTENTIONS

A question Steinbeck does not address in his guidelines for reader expectations and responses to *Grapes* is that of the novel's aesthetic merit—whether or not it is good art. Even though it has been assessed as one of the top ten books of the twentieth century and given status as a classic, some still question its artistry. Together with related questions, in approaching this question of its art, it is necessary first to explore critical response in the light of what Steinbeck intended to do in the novel as revealed in his own guidelines for reading it—especially its designed impact on readers and its meticulously balanced structure and meaning. For although some critics have been so strongly affected by the novel that their response to it reveals as much or more about themselves as about the text itself, their criticism nevertheless demonstrates the fulfillment of Steinbeck's intentions to involve readers. Do his intentions for *Grapes*, however, translate into art? How should we evaluate the negative and positive criticism? Addressing these questions, we shall find that *Grapes* withstands the test of time—its mythic story a part of our national heritage and identity as Americans.

In a 1939 review for *The Boston Herald*, Charles Lee demonstrates clearly the close relationship between Steinbeck and his reader: "Steinbeck has seen clearly, felt intensely, written passionately. As a result, the reader is absorbed, shaken, and convinced."[5] In his 1996 *Steinbeck's Typewriter: Essays on His Art*,[6] Robert DeMott maintains that such an empathic effect on readers results from Steinbeck's "participatory aesthetic," in which the writer, the reader, and the text are all intricately involved. As DeMott points out, "reading *Grapes* is not a passive activity; indeed, . . . making sense of the novel . . . becomes the reader's task" (177). And Steinbeck intended that readers bring to this task their hearts as well as their minds—a vulnerability leading to an absorption in this story that leaves them "shaken and convinced" of its truth.

Tracing the pattern of *Grapes* criticism across time in the introduction to his 1997 *"The Grapes of Wrath": Text and Criticism*, Peter Lisca finds that for fifteen years after the publication of *Grapes*, responses were similar to that of Lee—more "assertive" than analytical. Responding to a novel that many of them considered more social documentary than literature, critics tended to record their own emotional reactions rather than to analyze and explicate the text itself. Still, Steinbeck's aesthetic of reader participation is to an extent fulfilled here in that these critics record what *Grapes does*, but in a final analysis of the novel's aesthetic merit, critics must consider what *Grapes is* as well.

Focusing on what *Grapes does*, to illustrate, the titles of Charles Lee's two 1939 reviews of *Grapes* for *The Boston Herald*, one in April and the other in June, show his reactions to the novel: "*The Grapes of Wrath*: The Tragedy of the American Sharecropper" and "*The Grapes of Wrath* Tops Year's Tales in Heart and Art." Viewing himself as the average reader, Lee states that he is compelled to believe Steinbeck's story even though he does not want to. Absorbed, shaken, and convinced of its truth, he calls on those who love their country and its people to read *Grapes* (7). Although in his June review Lee goes further to rank it as "one of the few perfectly articulated soarings of genius of which American literature can boast," he does not substantiate his claim (9).

Similarly, 1939 reviewer Fritz Raley Simmons of the *Greensboro North Carolina Daily News* makes assertions without analysis, declaring that

Grapes makes people "think and think hard."[7] And, like Lee, he ranks Steinbeck as "one of the ablest if not the ablest writer" of the day, asserting that "his characterizations are superb" and that "there is majesty in the alternate chapters of this book." While he does not analyze either the characterization or the interchapters of *Grapes*, however, he does analyze his own experience in reading it, metaphorically comparing his reading "the first chapter of 'The Grapes of Wrath'" to listening to "a sonata in a minor key." Taken in by the novel's emotional pull, he concludes that "it gets you" (6). The 1939 reviewer John Selby also attests to the novel's power to lift readers "into the stream which flows from the author," enabling them to share in an "experience at living."[8] To a similar effect, in his "Books" column for the *Cleveland News*,[9] David H. Appel finds himself left "breathless" in the wake of the "burning intensity" of the novel's powerful "tenderness, pathos and even harshness" (12).

While Woodburn R. Ross's 1949 "John Steinbeck: Naturalism's Priest,"[10] looks beyond the art of *Grapes* to the role of its writer in his oxymoronic view of Steinbeck as "naturalism's priest," he draws upon both the text's power to involve readers and the role of the Steinbeck persona within the text. Since naturalism acknowledges nothing supernatural, Ross surveys Steinbeck's empirical bent, his desire to tell what *is* as clearly and as simply as possible. But he astutely sees Steinbeck's "priestly" role as well. Since a priest does deal with the supernatural, Ross observes that Steinbeck depends as much upon "intuition and affections" as he does upon reason and observation (438). The two sides of Ross's oxymoron, "naturalism" and "priest," are not, then, mutually exclusive, for they show a healthy tension between the scientific precision of the "naturalist" or "realist" and the gentle, intuitive, affectionate heart of Steinbeck as "priest." His oxymoronic measure of a literary artist, then, provides valuable insight on both the writer and the text of *Grapes*—in which social documentary blends with aesthetic vision.

Negative critics and reviewers are assertive as well, but, like those more positive, they may analyze the relationship among the reader, the text, and the writer. Ironically, both negative and positive critics attest to the novel's power to draw readers into its story—an effect Steinbeck intended. Bartlett Randolph's "The Book of the Day," for example, finds fault with the novel's structure, style, and content, proclaiming it to be "a prolonged scream" from beginning to end and comparing the reader to a bird "hypnotized by the snake—he hates it but he cannot tear himself away from it."[11] Without substantiation, Rascoe Burton's April 17 review, "But . . . Not . . . Ferdinand," for *Newsweek*[12] castigates *Grapes* for a lack of organization. Later, he will label it as "propaganda" and accuse Steinbeck of "superficial observation" and incorrect and tasteless dialogue. He also assures *Newsweek*'s audience that *Grapes* is "a bad book" (38). More assertive than analytical, Burton does not back up his statements with evidence or examples.

Although Ray Lewis White's 1983 "*The Grapes of Wrath* and the Critics of 1939,"[13] a bibliography of "108 American reviews . . . from 1939" is highly valuable, he is not content to document 1939 reviews but goes further to imply a continuing "decline" in Steinbeck's reputation (134). Such an implication is not only more assertive than analytical, it is also of questionable value because of the limited scope of his study to the reviews of 1939. And he may have given undue weight to negative critics such as Rascoe Burton who wrote for the highly influential *Newsweek* magazine. Interestingly, on the point of the durability of Steinbeck's writings and reputation, the highly regarded British scholar Roy Simmonds,[14] author of articles, a monograph, and several books on Steinbeck, predicts that Steinbeck's "work will date neither as rapidly nor with such finality as the work of some of his more stylistically daring and currently more highly regarded contemporaries." Comparing the breadth of the studies of White and Simmonds, it seems that the greater weight should be given to the assessment of the latter.

Like Ross's discussion of Steinbeck as "Naturalism's Priest," George F. Whicher's 1951 "Proletarian Leanings"[15] attempts to classify *Grapes*, in this case as a proletarian novel. He does not, however, have an adequate measure to lead him to this conclusion; nor does he have criteria to substantiate his conclusion. For after a discussion in which he praises the authentic character of Ma Joad and the power of some descriptive and dramatic passages, he castigates Steinbeck for his cleverness in creating "effects" that leave readers "feeling let down" (960). Unlike Frederic I. Carpenter, who measures *Grapes* as a literary work by its creation of a "moving picture" that provides a way of looking at the world, Whicher's tone throughout is assertive and impressionistic, his article lacking the objective criteria essential to the measure of a literary work.

Some critics not only lack an appropriate aesthetic measure for *Grapes*, they also seem not to have read the novel very well. As Lisca has pointed out, therefore, their observations are more hysterical than analytical (*Grapes* 557). Such is the case with William Fuller Taylor's 1959 "*The Grapes of Wrath* Reconsidered,"[16] in which he accuses Steinbeck of arousing "interclass hatreds" and castigates critics who find Christian and American theological and philosophical roots in *Grapes* (144). Evidently, Taylor does not look very carefully at Ma Joad's all-encompassing love, at the obvious parallels between their journey and that of the children of Israel as they fled Egypt, or at biblical and national echoes throughout the novel.

Like Taylor, Harold Bloom's introduction to the 1988 *John Steinbeck's "The Grapes of Wrath,"*[17] and Leslie Fiedler's 1990 "Looking Back after Fifty Years"[18] disparage Steinbeck, his critics, and *Grapes* in impressionistic discussions that leave the reader more with a sense of how these critics feel in the presence of this text than with an explication and enlightened discussion of it. Both label Steinbeck scholars as "middlebrows," by implication placing themselves in the position of "highbrows," and both find themselves uncomfortable with *Grapes* and with the ethos of the Steinbeck persona in the text. With little or no substantiation and no appropriate aesthetic measure for *Grapes*, they nevertheless speak as though theirs is the last word to be spoken on this novel, leaving no room for a scholarly dialogue. Evidently, there can be no meeting of minds when a critical hierarchy of middlebrows and highbrows has been arbitrarily declared and when critical responses are impressionistic rather than analytical. Agnes McNeill Donohue's 1968 preface to *A Casebook on "The Grapes of Wrath,"*[19] acknowledges emotive responses like those of Bloom and Fiedler, maintaining that "reactions" to *Grapes* "are rarely temperate" (vii).

Sadly, in his 1994 "Steinbeck 2000" in *John Steinbeck's Fiction Revisited,*[20] the highly regarded Steinbeck scholar, Warren French, bases his final evaluation of *Grapes* on Bloom's negative assertion that Steinbeck is "not one of the inescapable American novelists of our century." Following Bloom's reductive stance, French tries to ascertain "why one is . . . *compelled* 'to be grateful' for *The Grapes of Wrath* [emphasis added]" (133). (Note French's use of the word *compel*, an acknowledgment of the novel's power to move readers even as he proceeds to downplay the novel's standing as a work of art.) No favorable outcome is possible following such an acceptance of Bloom's assessment. Still following Bloom, French asserts "that one thing that remains in Steinbeck's work is its 'fairly constant popularity with an immense number of liberal middlebrows, both in his own country and abroad.' " And, with Bloom, falling into the fallacy of arguing by association, French finds *Grapes* "in one sense a magnificent failure" because so many "liberal middlebrows" appreciate it (135). Such far-fetched claims are unworthy of Bloom and French, both of whom know better than to put forth unsubstantiated claims with no sound theoretical base.

In a similar vein, Harry Thornton Moore's 1939 *The Novels of John Steinbeck: A First Study,*[21] had found fault with the novel's structure and plot because the Joads do not "fight back," thus depriving the story of forcefulness and dramatic impact (68–69). Although Moore attempts an analysis of *Grapes* here, he tries to use a dramatic measure of forcefulness and conflict that do not fit this novel. Even though the novel does have tension and drama, they tend to be internal, of the spirit, rather than outward, as the Joads learn to look upon needy strangers as family members to be cared for. Still, Moore does see mythic qualities in *Grapes* that at times make it seem like an epic, and on this basis he proclaims Steinbeck to be the novelist who is becoming "the poet of our dispossessed" (70, 72).

In all of these responses to *Grapes*, Steinbeck achieves a vital part of his intentions, for, whether the assessment is negative or positive, each critic or reviewer has been involved with the migrant experience. Still, more is required of a literary work than reader or critic involvement with its story. But how does the critic measure the aesthetic merit of a novel such as *Grapes*, which in a real sense is truly at one and the same time a classic literary work of art and a social documentary?

ASSESSING *GRAPES* IN LIGHT OF THE TEXT: IN SEARCH OF AN AESTHETIC MEASURE

By considering questions of characterization, style, and structure, Peter Lisca's 1957 "*The Grapes of Wrath* as Fiction" looks closely at the text itself and shows how those materials out of which the novel is made contribute to reader response. While this novel is designed to involve the readers' emotions, he maintains, and arouses their indignation over the treatment of fellow human beings, it rises above propaganda and sentiment. Rather, it is by means of the Steinbeck aesthetic itself that these empathic responses arise. In other words, *Grapes* has the power to move the reader because of the artistic mold in which it is cast, bringing it closer to the romantic view of sublimity than to the modern disdain of sentimentality (*Grapes* 578, 587). Lisca's 1969 "Steinbeck and Hemingway: Suggestions for a Comparative Study"[22] similarly finds that "both writers are notable for the depth of esthetic feeling . . . and their great ability to express it" (17).

The implication here is that "esthetic feeling" in a work of art is an essential component and is not necessarily sentimentality at all but rather a way to involve readers' hearts as well as their minds.

But what should the reader or critic look for specifically in this text? Steinbeck himself addresses this question in "Suggestions for an Interview with Joseph Henry Jackson" of the *San Francisco Chronicle*. His suggestions for conversations with critics all center around the text itself: What are the novel's themes? How does it address human needs? How does it fit with other works of literature? What material does the writer cover—for example, Steinbeck's own emphasis on the plight of those who are impoverished or downtrodden? (*Grapes* 541). The writer's own role, Steinbeck states, is twofold: to present clearly things as they are and to predict the outcome if there is no change of heart and policy.

Donohue's *Casebook* faces the question of how *Grapes* should be read head-on, for she encourages students to read the novel closely, bringing to it their own measure and theory of good literature (vii). Across time, such close reading, paying attention to the text, and discovering appropriate measures have elevated *Grapes* to its current status as a classic. The most instructive criticism of *Grapes* as a text, as Donohue implies, begins with an appropriate aesthetic theory. Critical responses that center on the text and begin with an appropriate aesthetic measure may be considered under three categories: close readings that are based on theme, style, or theory; comparative studies; and worldviews that are depicted in moving pictures.

Close Readings: Thematic, Stylistic, Theoretical

Because *Grapes* was viewed primarily as social documentary and popular reading matter, there were few analytical studies in the fifteen years following its publication, leaving a critical vacuum that brought into question the novel's aesthetic merit (*Grapes* 548). Part of the problem here is that while *Grapes* draws on numerous literary precedents—such as biblical parallels between the Joads' dispossession and the flight of the children of Israel from Egypt and techniques in the interchapters adapted from the writings of Henry Fielding and John Dos Passos—it is unique. As John Milton's seventeenth-century poetry stands alone among that of the metaphysicals and Cavaliers of his day, Steinbeck's *Grapes* stands alone, a literary monument. But how should it be assessed? As Steinbeck himself has suggested, the critic's primary focus should be on the text itself.

Basing his observations on a close reading of the text, in his 1989 "The Squatter's Circle in *The Grapes of Wrath*,"[23] John H. Timmerman focuses on the reversal of male and female roles in *Grapes* as revealed in changes that take place in the male circle of authority, in which men crouch together on their haunches or heels to decide what to do next. Typically, women and children stand behind the circle, waiting for the men to decide what to do. With great empathy Timmerman shows how this circle evolves until a point near the end of the novel when Pa is crouched in fetal position, watching Ma fry potatoes. This is one of Steinbeck's cinematic scenes frozen in time, which depicts the pathos of Pa's isolation and increasing helplessness. Now he is watching her as she resolutely goes about her daily tasks. Such a textual study serves to highlight the artistry in the use of details—fulfilling a concern and objective documented in the journals that Steinbeck kept while writing *Grapes*.

DeMott's 1996 " 'This Book Is My Life': Creating *The Grapes of Wrath*" in *Steinbeck's Typewriter*, another close reading, approaches the question of aesthetic measure by exploring the relationship between the writer and his text. He observes that Steinbeck's involvement with the problems of the migrants wounded him deeply, resulting in the creation of a highly em-pathic persona in *Grapes* who is actively and persuasively engaged in the story of dispossession and impoverishment. DeMott believes further that this persona's "creative, interior, or *architextual* level of engagement is the elusive and heretofore unacknowledged fifth layer of Steinbeck's novel," (183–85). Drawing on materials in the accompanying journal that Steinbeck kept while writing *Grapes*, DeMott backs up his claim persua-sively, especially in recalling the journal entry in which Steinbeck envi-sions Tom Joad actually entering his room, after which he returns to the writing task with renewed vigor.

Christopher S. Busch's 1994 "New Directions for Steinbeck Studies"[24] gives guidelines for close readings and research that needs to be done on "the influences of realism, naturalism, and romanticism on Steinbeck's unique aesthetic and with regard to Steinbeck's literary 'heritage,' that is, his thematic and stylistic relationships to writers who preceded and fol-lowed him" (154).

Busch thus offers a direction and beginning point for further studies. The publication of other scholarly tools, such as Jackson J. Benson's 1984 biography, *The True Adventures of John Steinbeck, Writer;*[25] Robert DeMott's 1984 *Steinbeck's Reading: A Catalogue of Books Owned and Borrowed;*[26] and Robert B. Harmon's 1990 *"The Grapes of Wrath": A Fifty Year Bibliographical Survey,*[27] all provide materials essential to the student who wants to follow up on Busch's suggestions for approaches to Steinbeck's art.

Nicholas Visser's 1994 "Audience and Closure in *The Grapes of Wrath*"[28] looks at the rhetorical question of audience, exploring how "radical novels . . . gain access to an audience" since their primary readers are going to come from the middle class (20). Somehow the writer must convince these read-ers that the novel is essentially true. If they are not assured of its truth, Visser suggests, then they cannot find meaning in the novel (27). In order to reach this audience, Visser believes, Steinbeck had to tone down the ending so that it was not radically political. Hence, he maintains that Steinbeck unavoidably distorted the novel's message. Like Emily Dickinson, however, Steinbeck has a poetic view of truth, aware that in or-der for people to understand at all, the truth must be told "slant"; otherwise, they may not be able to bear it.

Focused sharply on the text itself, John Ditsky's 1989 "The Ending of *The Grapes of Wrath*: A Further Commentary"[29] brings a poet's mind, eye, and heart to bear on *Grapes*. His comments are an extension of the art of

Grapes itself, elucidating the text, showing us at what point art and myth become one.

> The narrative of the Joads has nowhere to go after Rose of Sharon draws the camera into focus upon that mysterious smile, then holds the pose while the camera backs away . . . to make it clear that she has become the world's true center. . . . It is Woman picking up the pieces of the American dream and holding the man-caused shards together, the seams invisible. The power to work this miracle is implied in Rose of Sharon's smile. It is an Eastern smile, a smile of understanding, in this ultimate Western book. She has got it all now. All the lines of narrative come to focus in her; like light, they prism in her. (123)

Ditsky concludes by comparing Rose of Sharon to the Virgin Mary in the New Testament, the one nursing one of God's children and the other, his Son. Ditsky shows that in *Grapes*, as in the Hebraic and Christian Scriptures, then, the victory falls not to the strong, but to the faithful.

In " 'This Book Is My Life': Creating *The Grapes of Wrath*" in *Steinbeck's Typewriter*, DeMott, like Lisca and Joseph Fontenrose, focuses on language and style, maintaining that this novel "is not narrated from the first-person point of view, yet the language has a consistently catchy eyewitness quality about it; and the vivid biblical, empirical, poetical, cinematic, and folk styles Steinbeck employs demonstrate the tonal and visual acuity of his ear and eye" (175). DeMott finds that Steinbeck's creation of such an amalgram of styles draws on the very essence of his "being," not just his intellect. As an example, he cites "the tempo" in interchapter 25's jeremiad that "indicates the importance of musical and harmonic analogies to the text." His discussion further elucidates this musical analogy as it applies to *Grapes* as a whole. "Steinbeck's . . . fusion of intimate narrative and panoramic editorial chapters enforces a dialogic concert. Chapters, styles, and voices all speak to each other, set up resonances, send echoes back and forth—point and counterpoint, strophe and antistrophe—as in a huge symphony of language whose total tonal and spatial impression far surpasses the sum of its discrete and sometimes dissonant parts" (175). Skewing and avoiding the question of the aesthetic standing of *Grapes* by labeling Steinbeck scholars as "middlebrows," French and Bloom skirt the issue. Ditsky and DeMott themselves enter into its story, however, extending and elucidating its meaning by discussions of *Grapes*' mythic and musical qualities.

Bringing current literary theory to bear on *Grapes*, Chris Kocela's 2000 "A Postmodern Steinbeck, or Rose of Sharon Meets Oedipa Maas"[30] explores some "well-studied aspects of the novel in light of some recent influential theories of postmodernist fiction." First, he argues that "Steinbeck's use of the interchapters exemplifies a postmodern strategy of 'frame-breaking,' whereby differences between history and fiction are established within the text only to be problematized, alerting the reader to the difficulties of historical and political representation" (248). Second, he draws on Deborah Madsen's theory of "'postmodernist allegory' to examine how the problematic divide between history and fiction is further broken down by Steinbeck's superimposing of biblical and fictional worlds on the plane of the Joads' story" (248). And third, he explores "Steinbeck's influence on, and continuity with, a later generation of American writers," comparing *Grapes* to Thomas Pynchon's *The Crying of Lot 49*. Interestingly, in an endnote Kocela goes further, suggesting *Grapes* as a possible influence on the film trilogy *Star Wars*.

The search for an aesthetic measure of *Grapes* has come a considerable way since the long fifteen years following its publication in 1939, when it was viewed primarily as social documentary and popular reading matter. Although it is now recognized as a classic, there are still those critics who only grudgingly acknowledge that status, but most of these negative responses continue to be more emotive than analytical—documenting the critics' reaction to the novel rather than an explication of the novel itself. But there is abundant evidence that *Grapes* stands up to critical scrutiny, for scholars have found appropriate measures of its aesthetic merit that range from the comparative to the thematic, from Steinbeck's spatial imagination to his writing style, from feminist to postmodern, and more. Tetsumaro Hayashi, longtime editor of *Steinbeck Quarterly*, has worked diligently toward such an end, always looking to the future, always hoping for someone to "carry the torch" for Steinbeck studies. In his 1990 *Steinbeck's "The Grapes of Wrath": Essays in Criticism*,[31] he states his aspirations. "May our new generation of Steinbeck students and scholars blessed with more primary and secondary published sources, more critical and biographical materials, and more published research materials, find a greater enjoyment in reading, discussing, and writing about Steinbeck's enigmatic literature, appreciating and understanding his magic as an artist and craftsman."

While readers, students, and scholars, however, are now "blessed" with more secondary source material, they would still do well to heed Donohue's admonition to her students to read the novel closely and carefully, creating their own theory of good literature by which to measure *Grapes'* aesthetic worth.

Comparative Studies

Frederic I. Carpenter's 1941 "The Philosophical Joads"[32] acknowledges the "narrative power" of *Grapes* to draw readers into the story and also offers an aesthetic measure by which to evaluate it (*Grapes* 563). Comparing Steinbeck to Nathaniel Hawthorne, Herman Melville, Mark Twain, Sinclair Lewis, and Ralph Waldo Emerson and defining art as a pictorial depiction of an action that criticizes human behavior and provides a way of looking at the world, Carpenter observes that *Grapes* preaches a positive worldview and condemns the conservative fear of challenging the status quo. Based on these concrete comparisons, he finds that *Grapes* strikes out into new territory, uniting Emerson's transcendental mysticism; Walt Whitman's democratic, populace poetry; William James and John Dewey's pragmatism with a Christianity that emphasizes action in this world (*Grapes* 563). Carpenter engages *Grapes*, then, on a theoretical level, giving a new direction for criticism and moving away from the assertive to the analytical—from what the novel *does* to what it *is*. Still, when he chooses the word "preach" to describe what *Grapes* does, he recognizes Steinbeck in his persona as bard and his readers as those compelled to listen, whether or not they respond positively. Basing his study thus on sound aesthetic theory that grapples with the question of what *Grapes* is as a work of art, Carpenter has established grounds for a critical dialogue.

Adding Thomas Jefferson's agrarianism to Carpenter's comparison between *Grapes* and Emerson, Whitman, James, and Dewey in 1947, Chester E. Eisinger's "Jeffersonian Agrarianism in *The Grapes of Wrath*"[33] expands Carpenter's discussion of the impact of transcendentalism, democracy, and pragmatic philosophy in *Grapes* (149). Like Carpenter, he analyzes *Grapes*; however, he also responds to the novel with empathy for the downtrodden portrayed in its pages, speaking in first person to recommend a Christian world in which Americans assure the rights, safety, and dignity of its citizens (154).

Stephen Railton's 1990 "Pilgrim's Politics: Steinbeck's Art of Conversion"[34] draws on comparison and contrast and the classical concept of necessity, or inevitability, in his discussion of one of the novel's major themes, that of conversion. Comparing the Joads' journey to that of Saul in the Acts and Christian in John Bunyan's *Pilgrim's Progress*, Railton maintains that one of the primary themes in *Grapes* is conversion and that "thematically Route 66 and the various state highways in California that the Joads travel along all run parallel to the road to Damascus that Saul takes in Acts, or to the Way taken by Bunyan's Christian in *Pilgrim's Progress*" (29). Like Saul and Christian, the Joads inevitably move from one point to the next with no alternative action open to them: "Again and again what will happen next is made narratively inescapable." Their plight, Railton suggests, moves readers to a reaction against such oppressive circumstances, arousing them "toward action to change the status quo" (32). Thus placing *Grapes* within the context of previous literary and biblical themes and using the classical concept of necessity—with events following one another in logical and inevitable sequence—Railton provides a persuasive and insightful study of the novel.

Barry Maine's "Steinbeck's Debt to Dos Passos,"[35] compares *Grapes* with Dos Passos's *U.S.A.* He finds that the interchapters in *Grapes* and the "Camera Eye" sections in *U.S.A.* do bear some likeness but that the two works differ significantly in substance. Dos Passos's novel is more naturalistic, with human beings subject to historical forces; Steinbeck's is more visionary and prophetic, with human beings enduring and triumphing over history. The differences between the two novels, then, go beyond the substantive, for, as Maine points out, "As much as it is form it is vision that separates and distinguishes these two writers of the Depression era" (26). Note here that Maine's aesthetic measure for the two texts centers on the texts themselves—on their content, style, tone, and view of the human condition.

Another comparative study, Abby H.P. Werlock's 1992 "Poor Whites: Joads and Snopeses,"[36] places Steinbeck's Joads alongside Faulkner's Snopeses, finding them to have significantly "different literary archetypes and divergent views of Christianity." While Jackson J. Benson believes the Joads to be an "idealized view of common man," Werlock points out, "in *The Hamlet* . . . the narrator seems to approve the view of Snopeses not merely as inhuman, but as varmints, animals, reptiles" (64–65). She finds the two authors alike, however, in the end result of their depiction of the Joads and Snopeses. "Both authors successfully employ their chosen 'families' to make a similar point: Steinbeck and Faulkner articulate a resounding 'No' to exploitation and totalitarianism and an emphatic 'Yea' to the rights and dignity of the ordinary individual" (71). With her measures of "literary archetypes and divergent views of Christianity," Werlock establishes an objective and persuasive measure for her comparison of the two novels.

A perusal of Tetsumaro Hayashi and Beverly K. Simpson's 1994 *John Steinbeck: Dissertation Abstracts and Research Opportunities*[37] reveals the aesthetic measures employed in these dissertations, along with "trends and new directions in Steinbeck scholarship" (xiii). Comparative studies, for example, include George Henry Spies III's "John Steinbeck's *The Grapes of Wrath*" and Frederick Manfred's *The Golden Bowl*: A Comparative Study,

Carl H. DeVasto's "The Poet of Demos: John Steinbeck's *The Grapes of Wrath* and Other Major Later Fiction," and Leslie Thomas Pollard's "*The Grapes of Wrath* and *Native Son*: Literary Criticism as Social Definition," among others. In addition to these comparative studies, these dissertations show the relationship of *Grapes* to Steinbeck's other novels and explore his view of America.

Worldviews in Moving Pictures

Carpenter's comparative study of Steinbeck, Hawthorne, Melville, Twain, Lewis, and Emerson offers a definition of art as a picture in motion that criticizes human behavior and provides a way of looking at the world—a measure other critics draw upon as well. Joseph Fontenrose's 1963 "*The Grapes of Wrath*" in *John Steinbeck: An Introduction and Interpretation*,[38] for example, arrives at a theory to measure *Grapes* that is reminiscent of Carpenter's, for he finds in the novel "a vivid picture of something that happened and a feeling tone" (60). He adds to Carpenter's theory, however, a study of Steinbeck's style of writing that finds it suited to the content and, on this basis, declares "some . . . interchapters are masterpieces in themselves" (69).

Saddened by negative criticism that he had to record in his 1969 edition of *Steinbeck and His Critics: A Record of Twenty-Five Years*,[39] E.W. Tedlock Jr. draws on ancient measures—truth and beauty—to provide "one insight" into Steinbeck's art: "There is at time in Steinbeck an experience that I think of as purely existential and native or basic to him, beyond cavil. It can be seen in a note of his on an early morning encounter with some farm laborers camped by the road. The note is of great objective purity, and is also most humanly attractive, . . . so beautifully natural and yet so vulnerable" (v).

Tedlock's insight is reminiscent of Carpenter's measure of art as a "moving picture" that gives readers a worldview, for here he sees Steinbeck's art as "an experience." Further, he finds truth in what he calls Steinbeck's "note . . . of great objective purity"—his ability to stand back and to see things as they actually are—and he finds this "note" to be "beautifully natural and . . . vulnerable." Tedlock explores questions of the beauty and vulnerability of the human experience in Steinbeck's art, then, and finds them truly expressed (v).

Although Robert Murray Davis's 1990 "The World of John Steinbeck's Joads"[40] shows that Steinbeck's portrayal of the Oklahoma landscape was not accurate, he does not find this inaccuracy a grievous fault. Rather, he applauds Steinbeck's ability to depict "what it means to be an Oklahoman

... [and] what it means to be human." Like Carpenter, Davis finds in *Grapes* a moving picture with a worldview and, like Tedlock, finds truth and beauty in Steinbeck's poetic creation of "characters and their world from the inside out" (404).

George Henderson's 1989 "John Steinbeck's Spatial Imagination in *The Grapes of Wrath*: A Critical Essay,"[41] a cross-disciplinary study, brings a new perspective to Steinbeck studies—that of the social geographer. Following from his thesis that explores "how meaning is produced, controlled, and disseminated with regard to social and workaday space," he finds that in *Grapes* Steinbeck establishes "a problem . . . of that recurrent human condition . . . shaped by historical and social contingencies . . . [so that] it is from social and geographical relationships that meaning radiates, rather than from an individual character or action" (212). Like Carpenter, Henderson believes a work of art should give readers a picture of what it means to be human and a worldview. *Grapes*, he maintains, provides such a picture and such a view. He goes further to establish how character contributes to this view. To illustrate, "Ma Joad" rises "from the ashes of a burnt-out household, the vehicle for Steinbeck to expose the pitfalls of patriarchy" (221).

STEINBECK'S MYTHIC AMERICA: *GRAPES* FOR OUR TIMES

In the foreword to his 1966 *America and Americans*, Steinbeck states that this text "is inspired by . . . a passionate love of America and the Americans."[42] The same statement is true of *Grapes*, in which his "passionate love" is evident in his narrative persona, in his characters such as Ma Joad, Tom Joad, and Jim Casy, and in his story that has become a part of the nation's mythic identity. For Americans may be defined even now as both the heroic, suffering poor who learn to share from meager resources and the greedy "owners" who leave the needy to fend for themselves; and both still travel side by side along a mythic Route 66. And today's readers are still drawn to this mythic representation of the "good guys" and those who are not good. Studs Terkel's 1989 "We Still See Their Faces,"[43] the introduction to Viking's 1989 edition of *Grapes*, to illustrate, states that Steinbeck was "driven," possessed by "an almost messianic urgency" in writing *Grapes* and is now a "constant companion" who urgently addresses readers through his text (xv). As the 1939 reviewer Fritz Raley Simmons asserts, "It gets you."

What is there about *Grapes* that gives it relevance not only to Americans but also to people in countries all over the world? Perhaps the 1939 "*The Grapes of Wrath*: The Tragedy of the American Sharecropper" by reviewer Charles Lee provides the key to answer this question: "*The Grapes of Wrath* will irritate the complacent, but excite the compassionate. I hope every congressman reads it and everybody in America who loves his country and his fellowmen" (9).

Because *Grapes* does not leave its readers unmoved, Lee suggests that reading it is the beginning point to bring about a change toward more "compassionate" and loving leaders and citizenry. This is the simple, but not simplistic, theme of *Grapes*, which addresses the question of how to live in this world as well as how to live in America. The answer for Steinbeck is to live as if people really mattered—an answer and theme pertinent to any culture in any era.

We are still left with the question of what *Grapes* has to say to America today. If this novel has in truth become a part of the American identity, who are we in the light of its story? And what does Steinbeck imply will be the outcome of our taking on this identity? He addresses these questions in later works—especially in *East of Eden, The Winter of Our Discontent, Travels with Charley in Search of America*, and *America and Americans*. Considered together with *Grapes*, the two fictional works—*Eden* and *Winter*—have the timing and effect of an epic trilogy. For *Grapes* begins the American story *en medias res*, in the middle of things, with the vast migration instigated by the Oklahoma Dust Bowl. *Eden* takes a backward turn to the historical beginnings of the Salinas Valley that was first inhabited by the American Indians, then by the Spanish, and finally by the Americans. *Winter* takes the story into modern times, but with echoes of an Arthurian England, dealing with the moral decay represented in the television quiz show scandals of the fifties. Taken together these three novels have an epic scope that encompasses the moral moorings of America—an oxymoronic view that shows the nation's dark as well as its light side, highlighting a greedy self-absorption and a warm magnanimity. The hero who walks through all three novels is an ordinary, everyday Every American, who is flawed but capable of transcendence.

Such a view makes an uncomfortable demand on all Every Americans, for it insists that they rise above their faults, respond to the needs of those about them, and carry on a heritage of freedom and responsibility. Unlike Cain, Steinbeck implies, with attention, love, and generosity, they must take on the role of their "brother's keeper." These later novels, then, fulfill Moore's 1939 foresight in *The Novels of John Steinbeck: A First Study*, in which he suggests "*The Grapes of Wrath* is packed with meanings that may be partly understood in terms of his previous tendencies, though there are new beginnings which may lead to future developments" (66). The "new beginnings" are incipient in *Grapes*, a novel that has established itself as a part of a nation's heritage, its conscience, and its myth. It has a haunting quality that does not vanish across time but lingers, reminding Americans of who they are and who they might be, if they choose. The "future developments," as depicted in *Eden*, show Americans they have the freedom to choose a higher way. Further, as these "developments" are portrayed in *Winter*, they imply the possibility of transcending over a dark alter ego and finding light for the way ahead.

Who are we Americans, then? In defining himself, Steinbeck defines us as well. In *Travels with Charley in Search of America*, he reveals a sense of self that is intertwined with his identity as an American, declaring America to be "the macrocosm of microcosm me,"[44] and we could expand the declaration to include us all. America is the macrocosm of the microcosm of the Every American. Steinbeck's dream of who we are as Americans was verified in the horrors of the national tragedy of September 11, 2001, when terrorists flew airplanes into the two towers of the World Trade Center and the Pentagon and when a few passengers on another hijacked airplane chose to cause it to crash in a Pennsylvania field rather than into another national building, sparing who knows how many lives. In the midst of horror, the heroism of these passengers, of New York City's firemen and policemen, and untold others revealed humane, loving, attentive Every Americans, and no one would now dare call these descriptions sentimental. And the unselfishness of restaurants that prepared and delivered meals without charge to rescue workers and of countless others who gave of themselves attest to a genuine and generous outpouring of love for America and its people. Individual stories bring pride to our hearts and tears to our eyes—the two women, for example, who carried a fellow worker in a wheelchair down sixty-eight flights of stairs to escape their tower's conflagration, not counting the cost if the endeavor had failed. Some of the stories we will never know. As Steinbeck always believed—and was labeled sentimental for that belief—Americans can transcend their faults. He had faith that the people of his country were capable of being loving, generous, and good. He was right. September 11, 2001, has answered the question of who we Americans are: one nation, under God, indivisible. Steinbeck knew that all along.

Feminist critic Helene Cixous was surprised to discover that in order to understand the writing of "the Brazilian writer Clarice Lispector," a person must pay attention and look for love: "And there, there is the treasure of events: we have only to love, to be on the lookout for love, and all the riches are entrusted to us. Attention is the key."[45] This observation is the key to understanding Steinbeck's writing as well: pay attention, and "be on the lookout for love." Having left behind us forever the age of irony and aloof detachment, Americans can better understand the elegant simplicity of this admonition. There is something so right about it now that national tragedy has trimmed away the nonessentials. As shallow, young Rose of Sharon in Grapes is transformed into a modern Madonna, as Cal in Eden learns that he must make his own choices and stand on his own feet, and as Ethan in Winter turns away from greed to embrace a higher way, so Steinbeck's Every Americans can live up to their nation's ideals.

As Donohue maintained in Casebook, Grapes is closely tied to the American psyche: "This novel has survived a 'rhetoric of praise and blame' and has come to be known as an American classic. To follow its turbulent history . . . is to make an excursion into American literature, history, myth, culture, and dream. It is a journey as perilous as that of the Joads to a shattered Eden known as American success" (vii).

Similarly, in Steinbeck's Typewriter DeMott recognizes the mythic reflection of this American psyche in Grapes, finding this novel to be "a tale of dashed illusions, thwarted desires, unconscionable suffering, and betrayed promises—all strung on a gossamer thread of hope" (194). Grapes is uniquely American, then, revealing who we Americans are, warts and all, but always with the investment of Steinbeck's faith in us and hope for us to live up to our national ideals. We have arrived now at the frontier that he envisioned, but it is an inner and spiritual frontier. And this is not a bad place to be, for America's greatest wealth has always been in the spirit of its people—not in its money, or its vast land, or its goods.

NOTES

1. Peter Lisca, with Kevin Hearle, eds., John Steinbeck, "The Grapes of Wrath": Text and Criticism (New York: Penguin Books, 1997), 446–53. Hereafter references to this work will be cited parenthetically within the text, identified as Grapes with pertinent page numbers. The original article by Lisca appeared in Viking's 1972 edition, reprinted from PMLA LXXII (March 1957), 269–309.

2. Viktor E. Frankl, Man's Search for Meaning: An Introduction to Logotherapy, 3rd ed. (New York: Simon and Schuster, Inc., 1984), 134.

3. In postmodern terms the text is more "writerly," or "scriptible," than it is "lisible," or "readerly." In a scriptible text a reader must participate in the making of meaning whereas in a more lisible text the reader discovers meaning. For example, in the conclusion of Jazz, Toni Morrison addresses and challenges the reader to "remake" her book: "You are free to do it and I am free to let you because look, look. Look where your hands are. Now" (229). Similarly, Steinbeck leaves his readers with a final tableau, a frozen cinematic shot, with neither a resolution nor even a prescription for a resolution.

4. See note three above.

5. Charles Lee, "*The Grapes of Wrath*: The Tragedy of the American Share-cropper" and "*The Grapes of Wrath* Tops Year's Tales in Heart and Art," reviews in *Boston Herald*, 22 April 1939, sec. A, p. 7 and 17 June 1939, sec. 1, p. 9. Here-after references to this work will be cited parenthetically within the text.

6. Robert DeMott, *Steinbeck's Typewriter: Essays on His Art* (Troy, New York: The Whitson Publishing Company, 1996), 186. Hereafter references to this work will be cited parenthetically within the text.

7. Fritz Raley Simmons, "Farm Tenancy Central Theme of Steinbeck," *Greensboro North Carolina Daily News*, 16 July 1939, sec. D, p. 6. Hereafter refer-ences to this work will be cited parenthetically within the text.

8. John Selby, "Books," *Daytona Beach News-Journal* (Fla.), 14 April 1939, p. 10.

9. David H. Appel, "Books," *Cleveland News*, 15 April 1939, p. 12.

10. Woodburn R. Ross, "John Steinbeck: Naturalism's Priest," *College English* (May 1949), 432–38. Hereafter references to this work will be cited parentheti-cally in the text.

11. Bartlett Randolph, "The Book of the Day," *New York Sun*, 14 April 1939, p. 17.

12. Rascoe Burton, "But . . . Not . . . Ferdinand," *Newsweek* 13 (17 April 1939) and 13 (1 May 1939). Hereafter references to this works will be cited par-enthetically within the text.

13. Ray Lewis White, "*The Grapes of Wrath* and the Critics of 1939," *Re-sources for American Literary Study* 13 (Autumn 1983), 134–64. Hereafter refer-ences to this work will be cited parenthetically within the text. See also Joseph McElrath, Jessie Crissler, and Susan Shillinglaw, eds., *John Steinbeck: The Con-temporary Reviews*. Contemporary Reviews Series (New York: Cambridge Uni-versity Press, 1996).

14. Roy Simmonds, *Steinbeck's Literary Achievement*, Steinbeck Monograph Series, no. 6 (Muncie, Ind.: John Steinbeck Society of America/Ball State Uni-versity, 1976).

15. George F. Whicher, "Proletarian Leanings," in *The Literature of the Ameri-can People: An Historical and Critical Survey* (New York: Appleton-Century-Crofts, Inc., 1951), 959–61. Hereafter references to this works will be cited parenthetically within the text.

16. William Fuller Taylor, "*The Grapes of Wrath* Reconsidered," *Mississippi Quarterly*, XII (Summer 1959), 136–44, reprinted in Agnes McNeill Donohue, A *Casebook on "The Grapes of Wrath"* (New York: Thomas Y. Crowell Company, 1968).

17. Harold Bloom, ed., *John Steinbeck's "The Grapes of Wrath,"* Modern Criti-cal Interpretations Series (New York: Chelsea House Publishers, 1988).

18. Leslie Fiedler, "Looking Back after Fifty Years," *San Jose Studies* XVI, no. 1 (Winter 1990), 54–64. Hereafter references to this work will be cited parentheti-cally in the text.

19. Agnes McNeill Donohue, *A Casebook on "The Grapes of Wrath"* (New York: Thomas Y. Crowell Company, 1968), vii. Hereafter references to this work will be cited parenthetically in the text.

20. Warren French, "Steinbeck 2000," *John Steinbeck's Fiction Revisited* (New York: Twayne Publishers, 1994), 132–38. Hereafter references to this work will be cited parenthetically within the text.

21. Harry Thornton Moore, *The Novels of John Steinbeck: A First Study* (Chicago: Normandie House, 1939), 68–69. Hereafter references to this work will be cited parenthetically within the text.

22. Peter Lisca, "Steinbeck and Hemingway: Suggestions for a Comparative Study," *Steinbeck Quarterly* (Spring 1969), 9–17. Hereafter references to this work will be cited parenthetically within the text.

23. John H. Timmerman, "The Squatter's Circle in *The Grapes of Wrath*," *Studies in American Fiction* (Autumn 1989), 203–11.

24. Christopher S. Busch, "New Directions for Steinbeck Studies," in *John Steinbeck: Dissertation Abstracts and Research Opportunities*, Tetsumaro Hayashi and Beverly K. Simpson, comps. (Metuchen, N.J.: Scarecrow Press, 1994).

25. Jackson J. Benson, *The True Adventures of John Steinbeck, Writer* (New York: Viking Press, 1984).

26. Robert DeMott, *Steinbeck's Reading: A Catalogue of Books Owned and Borrowed*, Garland Reference Library of the Humanities, vol. 246 (New York: Garland Publishing, 1984).

27. Robert B. Harmon, with John F. Early, *"The Grapes of Wrath": A Fifty-Year Bibliographical Survey* (San Jose, Calif.: Steinbeck Research Center, 1990).

28. Nicholas Visser, "Audience and Closure in *The Grapes of Wrath*," *Studies in American Fiction* 22:1 (Spring 1994), 19–36. Hereafter references to this work will be cited parenthetically within the text.

29. John Ditsky, "The Ending of *The Grapes of Wrath*: A Further Commentary," *Critical Essays on John Steinbeck's "The Grapes of Wrath,"* ed. John Ditsky (Boston: G.K. Hall & Co., 1989), 116–123, reprinted in Peter Lisca, with Kevin Hearle, eds., *John Steinbeck, "The Grapes of Wrath": Text and Criticism.* Hereafter references to this work will be cited parenthetically within the text.

30. Chris Kocela, "A Postmodern Steinbeck, or Rose of Sharon Meets Oedipa Maas," in *The Critical Response to John Steinbeck's "The Grapes of Wrath,"* ed. Barbara A. Heavilin (Westport, Conn.: Greenwood Press, 2000), 247–66. Hereafter references to this work will be cited parenthetically within the text.

31. Tetsumaro Hayashi, *Steinbeck's "The Grapes of Wrath": Essays in Criticism*, Steinbeck Essay Series, no. 3 (Muncie, Ind.: Steinbeck Research Institute/Ball State University, 1990), viii–ix.

32. Frederic I. Carpenter, "The Philosophical Joads," in *College English II* (January 1941), 315–25, reprinted in Lisca and Hearle, eds., *John Steinbeck, "The Grapes of Wrath": Text and Criticism* (New York: Penguin Books, 1997). Hereafter references to this work will be cited parenthetically within the text.

33. Chester E. Eisinger, "Jeffersonian Agrarianism in *The Grapes of Wrath*," *The University of Kansas City Review* XIX (Winter 1947), 149–54. Hereafter references to this work will be cited parenthetically within the text.

34. Stephen Railton, "Pilgrim's Politics: Steinbeck's Art of Conversion," *New Essays on "The Grapes of Wrath*," ed. David Wyatt (Cambridge, 1990), 27–46. Hereafter quotations from this work will be cited parenthetically within the text.

35. Barry Maine, "Steinbeck's Debt to Dos Passos," *Steinbeck Quarterly* 23:1–2 (Winter/ Spring 1990), 17–27.

36. Abby H.P. Werlock, "Poor Whites: Joads and Snopeses," *San Jose Studies* 18:1 (Winter 1992), 61–71. Hereafter references to this work will be cited parenthetically within the text.

37. Tetsumaro Hayashi and Beverly K. Simpson, comps., *John Steinbeck: Dissertation Abstracts and Research Opportunities* (Metuchen, N.J.: Scarecrow Press, 1994).

38. Joseph Fontenrose, *John Steinbeck: An Introduction and Interpretation* (New York: Barnes & Noble, Inc., 1963), 67–83. Hereafter references to this work will be cited parenthetically within the text.

39. E.W. Tedlock Jr., *Steinbeck and His Critics: A Record of Twenty-Five Years* (Albuquerque: University of New Mexico Press, 1969), v. Hereafter references to this work will be cited parenthetically in the text.

40. Robert Murray Davis, "The World of John Steinbeck's Joads," *World Literature Today: A Literary Quarterly of the University of Oklahoma* 64:3 (Summer 1990), 401–04. Hereafter references to this work will be cited parenthetically in the text.

41. George Henderson, "John Steinbeck's Spatial Imagination in *The Grapes of Wrath*: A Critical Essay," *California History* 68:4 (Winter 1989/90), 211–23. Hereafter references to this work will be cited parenthetically within the text.

42. John Steinbeck, *America and Americans* (New York: The Viking Press, Inc., 1966).

43. Studs Terkel, "We Still See Their Faces," introduction to *The Grapes of Wrath* (New York: Viking Penguin Inc., 1989), v–xx.

44. John Steinbeck, *Travels with Charley in Search of America* (New York: Viking Penguin, Inc., 1962), 209.

45. Biddy Martin, "Teaching Literature, Changing Cultures," *PMLA* (January 1997), 7–25.

2   Content

Chapter 1 of *Grapes* is an expository chapter that foreshadows and establishes *tone, setting, characterization, theme, voice of the narrator,* and *role of the reader.* From the very first sentence, the story is quintessentially American, the opening scene set in Oklahoma—a microcosm of a nation's ravage and greed that takes its toll on people and land alike. This story is told in the voice of an omniscient, indignant, and compassionate narrator who participates by relating firsthand to the pain and suffering with which people and land are afflicted. Through his eyes, the reader, too, shares in this American experience.

Although the narration appears to be an objective description of the land, in tone it is so sympathetic to the environment that the land itself becomes a character as important to this story as the people. Focusing first on the land and then on the people, this description sets a mood of impending disaster. The opening sentences establish the land as already lying wounded, vulnerable, and helpless before mechanical and human exploitation, as well as to natural forces of erosion when it is left exposed to the elements. Steinbeck describes "the last rains" as coming "gently," not cutting earth that is already "scarred."[1] There is a strong implication, however, that plowing is continuous, crossing and recrossing "the rivulet marks," oblivious to damage inflicted on the land (*Grapes* 3). Had these final rains come in torrents rather than gently, then erosion would have increased the damage, washing away soil left bare by human manipulation.

By the use of color, image-creating verbs, and repetition, Steinbeck draws a picture of the devastation left in the wake of the Oklahoma Dust Bowl: "The *red* country" and "the *gray* country" become "*pale, pink* in the *red* country and *white* in the *gray* country." The *green* of the corn begins to give way to "*brown* lines" that "widened and moved in on the central ribs." Sometimes Steinbeck employs the verb and noun forms of a word, emphasizing by both image and repetition: "The surface of the earth *crusted*, a thin hard *crust.*" Most often, however, the verb itself carries the weight of the description: "The earth *dusted* down in dry little streams. . . . The sharp sun *struck* day after day. . . . The weeds *frayed* and *edged* back from their roots. . . . The dirt crust *broke* and the dust *formed.*" And, most effectively, he repeats the image verb so that its impact is compounded: "Every moving thing *lifted* the dust into the air: a walking man *lifted* a thin layer as high as his waist, and a wagon *lifted* the dust as high as the fence tops, and an automobile *boiled* a cloud behind it" (*Grapes* 5). The image intensifies here as "lifted," a fairly innocuous term, is replaced by "boiled," giving a sense of the choking quality of air filled with churning dust.

Color, light, darkness, image-creating verbs, and repetition join ominously as Steinbeck completes this picture of devastation: "The dawn came, but no day. In the *gray* sky, a *red* sun appeared, a *dim red* circle that gave a little *light, like dusk*; and as that day advanced, the *dusk* slipped back toward *darkness*, and the wind *cried* and *whimpered* over the fallen corn [emphasis added]" (*Grapes* 6).

Here "red" is no longer associated with the normal color of "the red country" but is rather the color of the sun at first partially concealed by dust and then blackened out. A personified wind cries and whimpers in grief over the dead corn. With these images of darkness, crying, whimpering, and sorrow, the setting, tone, and character of the land are thus set, ready for the introduction of human beings.

Following this dark scene of an earth in mourning, Steinbeck depicts the human misery inherent in living in such a setting, describing people who huddle inside their homes. When they emerge from this shelter, they shield themselves from the dust by covering their noses with handkerchiefs and their eyes with goggles. Steinbeck intensifies this scene again by image verbs: the light of the stars cannot "pierce" through the dust; lights from the houses do not "spread" past their own yards; cloth is "wedged" into the cracks of windows and doors; and the sun "flared." He describes the children as unnaturally still—no running or shouting—and the sun's redness is metaphorically compared to blood. Generalized rather than particularized, "the people" in this opening chapter nevertheless engender a reader's sympathy with their plight (*Grapes* 6–8).

With the cessation of the wind, they come out of their houses—the men to survey the damage to the corn, the women to wait beside them, observing their faces to determine whether or not they are holding up. For the men mattered more to the wives than the failed crops. The children similarly examine the faces of their parents to see whether or not they are still strong. Assured finally that the spirits of the men are not broken, the women return to their housework, and the children return quietly to their games. The last sentence is oxymoronic, portraying a tumultuous stillness as the men sit still, trying to figure out their next move. Cinematic in effect, the scene freezes with the sitting men in the forefront—the only action an inner and private one.

If this one chapter were all that Steinbeck ever wrote about the Oklahoma Dust Bowl, it would still stand as a literary monument, a poetic landmark of a period in American history. True, it does not tell a particularized story, but it does set the tone and establish the mood of these desperate times. It does so in the voice of a narrator who knows and cares intensely about the plight of both the land and the people who inhabit it. He knows the wounding of the earth as it lies prey to erosion by rain, wind, and plow. He knows the anxiety of the women as they stand by their men, waiting to see whether or not their spirits are broken this time; of the children as they observe parents weighed down by natural disaster and exploitation; and of the vigorous, work-hardened tenant farmers—forced to sit, though unaccustomed to stillness, and to figure what to do.

The first, most immediate link between this expository chapter , which portrays the general backdrop of the dust bowl's impact, and the next chapter, which begins the saga of the Joad family, is the use of color. But verbs, repetition, and scenic similarities likewise serve as links.

Vestiges of Steinbeck's use of color, image-creating verbs, repetition, and scenic similarities link this first narrative of the Joad family to the preceding general chapter 1. In place of "the red country" and a "sun as red as ripe new blood" depicted in the general chapter, "a huge red transport truck" stands parked before a small roadside restaurant (*Grapes* 5, 7, 9). Steinbeck establishes a sense of immediacy from the outset—the truck stands "in front of *the* little roadside restaurant," not "*a*" restaurant (*Grapes* 9). The impact of this choice is significant, drawing readers into a specific place at a specific point in time, in effect taking them there to witness the story firsthand. As image verbs depict the disaster in chapter 1, enabling readers to see, feel, and understand the dust bowl more fully, in chapter 2 they describe the inside of this restaurant, with scenic and cinematic effect: "a . . . fan *turned*"; "flies *buzzed*"; "the truck driver . . . *rested* his elbows on the counter"; "the flies *roared*"; "the coffee machine *spurted* steam [emphasis added]" (*Grapes* 9). Whereas "the men" in the concluding scene in chapter 1 "sat still—thinking—figuring," so the truck driver sits in this opening scene of chapter 2, his "smart listless language" parallel to their silence, and the stasis of the final scene in chapter 1 is replaced by an almost absurd roaring of flies and spurting of steam from the coffeepot. Note the specificity of the choice of "*the* coffee machine" rather than "*a*," drawing readers into an immediate scene (*Grapes* 8–9).

An important theme is introduced with the advent of Tom Joad, who is not identified, however, until about the middle of the chapter. Paroled from the McAlester State Penitentiary after being imprisoned for four years for manslaughter in self-defense, he is returning home and asks the driver of the red truck for a ride. Going against company policy, the driver yields to Tom's manipulative plea that he prove himself "a good guy" and gives him a ride. Such hospitable behavior is a key theme in *Grapes* and a family characteristic of the Joads. This opening narrative in which a truck driver proves to be "a good guy" points forward toward the very heart of *Grapes* as well as to a theme that runs through ancient Greek and Hebrew literature: those who are hospitable endear themselves to the gods, to God (*Grapes* 11).

The theme of hospitality as a defining quality of this family, then, is key and runs through the entire novel, to the end where the Joads—finally destitute with no work, no food, no shelter other than a barn, and winter upon them—still behave in character. There are other dialogic links in addition to color, image verbs, repetition, and theme.[2] In chapter 15, an interchapter, the setting is likewise a restaurant, with a waitress, a truck driver, and a slot machine. Just as Tom Joad needs a ride in chapter 2, a migrant man with two children needs bread in chapter 15—and both needs are hospitably met. Similarly, the truck drivers in both chapters prove to be good guys.

One of the most famous chapters in *Grapes*, interchapter 3, depicts a land turtle's arduous journey across a highway. This interchapter's description of movement of life along the edges of the highway—the turtle, the seed heads, the burrs of grasses, weeds, and clover that lay ready to attach to anything passing—links to chapter 2's portrayal of Tom Joad, who is heading home with feet crammed inside yellow shoes, part of the attire provided by the prison on his release. There is likewise an oblique color connection among chapter 1's depiction of the red country and the bloodred color of the sun, chapter 2's red truck, and this chapter's "red ant" that gets under the turtle's shell, only to be crushed (*Grapes* 19).

And the good-guy, bad-guy theme continues as well. A woman swerves to avoid hitting the turtle, and a man in small truck aims to hit it, succeeding only in flipping it over onto its back. Righting itself, the turtle drags dirt over seeds loosened from its shell and continues doggedly on its way, its progress undeterred by the sliding dust. Symbolic of the Joads and all others now dispossessed, with "his fierce, humorous eyes" the turtle is personified and presented so sympathetically that it gives a sense of the oneness of all things and reveals a mystical view similar to that of Saint Francis of Assisi, who admonished, "Tread softly. The rocks, too, are thy brothers" (*Grapes* 18). As a fellow traveler, Steinbeck implies, the turtle also deserves to be treated hospitably and gently.

Again there is an oblique connection between interchapter and narrative as color carries over from chapter 3 to the Joad narrative in chapter 4, with the turtle's "yellow toe nails" echoed in Tom Joad's "new yellow shoes" (*Grapes* 19, 20). Similarly, chapter 4 echoes chapter 1's general portrayal of the conditions during the Oklahoma Dust Bowl, when the dust blows with the movement of everything living—as high as a man's waist as he walks. Tom Joad is also accompanied by a cloud of dust kicked up by his feet. Another link between interchapter 3 and narrative chapter 4 occurs when the generalized land turtle in chapter 3 becomes a specific land turtle in chapter 4, a gift Tom wants to take home with him for his young brother, Winfield. Also, the turtle in chapter 3 has "a horny beak," an image echoed in the later description of the preacher Jim Casy's nose that is "beaked and hard" (*Grapes* 19, 22).

In this chapter Casy shares the experience from which he has just come—one similar to the experience of Christ in the wilderness but with Emersonian overtones—as he philosophizes that perhaps everyone is part of one soul. Tom tells Casy of his four-year stay in McAlester for homicide. And both reminisce about shared experiences at religious meetings and with members of the Joad family—Granma's speaking in "tongues" and her Christmas card, earning Tom the nickname of "Jesus Meek"; Pa's breaking his leg Jesus-jumping over a bush; and Uncle John's making himself sick by trying to eat an entire pig (*Grapes* 29). They also discuss the ruined corn crop in the fields, and Tom reveals his own family's continual exhaustion of their forty acres of land, which they depend on for a livelihood, by depleting it of nutrients. Readers have seen the result of such depletion from the outset of *Grapes*. When Tom and Casy get within sight of the Joad house, they realize it is empty and abandoned.

Chapters 1 and 5 open with settings, in the first, land to which "the last rains" come gently and in the fifth, landowners that come closed off in their cars to survey the condition of the land (*Grapes* 6). As these men let the dust of the earth run through their fingers and on occasion drill to test the soil, the narrator creates images of ravage and rape, with land as the helpless victim of human exploitation. Coming to give notice of eviction, the landowners tell the tenants the land is worn-out from monocropping the cotton, which has robbed vital nutrients from the soil. Although the tenants know crop rotation might restore the land, the owners assure them it is too late and describe a monstrous bank that breathes profits and eats interests, demanding an ever-increasing supply. To the men's protest that cotton will destroy the land comes the owners' assurance that when the land will no longer produce cotton, they will then sell it for housing development. In this interchapter, as in chapter 1, the tenant men have come into the dooryards, while the women and children stand silently watching them. The owners are the new and complicating factor here, adding the insult of eviction to the pain of desolation the people already feel.

Signaled by a spacebreak on the page, the narrator's voice—sympathetic to the plight of the tenant people—now shifts attention away from them to the land that lies prey to further exploitation and rapine. And the tone of this voice shifts from sympathy to outrage as the principles of contour farming are disregarded, and tractors come onto the land, plowing in straight furrows, without regard to houses or fences that might be in their way. In two sentences Steinbeck uses the word "straight" four times to emphasize this disregard for people and land (*Grapes* 38). Images of rape become explicit as the narrator describes land controlled and mutilated by iron, creating one of the most hideous images in literature.

> Behind the tractor rolled the shining disks, *cutting* the earth with *blades—not plowing but surgery*, pushing the cut earth to the right where the second row of disks *cut* it and pushed it to the left; *slicing blades* shining, polished by the *cut* earth. . . . Behind the harrows the long seeders—twelve *curved iron penes* erected in the foundry, *orgasms set by gears, raping methodically, raping without passion*. The driver sat in his iron seat and he was proud of the *straight* lines [emphasis added]. (*Grapes* 38–39)

The driver of the tractor is a robot, at one with his monstrous machine—not connected to the land, with no love for it. Like Gerard Manley Hopkins who grieves because the land is denuded and "foot [cannot] feel, being shod," in harsh poetics Steinbeck grieves for an earth violated and in pain.

Signaled by another spacebreak, the narrator's voice now combines the two scenes: the tenants and the land that some of them have inhabited for generations. When the tenant men remonstrate with the tractor driver because he has demolished their well, he responds that he had to keep his rows straight. The driver assures them that he is not the one responsible, that he only follows orders. Goggled and masked, he goes on his way, plowing in straight rows, knocking over a house, with the helpless tenants staring after him.

The Joad narrative continues in chapter 6, opening at the point at which interchapter 5 leaves off, with a tractor driver crushing a tenant house as the family watches. In chapter 6 Tom and Casy stand on a hill and look down at the Joad house—crushed in one corner and knocked off its foundation. Tom quickly assesses the scene, assuming that the family is gone or dead because the front door gate is standing open, and Ma always kept it closed to guard against intruding pigs, as one had gotten into a neighbor's house and eaten the baby.

The narrator catalogs the things left behind—debris left by children throwing rocks through the windows, various worn-out or discarded household items, and personal castoffs. He catalogs as well those things that are not there: no furniture in the kitchen, no stove, no bedroom furniture, nowhere to sit. Tom and Casy sit on the edge of the front porch, feet resting on the step, alternately focusing on past memories evoked by the place and then on figuring out why it has been laid to waste. Casy points out the place where he had baptized Tom, who was clinging fiercely to a little girl's pigtail all the while. Tom believes there may not be any neighbors around either, because a lean gray cat is still hanging around rather than moving on to another house.

The colors red and yellow, or gold, echo again in this chapter, connecting it to previous accounts. To illustrate, the sunset is a mixture of red and gold; the sun itself is red; Tom puts on his yellow shoes again; the dust glows red in the sunset; the sun is red as it slips over the horizon; after the sun sets, it leaves behind a bloodred fragment of cloud; and the blood of Muley's father is still on the ground where a bull had gored him to death. Further, there is the glow of the firelight and the lights of the approaching superintendent's car. Luridly and forlornly, these images mingle with the description of the mechanical rape of the land in interchapter 5. Human beings are dispossessed, and all nature grieves and suffers before the all-powerful, monstrous bank that breathes profits and eats interest.

The turtle again appears as Tom sets it free to continue its journey to the Southwest—a symbol of the resilience, determination, and courage of people who must likewise take this southwest journey. The image of interchapter 3's turtle with its "horny beak" links obliquely to the description here of "Muley's mouth . . . [with] a little parrot's beak in the middle of his upper lip," thus showing the interrelatedness of all things (*Grapes* 18, 50).

Muley's story of the dispossession of the Joads and their neighbors likewise links to chapter 5's depiction of the dispossession of the nameless tenant farm family. And Muley's sharing of his supper of newly killed rabbits with Tom and Casy is a thematic link to Tom Joad's exhortion to the truck driver to be "a good guy" by giving a ride to a stranger in need in chapter 2. Like the biblical distinction between sheep and goats, this key theme of hospitality that distinguishes the good from the bad runs throughout the novel.

The narrator's sympathetic portrayal of the land in interchapter 5 carries over into this chapter as Muley tells the story of the loss of his land, acknowledging that his family has misused and abused the soil. Fit only for grazing, the land has been depleted by cotton. It is evident that the Joads, the Graves, and their other neighbors have been forced into a westward flight to seek shelter, food, work, and a place to put down new roots and create a new home. Muley has already determined to stay behind, Tom worries because his parole requires residency in Oklahoma, and Casy now decides to go along, hoping that there will be room for him and an opportunity to preach along the way.

Evading the headlights of the superintendent's car and the spotlight by crouching in the cotton field, the three men head to Muley's favorite place to spend the night—a cave Tom and his brother, Noah, had dug as children. Muley sleeps in the cave, Tom settles on the ground, and Casy stays awake to puzzle over what is happening to him and to the people. As they rest, predatory birds fly over without making a sound—an aslant tie to the duplicity of the used-car salesmen, who are predators of a different stripe. In interchapter 7, the soundlessness of the birds is in contrast to the staccato babble of the sellers.

Chapter 7 opens with the voice of the narrator describing a used-car lot. In the last two sentences of the second paragraph down to the end of the third paragraph, this voice is interrupted by the staccato voices of used-car salesmen as they dupe the dispossessed tenant farmers into purchasing jalopies that are already worn-out. When the narrator's voice is heard again in the fourth paragraph and continues with the portrayal of used-car salesmen, there is another oblique tie to the predatory birds in chapter 6. The salesmen's eyes are like those of a hawk, sizing up the tenant families, looking for signs of weakness. In short fragments the narrator's voice, here coldly objective, intersperses with the sales pitch of the used-car lot. In effect, the narrator takes the reader to this place, displaying the essence of greedy owners who happily take advantage of dispossessed people forced to head across the country in search of a livelihood.

Chapter 8 echoes the previous chapters' depiction of the omnipresent dust during the Oklahoma Dust Bowl. As the chapter opens, although Tom and Casy cannot see the dust as they begin a predawn trek to Uncle John's place, they smell it and hear it as their feet in squeaky thuds break up dry dust clods as they walk. This narrative chapter is more directly tied to the previous interchapter by the Hudson sedan transformed into a truck that stands in Uncle John's yard. As Tom walks rapidly toward this hybrid vehicle, the dust rises up to his waist, a recurring image first introduced in chapter 1. And, as they hurry, the red of the sunrise is reflected in the redness of the feathers of two chickens in the yard. Later, even the dust under the truck where the two dogs are lying is red, coating their panting tongues. Al wears "red arm bands on his blue shirt" (*Grapes* 86). Threading through the novel, then, the color of red has a cumulative effect that is reminiscent of Homer's depiction of the rosy-fingered dawn in the *Iliad* and the *Odyssey*. Also, both the used-car lot and Uncle John's place have one-room houses—the one large enough for a desk, a chair, and a logbook for sales, and the other equally cramped for space, with a little lean-to as a kitchen.

In this chapter other members of the Joad family are introduced: Pa, Ma, Granma, Grampa, Noah, Al. Although he is showing signs of age, Pa, or Old Tom Joad, is still vigorous and almost boyish as he plans to surprise Ma with Tom's arrival. The portrayal of Ma's physical appearance, like Pa's, showing signs of age, gives way to a character study that establishes her as the true family head. The depiction of her traits reads like a biblical list of virtues: loving, joyous, peaceful, long-suffering, gentle, meek, kind. Granma, ferociously religious, and Grampa, lecherous and bellicose, together make a pair as grotesquely hilarious as ever graced a Shakespearean play for comic relief. Injured at birth when Pa had imprudently pried him from his mother's womb, Noah is different from other people, lacking passion of any kind. Al, the expert on car engines in the family, is Noah's opposite, described as "randy," always on the prowl in search of girls.

By his grace at breakfast, Casy's character is more fully developed, revealing a philosophy and theology that is half Christ's temptation in the wilderness and half Ralph Waldo Emerson's transparent-eyeball transcendentalism, which finds oneness, wholeness, and holiness in life itself. After breakfast the men gather, and Pa outlines their assets as they get ready for the journey to California in search of work and a new home: two hundred dollars and a sedan converted into a truck to carry people, clothing, and household essentials.

Another interchapter, chapter 9, is complementary to chapter 7's dramatic portrayal of a used-car lot, with a litany of people's loss not only of their livelihood but also of their past and their very identity: plow and harrow, seeder and hoe, a team of horses whose mane a little girl used to braid and adorn with red ribbons, household furniture, and mementos from a past from which they are being severed. As the novel reveals, people's lives are tied to and intertwined with place and time, and these people are losing their roots.

Again the narrator's voice is interspersed throughout the chapter, here alternating with the voices of dispossessed men, women, and children as they are uprooted and forced to leave behind a vital part of their lives. Again there are oblique color connections as well as complementary episodic ones—the red ornament for the horse's brow, reminiscent of the red ribbon the little girl used to tie on the horse's mane, and, metaphorically, the red earth to which the very identity of these tenant families turned migrants is tied. The goods they cannot take, they burn. Frenzied, they pile in cars weighted down with essentials for living and drive away, leaving dust hanging in the air. Steinbeck juxtaposes the word "dust" at the end of one sentence and the beginning of the next, thereby giving it double emphasis and import as an ever present enemy that adds insult to the physical and psychic injuries already inflicted. The tenants must go; the dust remains, echoing insistently and persistently through these Oklahoma chapters in the first third of the novel.

Narrative chapter 10 dramatizes and makes particular interchapter 9's litany of loss as the Joad family experiences their transformation from tenant farmers to migrants, with the Hudson truck now the center, the moving home, around which the family gathers. Ma is now the one who goes through boxes of letters and keepsakes, most of them to be left behind. Chapter 10 obliquely links to previous chapters as dust and color combine, with the Hudson leaving behind "a high whirling column of red dust" and with "windows reddening under the first color of the sun" as the Joad family leaves a familiar life behind and faces the unknown (*Grapes* 133, 156). Later an image that is to recur and that foreshadows the novel's end first appears as an identifying epithet for the pregnant girl, Rose of Sharon. Her smile here is "self-satisfied" and "complacent"—in the end to be transformed into "mysterious" as she both partakes of and gives the sacrament of suffering (*Grapes* 101).

In narration and dialogue the remainder of the Joad family comes on the scene, together with fuller development of all of the primary characters. Tom sounds like the preacher of Ecclesiastes as he advises Ma not to worry about the unknown that lies ahead on their journey to California but to take one day at a time. And Ma maintains that Casy appears to have been baptized because he has the appearance of one able to see through things. Casy is troubled because the whole country is being emptied of its inhabitants and determines to go where the people are going, hoping to find happiness working in the fields alongside them. Ruthie is twelve, approaching adolescence, and Winfield is ten. With her ash-blond hair in a crown of braids around her head, Rose of Sharon is proudly and self-assuredly married and pregnant; her husband, Connie, nineteen, quietly capable, takes his place in the gathering of men who must figure out their next move.

Lonely and cut off from others by guilt, blaming himself for his wife's death, given to fluctuation of extremes in his appetites, and generous to children as his atonement for these lapses, Uncle John must nevertheless assume a position of leadership alongside the other men in this patriarchal family, with Pa as its titular head. Sixteen-year-old Al assumes a respected position of leadership because of his knowledge of automobiles, having chosen the Hudson with great care and an eye to its capability to stand up to the tortuous trip to California. The Hudson itself becomes a living entity whose condition must be constantly monitored, for it is now the center around which the family gathers.

At the men's tactical gathering with the women and children on the outskirts of their circle, Ma early on emerges as a moral leader in the family as Pa defers to her the question of Casy's going with them. Her hospitable response is at the heart of this novel's major theme of hospitality, a measure by which this novel separates good people from bad—like the biblical division between sheep and goats. Ma responds to Pa's query with the dignity of moral fortitude, maintaining that Joads and Hazletts do not turn hungry people away or pass by those on the road who need a lift—their families have never been this mean.

Deciding to leave before their meager funds run out, they slaughter the pigs, salt them down, pack up, and get ready to leave. Muley Graves comes to tell them good-bye but cannot be persuaded to join them, and Grampa decides that he is not going, so that Ma and Tom have to sedate him with cough syrup in a cup of strong black coffee. Although Ma resignedly looks straight ahead as they pull out, those on top do gaze back at Uncle John's house and barn in the reddening dawn, with Muley looking lonely and forsaken as he watches them leave.

Interchapter 11 supplies a fitting end to the Oklahoma section of the novel with images of cold tractors replacing warm horses and vacant and deteriorating houses. As chapter 10 closes with the Joads on top of the truck looking back at Uncle John's farm, interchapter 11 opens with houses and land left vacant as the migrants leave, thus tying the specific to the general as well as showing the aftermath of the dispossession of the tenants. The omniscient narrator contrasts a life that has just passed with the life that has come, pointing out that a vital relationship between humans and land has been severed with the coming of the tractors and agribusiness.

Reciting parts of the chemical makeup of humans and land—nitrates, phosphates, carbon—he maintains that both are more than chemistry or any of the elements by which they may be analyzed. On the one hand, knowledge and love foster an understanding between person and land that chemistry cannot, while on the other, cold chemistry leads to contempt for the person as well as the land. As the relationship to the land is severed, the human, too, is cutoff, no longer at home; and the tractor driver, a robot on a machine, has thus lost a vital part of his humanity.

There is a sense of immediacy as the narrator draws the deterioration of the empty houses across a time sequence, beginning with "the evening of the first day," moving to "when the night came," to "now there came a little shower," to "on a night," and "the midday sun" (*Grapes* 118). Meanwhile, the cats, which once meowed for human response, are now totally dependent on their own hunting and have become wild, not coming to the door any longer. The houses are now frequented by gophers, mice, weasels, and owls, whose destruction is relentless and rapid.

As chapter 1 opened the Oklahoma section and as chapter 11 showed the aftermath of the tenants' dispossession as reflected in the landscape, interchapter 12 opens the second major phase of the novel—the journey to California. The narrator's depiction of "the red lands and the gray lands" echoes chapter 1 and the color red that runs like a thread through the novel. The narrator's voice is that of a poetic bard, with the incremental repetition of "Highway 66" and "66" throughout (*Grapes* 119–23). Also, there is a mournful, repetitive refrain near the chapter's end, underscoring the plight of migrant children with insufficient sustenance. A little boy named Danny sits in the backseat of a migrant car, complaining of thirst and begging for a drink of water. Four times the bard repeats the boy's request for the most basic of human needs. Once more the dangerously overheated cars of the migrants take center stage as the men listen with fixed attention and apprehension to any fluctuations in the sounds of motors and tires, fearing a complete breakdown and the exhaustion of their already meager funds. And once more the owners and sellers take advantage of their plight, and the hot, thirsty child in the backseat must wait for his drink of water.

The chapter ends with an unbelievable, uplifting incident that actually happened, the narrator tells us, and it returns to a key theme of hospitality. Delightedly the narrator tells this story of kind, courageous people. A dispossessed man, his wife, and ten children with no car load their belongings on a homemade trailer and wait beside Highway 66 where a stranger stops to take them along with his own family. He pulls their trailer with seven of them on top, accommodating the other five in his sedan, and takes care of their needs for food and shelter on their trip to California. This story, the narrator concludes, helps us to hold on to faith.

Following two interchapters that close the Oklahoma section of the novel, chapter 13 introduces the journey section, the terrifying flight of thousands of migrants across the country on Highway 66. The Joads' experience with their Hudson links with the more generalized problems of other migrants. As the Joads leave Oklahoma, the fields in the scorching sun are red, creating a heat mirage of vibration. Al, like the generalized migrant men in chapter 12, listens closely for any changes in the sounds of the car that may indicate trouble.

The hospitality theme with which chapter 12 closes continues as Ma assures Al that their inclusion of Casy on this trip is a good thing. Their dog is killed when they stop for water and gas, leaving Rose of Sharon frightened that witnessing its death may harm her unborn child, but Ma reassures her, urging her not to be so centered on herself. When they camp for the night, they meet the Wilsons who lend their tent for Grampa's illness. When Grampa dies, Sairy Wilson gives them her quilt to wrap his body, and they bury him in a field alongside the road. Ma again reassures Rose of Sharon, who is frightened once more by death. The hospitality theme is furthered by neighborly sharing between the Wilsons, who offer their tent and a quilt, and the Joads, who offer their food and Al's expertise in car repair. They agree to travel together, each helping the other—an echo of the stranger in chapter 12 who takes a family of twelve with him to California, providing for their needs. But the chapter ends with an aura of gloom, sharply focusing on Sairy Wilson whose pain keeps her awake.

In the first of two sections, interchapter 14 echoes the stance of the wakeful Sairy Wilson bracing herself to endure her pain. Like Sairy, Western states are apprehensive and nervous as they brace themselves against inevitable change brought about by the influx of the dispossessed. This section also includes images of prisoners of war, killed like pigs and left bleeding on the ground, an oblique tie to the Joads' slaughtering of pigs and dead dog lying bleeding by the road. The narrator's voice is again that of a poetic bard, or a folksinger, biblical or Whitmanesque in tone and beat, with incremental repetition of selected key words and phrases: "nervous" and "results, not causes." Echoing words have the effect of poetic refrains: "and know it and know it. . . . This you may know" (*Grapes* 151–53). This bardic voice, although ominous in its depiction of human atrocities, is nevertheless hopeful and optimistic about the human potential to overcome.

The second section of this chapter also opens with the narrator's voice, drawing on the image of nervousness developed in the first section, cataloging the states involved in the mass migration, then shifting the scene to one dispossessed family. With this shift, the voice changes to that of the migrants themselves, who address the reader directly, explaining what has happened to them. They admit that if they owned the tractor, it would no longer be an enemy, but as it is, the tractor's use is the same as a tank's in wartime, driving them off the land. Again there is a shift in voices as the narrator depicts the loneliness and bewilderment of one person, one family. Joining with others, however, alleviates the perplexity and isolation as they help one another, consoling and sharing meager resources. As in earlier chapters and in those to follow, the needs of the migrant children receive prominent attention, with one family giving away a treasured blanket that had belonged to a mother who is probably dead, to provide warmth for a sick baby.

In a paragraph of direct address to those who own the necessities of life, like the biblical prophet Nathan who points the finger of blame at King David, this bardic narrator warns that these owners must seek to discover why this swarm of people has come across the country in search of a home. He likewise warns that there will be dire consequences for withholding sustenance from starving people. With a poetic envelope effect, the speaker comes back full circle to the image of the nervous West as he observes "a half-million people moving over the country; a million more, . . . ten million more." The chapter closes with a cinematic image of tractors plowing empty land.

Interchapter 15 is both structurally and thematically the center of the novel. The focus shifts from the previous chapter's panoramic depiction of the westward movement of millions of homeless people to one hamburger stand and one migrant family's experience there. The narrator's tone has shifted, too, from bardic prophecy of gloom to journalistic description of "hamburger stands" along Highway 66, cataloging their contents, advertisement posters, jukebox sounds and hissings of the griddles as hamburgers fry. Here hospitality is for sale, but the waitress and cook, Mae and Al, prove to be on the side of good people as they provide a migrant man with bread and his children with candy canes at reduced prices. The red stripes on the peppermint candy sticks obliquely echo the red thread running through the novel.

With the journalist's eye for detail, the narrator records for the reader the names of the large, fine cars: Cadillacs, Zephyrs, La Salles. These cars cruise easily past the migrants' loaded down, fixed up jalopies, half truck, half car. He describes the women in these large cars as self-satisfied, self-centered, "sullen," and "pouting" and the men as "worried," "restless," trying to convince themselves that their business is honest, not corrupt. The waitress, Mae, calls them "shitheels." Although she and Al are generous to the migrant man in his need, Al displays shoddy moral fiber as he plays out the slot machine that is about ready to deliver a win, placing the retrieved money in the cash register. The businessmen's and the cook's dishonesty stands in contrast to the theme of hospitality, with vice running alongside virtue here as elsewhere in the novel. Like those who pass by on the other side in the parable of the good samaritan, well-heeled travelers whiz "viciously" past the migrants on Highway 66—culpable for passing by the needy strangers among them. Those who turn aside and refuse to see their plight, this bard implies, share in a dreadful guilt (*Grapes* 155–56, 163).

Narrative chapter 16 links to interchapter 15 in its sharply defined contrast between travelers and migrants. In the closing line of interchapter 15, the cars of the travelers are whizzing along viciously on Highway 66; in the opening line of chapter 16, the Joads and the Wilsons are crawling westward. The contrast here is between both people and mode of travel. The adverb "viciously" describes not cars but passengers, who by implication are self-centered, self-satisfied, inhospitable, oblivious by choice to the desperate plight of those traveling with them. Whereas the rich cars whiz by, the cars of the migrants "crawl"—a verb used like a refrain throughout the novel. Turtles, Joads, Wilsons, cars, people, and trucks all crawl. The poetic impact of this repetition throughout the novel is incremental so that the laborious, enforced movement becomes relentless, inexorable. In order to survive, these migrants must keep crawling toward California, where they believe their hopes for the future lie.

Henry Thornton Moore proclaims Steinbeck to be "the poet of our dispossessed,"[3] and this chapter's incremental repetitions and bardic narrative voice contribute to the reader's impression at times that this novel has much in common with great epic poetry and that Steinbeck is indeed a poet. This poetic repetition and tone may be observed in a passage that maps out the progression of the migrants' journey, with linebreaks added here for illustrative purposes.

The land rolled like great stationary ground swells.

Wildorado and Vega and Boise and Glemio.

That's the end of Texas.

New Mexico and the mountains.

In the far distance,

waved up against the sky, the mountains stood.

And the wheels of the cars creaked around,

and the engines were hot,

and the steam spurted around the radiator caps.

They crawled to the Pecos river, and crossed at Santa Rosa.

And they went on for twenty miles (*Grapes* 164).

The sweeping immensity and grandeur of the land and the courage of the migrants in making a journey for which they are ill equipped likewise speak to the heroic, epic qualities of *Grapes*.

As the Joads' truck and the Wilsons' "touring car" head westward, Rose of Sharon shares with Ma Connie's dreams of studying to get ahead and their hopes of having a house to live in and a doctor for their baby's birth. Ma realizes that these dreams have no substance. When the Wilsons' car breaks down, Al pulls up beside "a huge *red* billboard," his face turning an angry *red* [emphasis added]—ties to the use of red that runs from the beginning of *Grapes* with its red country to the end with petals torn from a bedraggled red geranium (*Grapes* 167).

Holding a jack handle, Ma threatens the men of the family if they try to break up into two groups, one to repair the Wilsons' car and the other to keep going toward California in the hope of getting work and settling down. Realizing that Ma will not back down, they yield to her demand that they stay together. At this point she becomes the substantive leader of the family. Although Pa seems to fade into the backgound, his role in the end reveals the emergence of an equitable relationship, with Pa and Ma working together for the good of the family. Al, Tom, and Casy stay to repair the Wilsons' car while those on the truck go ahead to find a place to camp. Granma's health worsens, and Casy shares his vision of helping the vast pilgrimage of migrants if he can. Although the proprietor of the camp where the truck parks will not allow the car to remain without pay, Tom stays long enough to hear a man returning from California tell of his failed search for work there. Again there is an oblique color tie, for the man has *red*, watery eyes from nervous giggling and coughing. Connie and Rose of Sharon sleep in the open, and Al stays behind with the family and the Wilsons while Tom, Casy, and Uncle John go to find a place to rest for the night, the car's headlights shining dimly on the road ahead.

Interchapter 17 echoes narrative chapter 16's implication that the migrants' cars as a whole are derelicts, with headlights that shine weakly, leaving the road ahead dim. Again the voice of a bard draws attention to the crawling cars of the migrants. He intensifies this crawling image by an analogy, comparing the cars to bugs that scuttle along by day and cluster together by night. But it is the cars, not the people, which are compared to bugs. These migrants are people who build a community and establish laws for their camping places, thus establishing social life and courtesies to guide their associations with one another. And he describes conversations in which they share memories of homes left behind and hopes, dreams, and aspirations for the future. He portrays as well their entertainments, guitar playing and singing. The ability to pick a guitar is "a gracious thing," he asserts—with the adjective "gracious" reflecting the whole scene that he has just drawn, for graciousness is an essential attribute of such community building (*Grapes* 200). The chapter's closing sentence is a poetic echo of the first sentence's analogy comparing their cars to bugs, with the cars again crawling, buglike, in contrast to the vicious whizzing of the big cars in interchapter 15.

Chapter 18 follows appropriately from the preceding general chapter, the image shifting easily from cars that crawl to the Joad family who slowly move west. The gracious community established by the migrants in the evening stands in sharp contrast to the harshness, even rudeness, of law enforcement officers who never offer help, but always move them on. Then the narrator poetically repeats the image verb that has come to show the persistence and doggedness of the westward migration: "They crawled. . . . And they crawled" (*Grapes* 201). They stop beside a river just over the Arizona border into California, looking backward at the murderous mountains just crossed and forward to the desert lying before them.

Bathing in the river, the men encounter a father and son who are returning from California. The man assures the Joads they will find no dependable jobs, only inhospitable people who want to be rid of them. He tells them about a newspaperman who owns a million acres near the coast, which are protected by armed guards, and about orchards of orange trees similarly guarded. Distressed by this account of conditions, Pa seeks advice from Uncle John, who responds pragmatically that there is no need thinking about it because they are already on their way. If there is work, they will work. If not, they will sit.

Noah decides to leave the family at this point, going off along the river alone. Granma is sick and delirious, but Ma rejects a Jehovite woman's offer to hold a prayer meeting for her. Insulted, the woman retires to her own tent to gather a prayer group anyway. Eerily this group howls, wails, and bays. Ma is shamed when Granma falls into an easy sleep. In response to a loud, rude marshal who calls them "Okies" and demands that they leave by morning, Ma angrily picks up a skillet and orders him to be silent (*Grapes* 214).

As Ma works to prepare for the night desert crossing, she prays for a suitable place where the family can rest, where she can wash clothes and cook meals, where they will not be as disheartened as they are now. Desperately ill, Sairy Wilson is unable to make the trip across the desert, and Casy reluctantly prays with her. In a scene reminiscent of the Israelites preparing for their flight from Egypt, the Joads eat standing up. They leave two dollars and a skillet of meat with potatoes for the Wilsons—another enactment of the theme of hospitality and gracious sharing.

At the gas station the attendants view the Joads as some inhuman species, too ignorant to recognize the foolishness and danger of trying to cross the desert at night in their noisy and decrepit old car. With an engine that is soon boiling, they go slowly through barren land that is white or gray. In a rhetorical color tie that runs obliquely through the novel, red contributes to a lurid scene of land burned by the sun and hills blackened like cinder, highlighted by the red glow of the sunset. Red is again repeated as time, space, and movement are juxtaposed: "The truck moved on into the evening, and the edge of the sun struck the rough horizon and turned the desert red" (*Grapes* 222). And as they cross this barren land, they think of the dying Sairy Wilson whom they had to leave behind.

On this final leg of the journey, Uncle John and Casy talk about sin; Connie and Rose of Sharon make love under the cover of darkness; and Ma tends to Granma, who dies during the crossing. When they stop for inspection, Ma tells the officers that Granma is sick and needs a doctor. Seeing Granma's white face, the officers let them go on. Heroically, Ma does not tell the family that Granma is dead until they get across the desert and crawl up the mountain, from which they can finally look down in awe on the riches of the enormous valley, with vineyards, orchards, and fields of grain. The recurring red motif appears here in the "red roofs" of houses and barns (*Grapes* 227). With forty dollars left, they set out to find a coroner so that they can bury Granma decently. Thus ends the second part of this three-part novel—the journey to California. What remains in the final third is the account of their experiences in what for them turns out to be a dystopia, rather than a utopia.

Interchapter 19 is part poetry, part history, part fiction. The poetic elements of this chapter are reminiscent of Walt Whitman's *Leaves of Grass*, the primary difference lying in Whitman's use of the poetic line and Steinbeck's use of the prose paragraph. Repetition is one of these poetic elements, with the word "land" occurring nine times in the first three paragraphs and its synonyms occurring six times: "earth" (used twice), "a rich acre," "the dear acres," and "farms" (used twice). Coordinate and parallel structures also contribute to the poetic effect, with four sentences beginning with "And" (*Grapes* 231–32).

History and fiction blend in this chapter, then, and create the kind of dramatic poetry that Aristotle declares to be truer than history because history is primarily a recording of facts whereas poetry gives a glimpse of what ought to be as well as what is. Steinbeck catalogs those who have possessed California: Mexicans; American "squatters"; "owners"; "little shopkeepers of crops"; industrial owners who "imported serfs" to work the land; and finally storekeepers who forgot the land altogether as they zealously guarded their margins of profit by exploiting workers (*Grapes* 231–32). In describing the plight of these workers, the observant narrator moves from the general to the specific, focusing first on homeless migrants. Then he telescopes the focus on one hungry, homeless couple with their emaciated children in their car, which is their only home. He follows the nameless, representative man's experiences from observing land that lies fallow and unused, a sin against his hungry children, to taking up citizenship in Hooverville camps for the impoverished and destitute on the edges of every town.

The conversations among these migrants are typical of those who had once considered themselves farmers of land that could be used to feed their families. But they will not be permitted access to such land here. Law officers protect the rights of landowners and stand guard over their property, ready to destroy any crops the migrants may try to raise surreptitiously or to shoot any of them who may try to take an orange from a pile dumped because of deflated prices. The chapter ends with a child dying from malnutrition. The migrants contribute from their meager funds for his burial and pray for sustenance for their own children, while the owners become more uneasy, realizing that a time will come when the praying stops.

This action-packed narrative chapter 20 moves from chapter 19's general account of the Hoovervilles to the Joads' first experience at a Hooverville encampment—a grotesque assortment of tents and improvised flotsam and jetsam gleaned from the city dump. Forced to leave Granma's body in Bakersfield for a pauper's burial, they encounter here an odd assortment of people as grotesque as their surroundings: a woman with braided gray hair, her face drawn and peaked, her eyes expressionless, her lips drooping slackly; a man with a beard who is demented from abuse; Floyd Knowles, a young man repairing his old Buick who has been searching for work for three weeks to no avail; hungry children who gather around

Ma as she prepares supper, hoping for a handout; a big woman who scolds Ma for preparing stew in front of her hungry children; and two carloads of discouraged migrants who return after looking for work.

In contrast, a contractor and deputy sheriff arrive in a new car, the contractor dressed in khakis and flannel and wearing a hat. The scene turns ugly when Floyd asks about the contractor's license and wages, prompting the deputy to claim that he saw Floyd at the scene of a robbery. In the ensuing fight, Floyd socks the deputy, Tom trips him, and the deputy misses a shot at Floyd, the bullet severing the knuckles from a woman's hand. To prevent the deputy's shooting again, Casy kicks his neck, and he falls unconscious. Casy insists that Tom and Al leave, taking on the full blame and getting into the car with the arresting officers.

The family's condition deteriorates precipitously from this point. Connie leaves. Feeling sad about Casy and his own sins, Uncle John goes off to get drunk. Ruthie and Winfield play at being drunk. The family has to leave this Hooverville before they are settled in, for the camp is to be burned in the night because of the incident with the deputy sheriff. Encountering a roadblock on their way out, Tom struggles to stay calm, to play the subservient in order to avoid trouble. In one of Ma's most notable speeches, she assures him that ordinary people like themselves will keep on going and that changes are coming.

The word "crawl," which has up to this point described the pace of the overloaded, decrepit vehicles of the migrants, here takes a different metaphorical twist as Tom assures Ma that the men at the roadblock have not succeeded in making them go north. "We still go where we want, even if we got to *crawl* for the right [emphasis added]" (*Grapes* 281). Here "crawl" describes the human spirit, forced into subservience and acquiescence, yet also silently rebelling. The final sentence in this chapter returns to the Hudson sedan's headlights that are so dim and weak that the Joads have to *feel* their way through the darkness. It is night, the highway lies black ahead of them, and the image drawn by the verb "feel" is that of a blind person who cannot *see* ahead and, therefore, must *feel* the way. Just as a blind person is uncertain of the terrain just ahead, so the Joads, like the children of Israel in their exodus, are homeless strangers in an unknown land, uncertain of what lies ahead.

Interchapter 21 is in the voice of a bardic storyteller. With incremental progression the story of the migrants moves from generalities to specifics, giving weight and emphasis to the relative stability of their previous lives as sharecroppers in contrast to the rootless wanderings that characterize their present lives. Arranging a passage to highlight its repetition and parallel structure shows the incremental design:

Those families *which had lived on* a little piece of land,

who had lived and died on forty acres,

had eaten or starved on the produce of forty acres,

had now the whole West *to rove in* [emphasis added] (*Grapes* 282).

Again the verb "rove" provides an image capturing the migrant experience, for those who rove have no set destinations, no goals. Blown about, with no roots to hold them, the migrants' plight is to go from one place to another in search of home and work, with no real sense of direction.

The bardic voice also speaks in metaphor. Again a passage is arranged to show poetic parallels:

The highways were streams of people,

and the ditch banks were lines of people (*Grapes* 282).

The noun "stream" then transforms into a verb that is repeated twice. With the addition of the verb "swarm" to depict their movement and of the concluding simile that compares their movement to ants, the voice gives the general impression of the unending, incessant movement of a hoard of people toward the West.

Along with this incessant movement, this chapter emphasizes the resulting changes in the migrants and in the clerks, storekeepers, farmers, banks, companies, and large landowners of the West. The latter group is frightened by the hunger and need of the multitude of people flooding into the West and determines to protect itself from the intrusion of strangers. In the midst of great wealth and plenty, which is largely being taken over by the large landowners, the migrants must endure their own hunger together with the unmet needs of their starving, ragged children. Echoing the novel's title, the bard observes quietly that their anger has begun fermenting.

The stranger motif runs throughout the novel, from Tom Joad's initial encounter with the truck driver in chapter two to the starving man in chapter thirty. It is a part of the theme of hospitality and echoes the biblical injunction of Christ: "I was a stranger, and ye took me in; naked, and ye clothed me." The motif and theme also fit with the ancient Greek beliefs in and prescriptions for civil and civilized behavior, for the god Zeus is the god of hospitality. And in the Bible are accounts of entertaining strangers who are in actuality angels. The solemnity of the bardic voice gives poetic emphasis to this universal theme.

Narrative chapter 22 takes up where chapter 20 ended with the Joad car's headlights dimly illuminating the black highway ahead. Late at night they finally arrive at Weedpatch Camp, modeled after a similar camp run by Tom Collins, to whom the novel is dedicated, along with Steinbeck's first wife, Carol. This camp is a high place in the Joads' experiences, and everything hereafter will be in stark, tragic contrast. Here Steinbeck provides a model of how things could be in a hospitable, well-run, well-equipped camp, with indoor plumbing and hot water. It is self-governed, with the migrants establishing and enforcing their own laws. In one of the warm, hospitable scenes that are interspersed among the horrors of dispossession and life on the road, Tom meets the Wallace family: Wilkie and Timothy Wallace, father and son, and Timothy's young wife, who carries a nursing baby under her shirt as she prepares breakfast. Highly memorable and symbolic, this scene brings together the novel's theme of hospitality and of the nurturing mother, a scene to be repeated in the novel's ending, with a twist both sacred and grotesque. The Wallaces share both their breakfast and their work with Tom, and their employer Mr. Thomas warns them of a plot to start a riot at the camp's Saturday dance, which will provide an excuse to shut down the camp.

In a moment of comic relief from the Joads' downward spiral, Ruthie and Winfield discover indoor plumbing. When Winfield inadvertently flushes a toilet, both children think that he has broken it. Ma especially revels in the readily available hot water, washtubs, and showers. When Jim Rawley, the camp manager, comes to call, her innate graciousness, kindliness, and hospitality come into play, and she is thrilled and proud because he takes a cup of her coffee and compliments her. She has become so steeled against cold inhospitality that she chokes back tears on being treated like a person again. Al is intrigued by a house trailer in which people can live wherever they stop, but Ma reiterates her desire for a small house.

The kindness and courtesy restore Ma's sense of familial identity, and she reminisces that the Joads have always been a proud people, not having to look up to anybody, that their great-grandfather fought in the Revolutionary War, and that they had been farmers until they had to go into debt. Since then, she muses, they have been downtrodden and dispirited, making it hard to retain their heritage of dignity and kindness. She states further that at this camp there are people just like themselves, that the manager has visited with her, complimented her coffee, and addressed her by the cherished title "Mrs.," so that once more she feels human.

A shadow is cast over the general sense of well being when a religious fanatic sees Rose of Sharon smilingly caressing her abdomen and the growing child within. She warns her against clutch-and-hug dancing, declaring that it is a sin that will cause her to lose the baby. Ma comforts her distraught daughter.

The Ladies' Committee comes for a lengthy visit to initiate the Joads into their circle's customs and rules. They tell them a story of Number Four's using so much toilet paper that they suspect theft. Overhearing this account, a woman tells them that her five daughters have had diarrhea from eating green grapes because they were out of food and money. She has been too embarrassed to tell the committee before. They scold her for letting her daughters go hungry, remind her of camp provisions for such emergencies, and send her to get groceries for her family. They also remind her that this is not charity because she will pay for the goods when she can.

When Ruthie bullies her way into the middle of a croquet game, all the children leave the court, and she is left to play alone. To her surprise Winfield joins the other children who stand back to watch her play, and she finally runs home in tears. The female supervisor warns them to be polite and let her play when she returns.

Looking for work, the men observe the beauty and fertility of California: walnut trees whose branches arch over the road, vineyards with clusters of grapes just beginning to form, peach trees with ripening fruit. But they also observe its protectiveness and inhospitality, with each orchard's entrance having No Help Needed and No Trespassing signs. In contrast to this ominous reception, Al stops to give a man a ride back to the camp. As they return, Uncle John moans about his aches and his sins, feeling that he ought to go away lest he bring bad fortune to the family. Encouraging him to stay with them, Pa reminds him that they have already lost too many people: Grampa's and Granma's death, Noah's and Connie's desertion, and Casy's imprisonment. Pa dreads telling Ma they have not found work, and Al reiterates his desire to go his own way to find work in a garage.

Ma and Rose of Sharon are elated after the visit from the Ladies' Committee because Rose of Sharon is to work in the nursery so that she can learn how to take care of babies, and Ma dreams about how nice it would be if the men find work so that she can provide better for the family's comfort. When the fanatically religious woman who upset Rose of Sharon returns, Ma threatens to strike her with a stick if she comes around again. Howling, the woman falls to the ground in a fit of hysteria. The manager has her carried to her tent, telling Ma that she is not well.

When they return, Pa is ashamed as he admits that they found no work. He and Ma reminisce about their experiences thus far on the road, about the home they have left behind, and about the signs in nature that always made them say winter is going to come early. When Pa goes to consult with Al about buying a tire, Uncle John, pessimistic as always, states flatly that there is no work and that maybe Tom did not leave for work at all—that perhaps he has gone off just as Noah and Connie did. Confidently telling him that Tom *is* working and *will* return in the evening, Ma sends John to find Pa and go to the store to buy something good for supper.

This interchapter 23 documents the simple pleasures of the migrants: jokes, storytelling, music, dancing, occasional movies or drinking sprees, baptisms. But it follows from chapter 22 with its opening depiction of the migrant men as they scuttle and scrabble in their desperate search for work, echoing the experience of the Joads and the other campers at the Weedpatch Camp. The voice of the bardic speaker's poetic account is broken by spaces into five sections. The first section is for the storytellers. One, who claims to have been recruited to fight Geronimo, tells the story of a young brave, who stood on the top of a ridge with his outline carved sharply in the sunlight, and describes the effects on those who shot him: the feeling that they have destroyed something better than themselves. Another recounts the plot of the movie he has just seen—a rich man and a rich woman pretending to be poor so that they can find someone to love them for themselves, not their money.

The second section is for the drinker and describes the experience of drunkenness when life becomes bearable though death is a close companion even in the stupor of sleep. The third section begins with an accolade to the harmonica: its multiple tones like a reed pipe, bagpipes, or an organ; its ready availability, kept in a pocket; its versatility, always with new possibilities of tone; its price, only a quarter, so that if it gets lost or broken, a person can buy another one. This accolade is followed by a similarly poetic description of a guitar that is of more value than the harmonica because it must be learned. It is also more highly valued because it is passed down from father to son, along with lessons on how to play it. Next in this small catalog of the migrants' musical instruments is the violin, or fiddle, more highly valued even than the guitar but harder to learn. The bard praises its shrillness that is like the wind and its longevity, for the instrument is rumored to last as long as four hundred years.

The three instruments join in a reel, and there follows another noteworthy passage that describes graceful, invigorated dancing. Note the effect of the poetic immediacy of the demonstrative pronouns pointing out the dancers—"*that* Texas boy" and "*that* Cherokee girl"—so that the narrator is an observer and commentator alongside the reader, in effect making both participants in the scene (*Grapes* 329). The fourth section depicts the preacher convincing the people of their sins and baptizing them. The children, newly baptized, wish to know what sins are so that they can try them out. The fifth section is a culminating description of migrants who seek pleasure along their journey.

In chapter 24 the narrative returns to the account of the Joad family's experience in the Weedpatch Camp, linked to the previous interchapter by the camp residents' preparation for a Saturday night dance and a catalog of activity: washing dresses, overalls, and shirts; bathing children; lighting the dance floor; adults bathing; braiding and ribboning hair; cleaning up after the evening meal; practicing the guitar, harmonica, and fiddle. (The latter links this chapter specifically to the previous chapter's accolades to these instruments, along with other, more oblique links, such as Jule Vitela, who is half Cherokee.) In addition, the Central Committee has laid intricate plans to thwart an attempt to start a riot, a preliminary to closing the camp. Interspersed with this activity is talk of shoddy treatment and poor accommodations outside the government camps. Although the chapter is generally upbeat, occasional ominous notes indicate that all is not well with the Joad family despite the hospitable atmosphere, good accommodations, and anticipated pleasures of the dance. Anxious to get to the platform where the dance is to take place, Ruthie and Winfield hurriedly eat a meager dinner.

Against the carnival-like backdrop of shrilling, whining music and the whirling movement of the square dancers, Tom and others on the Men's Central Committee quietly stifle and remove three men who are to be paid for disrupting the dance. Addressing these intruders, Ezra Huston, chairman of the five men who make up the Central Committee, echoes the words of Christ on the cross, stating that the intruders do not have any idea what they are doing—words that Casy, too, will later use as he pleads with the men who will kill him. In a squatters' circle, Pa and the other men talk about the change that is coming and the possibility of uniting against oppressors and accusers. The color red is again repeated, and here it also shifts in meaning to the philosophical label for a Communist, or "Red."

Interchapter 25 begins with visions of the lush beauty and fruitfulness of California in the spring, but ironically concludes with images of wastefulness, starving and dying children, and angry people. In bardic tones, its conclusion echoes the novel's title, referring to the migrants' increasing anger at their own helplessness. Between this depiction of a California paradise and the desperation of its migrants, an all-observing narrator praises the men behind the technological advances in agriculture. But the result is, on the one hand, an agribusiness that drives small farmers first into an engulfing debt and finally off their farms so that they must join the dispossessed migrants on the road. On the other hand, the result is the destruction of crops and farm animals to keep prices up—spraying kerosene on piles of oranges, burning coffee and corn, dumping potatoes into the rivers and guarding them so that no one can fish them out.

It is this destruction that leads to Steinbeck's famous jeremiad, a lament for children who die with pellagra because prices and profits on oranges are kept high, letting them rot rather than giving them to those who are starving. The narrator speaks in prophetic tones of a crime beyond words and a sorrow too deep for tears—bringing failure to topple over any successes. The "there is" structure of parallel sentences in this passage reverberates like a tolling bell and intensifies the horror of this scene of rotting food and starving children: "There is a crime," "There is a sorrow," "There is a failure" (*Grapes* 348–49). And with the bardic speaker, the reader observes and feels this horror. The anger with which this interchapter ends is a relief from the intensity of the suffering, for the grapes of the migrants' wrath are beginning to ripen, ready for harvest.

Chapter 26 returns to the Joads' story. Like an ancient Greek play—moving straightforward with a dire sense of inevitability—it covers almost seventy-five pages of an unrelenting, precipitously downward spiral in the Joads' condition. The deprivation and desperation of the migrants in the preceding interchapter have foreshadowed their circumstances. When the men cannot find work near the Weedpatch Camp, Ma insists that they figure out their next move because both food and money are almost gone. The growing anger of migrants forced to watch their children starve in the interchapter is echoed here as Ma purposefully annoys Pa to keep him from giving up. In contrast, she tells Tom that she depends on him, knowing that he will not give up, no matter what, telling him that she senses a special, higher calling for him, probably from God, although she does not say so directly. His closeness to and affection for Casy up to the time of his death and later determination to carry on Casy's mission of helping people are in accord with Ma's premonition.

Fearing for the well-being of her unborn child because she has not had sufficient milk, Rose of Sharon is depressed, and Ma discovers that she has been eating a chunk of lime concealed in her pocket. In a rite of passage showing that she is a woman now, Ma gives her a pair of treasured gold earrings and pierces her ears so that she can look forward to wearing them. She assures her daughter that there is a special meaning in this ceremony shared between mother and daughter.

Because the family is leaving Weedpatch in search of work, Al must say good-bye to a pretty blond girl, assuring her that he will return in about a month with plenty of money to take her to the movies. Pa and Uncle John have their good-byes to say as well, joining the nightly gathering of the men by the manager's office. Tom sits on the edge of the dance floor with

Wilkie and Jule, discussing the trials that they have endured since their dispossession. Ruthie fears that there will be no croquet game where they are going.

In the morning Ma awakens them before dawn, giving them each a biscuit as they climb into the truck, announcing regretfully that they have nothing else. Tom drives, looking longingly at the all-night restaurants with their bountiful supply of hot coffee. Another echo carries over from the preceding interchapter's portrayal of starving migrant children, as Ma tells Tom that they need to have a house before the winter rains come because of Winfield's fragile health. Tom assures her that they will get a house. As the men repair a punctured tire, a man drives up to tell them that peach pickers are needed at the Hooper ranch.

Hopeful, the Joad family heads north for the ranch. Ecstatic, Ma immediately begins to make a mental note of the groceries and supplies that she needs to purchase: coffee, flour, baking powder, meat, soap, milk. She daydreams about renting a house even temporarily. Al dreams of having a job as a mechanic in a garage and of going to restaurants and the movies every night. Tom hopes there will be enough money for tobacco.

Their mood changes, however, when a policeman stops them to ask their destination and puts them in a line of cars waiting entrance to the ranch. Two policemen on motorcycles fall in behind the line, and two policemen in front escort them past a crowd of angry people standing in a ditch. Two men with shotguns stand on guard at the entry to the ranch. The peach camp itself is composed of fifty little boxlike houses, each with one door and one window. Their assigned dwelling is dirty and smelly. Treatment in the orchards is no more favorable, with Tom's first box of peaches rejected because of bruising. Winfield and Ruthie must also work, although she complains of being tired, and Ma is delayed because Rose of Sharon faints. Together they pick twenty boxes, earning one dollar. With a credit slip for the amount earned in her hand, Ma goes to the ranch store, only to discover that prices are set high to take further advantage of migrants who cannot afford to drive into town for groceries. Carrying out the thematic thread of hospitality that runs through the novel, the storekeeper pays for the sugar that Ma cannot afford, assuring her he will get his dime back when she is given a credit slip for tomorrow's wages.

Curious about the angry crowd that they had passed on their way into the ranch, Tom decides to investigate after supper. Ma sends them all to wash up, although without soap, which she could not afford, and then rations out hamburger patties, potatoes, and bread—food that will not be enough to satisfy their hunger. Tom takes an ill-fated walk to discover why the people at the gate are so angry and why so many police are present.

Temporarily turned aside by a guard who tells him these people are "Reds" and refuses to let him pass, Tom pretends to go back to their assigned boxhouse, takes a circuitous route, and finds a group of men with Casy among them. Casy urges Tom to try to get those inside the camp to come out because as soon as their strike is broken, the price of picking a box of peaches will be two and one-half cents, not five. Tom teases him about talking so much, not really comprehending the situation that Casy describes. When deputies come to break up the group, Casy tells them that they do not know what they are doing—an echo of Christ's words on the cross—and one of them deals him a lethal blow, killing him outright.

Blind with rage, Tom takes the club from the deputy and hits him four times on the head, killing him. Tom then receives a glancing blow to the face and flees down the stream. He returns to the boxhouse where he spends an uneasy, painful night. The next morning Tom tells Ma what has happened and announces his intention to leave so that he does not bring trouble on the family. Ma insists that he stay with them, deciding that they must leave when night comes. Rose of Sharon is hysterical because of what Tom has done, and Ruthie comes running in to tell them that Winfield has fainted. Ma insists that Pa take the credit slip for the day's earnings to buy milk to go on Winfield's mush; she then sneaks some of it to Rose of Sharon.

Then they leave the Hooper ranch, with Tom hidden under a mattress arched high enough for him to breathe. As they journey on back roads, Ma, Pa, and Tom discuss ominous indications of an early winter. Seeing signs advertising for cotton pickers, they stop, planning to set up house in a boxcar. Tom hides in a woods nearby, and Ma agrees to leave food for him in a culvert.

Interchapter 27 carries over from the previous narrative with a generic migrant experience of picking cotton. It opens with an image of roadside placards and orange flyers advertising for pickers. The reader is drawn in by the sense of immediacy and presence in the narrator's voice: jobs for which the migrants have been so desperately seeking are now "*here*," "up *this* road" (*Grapes* 406). But this extended promise of relief from the downward spiral they are experiencing grows dim, as the owners of the fields charge the migrants a dollar for a bag to hold cotton.

The narrator's tone grows more positive as he depicts the experience of cotton picking in minute detail. From the positioning of the bags so that both hands are free to pick, to the gradual increasing of the bags' weight, to the talking and singing among the migrants until bags get quite heavy, to the picking hands moving skillfully among the cotton bolls, the narrator draws a moving picture that positions readers as insiders in this experience.

Readers hear the story of the woman who had a black baby and could not hold her head up any more. They observe that the migrants find joy in this work, pleasure in a job well done, contentment in the presence of their children.

But the experience is soured by the profound distrust between the migrants and the owners—the former suspecting incorrect scales, the latter suspecting stones in bags to weigh them down. Descriptions of the omnipresent cotton, which clings to everything and forms balls that the wind blows along the road, give way to the circular movement of the chapter, a return to the highway signs and orange handbills that draw more migrants: fifty, five hundred, rumors of a thousand more. The migrant voices grow plaintive, wishing that the work would last a little while longer, dreading the search for enough work to sustain their families. Then come the cold warnings: try to save some money, winter is fast approaching, there will be no work of any kind when it arrives. Attention shifts to the immediacy of their tiredness at the end of the day and their anticipation of supper, perhaps with biscuits if the wives are not too tired.

Dramatic irony fills this interchapter, for the reader knows more than the migrant does about the broader implications and foreboding in the observation that cotton will soon ruin the land. And the reader senses the underlying current of pathos and heartbreak because the land is being raped, exploited, and forsaken. Aspiring to own or rent land, the migrant says that a person can move somewhere else when the land is exhausted from cotton. Underlying this story of dispossessed people, then, is a concern for ecological responsibility. For Steinbeck, the ancient question "Am I my brother's keeper?" expands in *Grapes* to include "Am I the keeper of the earth as well?" It is a question that Steinbeck does not answer, leaving it finally in the reader's hands, as does Toni Morrison in *Beloved*, a novel ending with an address to the reader: "Look. Look what you have in your hands now."

Narrative chapter 28 begins where interchapter 27 ends, with the migrants' return after a day's work in the cotton fields, in the Joads' case to one end of a boxcar, shared with another migrant family, the Wainwrights, on the other end. Here Ma maintains some semblance of housekeeping with a makeshift oilcan as a stove, a floor on which she can unroll the mattresses at night, and their tarpaulin hung across the middle for a modicum of privacy. The picking lasts long enough for them to purchase a better stove and some clothing. As in the previous interchapter, however, more migrants arrive in search of work and put up their tents. As long as the work holds out, they can go to the store for groceries and supplies and occasionally something for which they hunger: meat and milk for Rose of Sharon, syrup because Pa wants pancakes, and Cracker Jacks for Winfield and Ruthie.

Mrs. Wainwright pushes the dividing tarpaulin aside and peers in to compare their day's earnings—the Joads' three dollars and fifty-seven cents, the Wainwrights' four dollars. Each woman is pleased and absorbed in her supper preparations when Mrs. Wainwright smells her bacon burning and Winfield interrupts. As Mrs. Wainwright runs back to her side of the boxcar to tend to her burning bacon, Ma pulls Winfield aside to hear his story of Ruthie's fight, resulting in her boasting to her tormentor that her brother Tom has already killed two people and will kill her, too. Dismayed, Ma leaves Rose of Sharon to tend the supper while she goes to warn Tom.

The scene before her meeting with Tom is one in which all nature seems to join her mourning: falling leaves, a rising wind, black clouds moving and erasing the stars for a time, a scattering of raindrops, the lonesome sound of a violin penetrating the night sounds. As Muley slept in a cave earlier, Tom has fashioned a cave among blackberry bushes, perhaps symbolizing rebirth. There Ma tells him what Ruthie has done and reluctantly advises him to leave. Ma feels his face in the darkness, finding a prominent scar and a crooked nose. In the darkness she feels his face again, this time for the sake of remembering, and insists he take seven dollars that she has put aside for him.

Sitting there in the darkness, Tom shares his memories of Casy's talk about his wilderness experience. Although he was not really listening at the time, he now understands that a person does not amount to anything alone, and he remembers Casy's quotations from Ecclesiastes that illustrate the concept of strength to be gained from a companion. To his mother's query how she is to know about his welfare, Tom responds with the now famous words echoing Ralph Waldo Emerson's concept of the oversoul, of which everyone is part. He promises to be wherever people are needy and to find the family when things have blown over, and they say good-bye.

Although Ma maintains an iron control and does not cry, as in John Milton's "Lycidas," nature seems to join in her mourning as it begins to rain. She meets a man looking for cotton pickers and assures him that her family will be glad to pick. They discuss the association's fixed rate of payment, agreeing that it crowds out poor people. Hospitably, Ma tells the Wainwrights about the opportunity for work and offers them a ride on their truck, splitting the gas money. Afraid that his daughter Aggie will get pregnant, Mr. Wainwright shares with the Joads his concern that she is going out with Al every evening. Ma assures him that either she or Pa will talk to Al, later apologizing to Pa for taking this initiative. But Pa, spending a lot of his time craving a home that is no longer his, is now indifferent when she takes charge of family matters. Ma tries to comfort and reassure him, but he is worried about the approaching winter and Rose of Sharon's imminent delivery. Dejected, discouraged, fearful for the future, he can think of no way out of their dilemma.

Ma assures him that they will just keep on going in spite of hunger, sickness, even death. Take each day as it comes, she advises. With Al's announcement that he is going to marry Aggie, get a job in a garage, and rent a house for the two of them, the family's worries grow more intense. Ma entreats him to stay with them until spring, but he is reluctant. Jubilant, Mrs. Wainwright looks around the curtain to be sure that they have heard the news, and the two women plan a celebration of the engagement, with pancakes and syrup. Rose of Sharon goes outside to crawl into the bushes so that she can avoid festivities that remind her of her own former happiness with Connie, who has forsaken them.

Ma awakens the family early the next morning, and Rose of Sharon insists on going with them to pick cotton. When they arrive at the farm, the barnyard is already filled with cars. The slow, pale dawn and the owner's heavy jacket, buttoned up around his throat, remind the reader of the imminent winter as the migrants scrabble for the little remaining work. There are so many of them that the owner predicts the cotton will be picked before noon. Racing with the looming rain clouds overhead, the migrants literally run from row to row, competing for the picking, and it is over by eleven o'clock, as the owner had predicted. And the rain begins, soon increasing to a downpour, as Rose of Sharon lies under piles of blankets, chilled and ill from the day's work and exposure to the elements. The narrator shifts from a narrow focus on the Joads to a broad focus on other migrants who are huddled in boxcars listening to the pelting rain.

The final interchapter, 29, corresponds to chapter 1's description of conditions during the dust bowl and the disastrous event surrounding the dispossession of tenant farmers and precipitating their flight to California in search of work and home. But this chapter's California setting during winter rains when there is no work places the migrants in an equally desperate situation. When floods come, the migrant men build dikes around the tents to no avail, and their cars are now shorted, the engines choked with mud. The migrants then flee on foot, to any barn that stands on a hill, to wait, cold, wet, and hopeless.

Occasionally their voices are heard in the midst of this objective account of their misery. Some go to seek help and return to report failure, their voices soft as they try to comprehend their plight: they are not eligible for relief until they have been in California for a year; the government promises help, but no one knows when it will arrive. But the most terrifying news is that three months will pass before there will again be work of any kind. The grayness of the clouds coming in over the ocean is reflected in the terrified faces of the migrants whose children cry because they are hungry and who are now prey to illnesses brought on and exacerbated by malnutrition and exposure.

Spurred by hunger, fear, and anger, desperate men and boys beg or steal food, and sheriffs respond by appointing more deputies and purchasing more rifles to guard against them. Local residents who had once been sympathetic to the needs of the migrants now view them with disdain and hatred. The downward spiral continues inexorably as the migrants are now exposed to the elements in barns that leak, where women with pneumonia give birth, and the old die curled up in fetal position. Fueled by desperation, men who are hungry attempt to steal the food their families need, ignoring the diligent guards.

As the tenant farmers in chapter 1 gather to figure out their next move, so these migrant men gather when the rains stop, squatting silently together to observe the flooded fields. When one speaks, the topic is the same—there is no work, money, or food. One muses over the contrast between the treatment of a team of horses that is well fed and cared for during the off-season and the treatment of human beings, like themselves. The terse response comes softly, quietly, that they are not horses, but men. And as they did in chapter one, the women watch the men intently for signs of anger to replace the fear in their faces. Gathering strength from one another, the men overcome their fear and grow angry. As in chapter 1, then, the women know that their men will not break under these pressures as long as wrath can replace fear, an echo of the novel's title. As an oblique symbol of triumph, the chapter ends with the grass greening at the opening of a new year, but, as the final chapter shows, this new beginning is a hopefulness that readers must envision for themselves because the novel ends with the Joads at the nadir of their journey. They have no home, no work, no food. But, paradoxically, as Rose of Sharon offers her breast swollen with milk for her stillborn child to a starving man in the barn where they have fled for shelter, the family has also reached its highest point of awareness and compassion. Readers, however, must come to this conclusion on their own as the narrator leaves no moral and no glimpse into the future.

The final chapter, 30, echoes the action of interchapter 29. But here the action is particularized with the Joads, the Wainwrights, and other occupants of the boxcars and tents trying unsuccessfully to shore up the bank so that the creek does not flood them. The interchapter is a prelude as well to Rose of Sharon's fevered illness and difficult labor, the birth of her stillborn child, and the family's flight to higher ground.

By incremental repetition the poetic narrator creates the experience before the reader's eyes:

> On the second day . . . *the rain poured down*. . . .

> On the third day the Wainwrights grew restless, . . . and *the rain
> drummed down*. . . .

> On the third day the sound of the stream could be heard above *the
> drumming rain* [emphasis added] (*Grapes* 435).

The spirits of the men are likewise dampened, and the children grow sullen. Cajoling Ruthie, Ma promises that they will soon have a home and a
dog and cat as well. With the early onset of Rose of Sharon's labor, Ma sends
Winfield and Ruthie to the other end of the boxcar with Aggie, but all
three of them creep back, hide behind the woodpile, and watch.

The men now have no choice but to try to shore up the banks of the
creek in an attempt to keep it from flooding the boxcars. But their efforts
are futile, for a fallen tree in the rushing waters tears out their embankment.
Al and the other men rush to move their vehicles to higher ground, but for
Al it is too late—the motor is flooded. Returning to their boxcar, the Joad
men find the smell of afterbirth, burning inside the stove, and the stillborn
infant in an apple box in a corner. The rain has let up enough so that they
can hear Uncle John crying.

Ma reassures a disconsolate Pa that he has done all that he could and
need not blame himself for the failure to hold back floodwaters that are
now lapping around the boxcars. Men who have helped Pa come angrily to
blame him because their cars are now destroyed. The narrator's coolly objective voice measures the pace of this final chapter by a continual report of
the rain that is the backdrop for this catastrophe. Now that it is beginning
to let up, he moves from the rain's whishing, to lightly scattering, to sweeping. And the bleak, somber grayness of the rain reflects the human loss, sorrow, and fear enacted in the Joads' boxcar.

In contrast to the bleakness of their situation, there is a moment of
epiphany, a triumph of the human spirit, in a hospitable exchange between
Ma Joad and Mrs. Wainwright. Echoing Emerson again—all of us as part of
one large soul—they thank one another for their friendship and help,
agreeing that they can no longer center on their own families but must continue to help anyone in need. Against the backdrop of catastrophe and
epiphany, the rest of the Joad saga plays itself out. While Mrs. Wainwright
keeps watch over Rose of Sharon, Ma sleeps fitfully, having nightmarish,
fearful dreams of Tom.

Taking lumber from the built-up sides of the truck, Pa and Al build a platform in the soon-to-be-flooded boxcar to make a place for the family above the water. When Uncle John is assigned the task of burying the still-born child, in a scene reminiscent of the Old Testament story of Moses in the bulrushes, he places the apple-box casket in the roaring waters of the stream, sending it on a mission: to rot in the street, its odor the message of distress. To Ma's dismay, Pa spends the last of their money on bacon and store-bought bread. As the floodwaters enter their boxcar, the downpour of rain begins again.

Echoing the language of the biblical story of creation in Genesis, "on the morning of the second day," the narrator tells us that Pa goes in search of food and returns with ten potatoes (*Grapes* 449). Since they are now penniless, the reader is left with the question of how Pa acquires these potatoes, but there are clues from the preceding interchapter in which desperate men with starving families steal food for them. Gender roles are reversed as Ma watches sulkily as Pa builds a fire, peels the potatoes, and cooks them. This reversal is even more striking as Ma then takes charge, insisting that they have to get Rose of Sharon and the children out of the flooded boxcar. Pa protests without conviction that they cannot leave, but in a quiet lull between rains, they do go, except for Al who remains behind with Aggie, the family's belongings, and the truck. Pa takes Rose of Sharon in his arms, holds her above the floodwaters, and sets her carefully down on the highway, still supporting her. In case Tom returns while they are away, Ma leaves Al instructions to tell him that they will return and that he is to be careful.

As they walk down the highway, with Rose of Sharon supported on either side by Ma and Pa, the rain begins again, at first lightly but then more heavily. As they head toward a barn on a hill, Ruthie and Winfield scuffle over a red wild geranium that Ruthie has picked, sticking its petals on her nose and forehead—the red thread that runs throughout *Grapes* thus coming full circle. At Ma's insistence that she share, Ruthie jabs a petal on Winfield's nose as hard as she can. Hearing the approach of a big storm, Ma and Pa, half dragging Rose of Sharon between them, hurriedly leave the highway, cross a ditch, and go through a fence before the furious storm reaches them. They can hardly see the barn through the blowing rain, and Pa must again carry Rose of Sharon. As they enter the barn, the storm rages furiously. Ma is grateful that there is hay for shelter and warmth, and they discover an anxious boy with his starving father, a man about fifty years old, who is sick and has not eaten in six days. He has given any available food to his son.

The Joads are in desperate need of dry clothes for Rose of Sharon who is wet, sick, and exhausted from childbirth. The starving man is in desperate need of food. The man's son offers "a dirty comfort" so that Ma can help Rose of Sharon out of her rain-soaked clothes and cover her against the cold. In a wordless exchange between mother and daughter, Rose of Sharon agrees to offer the only sustenance available. The rain now falling lightly, the boy and the Joads go into the tool shed, and Rose of Sharon breast-feeds the starving stranger. Here the scene closes and the novel ends, with Rose of Sharon's looking up to face the reader with a mysterious smile on her face. This very postmodern ending does not resolve the plight of the Joads or of the two strangers whom they encounter in the barn. Rather, this conclusion places the remainder of the story squarely in the hands and on the heart of the reader. It also leaves a powerful closing image of human compassion—giving what little one has to save another.

NOTES

1. Peter Lisca, with Kevin Hearle, *"The Grapes of Wrath": Text and Criticism* (New York: Penguin Books, 1997), 1. Hereafter references to this work will be cited parenthetically within the text, identified as *Grapes* with pertinent page numbers.

2. A dialogic link is one that establishes a dialogue between two separate parts. It is somewhat like a conversational dialogue between two people except that the "conversation" in *Grapes* occurs between the interchapters—or general chapters—and the narrative chapters. For example, general chapter 1's image of an unnamed man walking down the road, his feet stirring up dust that swirls waist high, and interchapter 3's symbolic turtle are both echoed in narrative chapter 4 as, accompanied by a dust cloud kicked up by his feet, Tom Joad walks down the road and picks up a turtle to take home to his younger brother, Winfield. Thus, a dialogic link—one characterized by dialogue—is established among these chapters. Similar links occur throughout the novel.

3. Henry Thornton Moore, *The Novels of John Steinbeck: A First Study* (Chicago: Normandie House, 1939), 68, 72.

3   Texts

Above all, Steinbeck was a poet.
    —Jackson J. Benson, *John Steinbeck, Writer* (1984)

As a writer and a journalist, John Steinbeck walked with his times—from the dust bowl of the thirties to World War II, the Vietnam War, and the television quiz show scandals that he saw as evidence of a nation's moral degeneracy. The genesis of *Grapes*, however, goes far beyond a journalist's keen eye for facts to include Steinbeck's concern for the impact of science, nature, and myth on the human experience. In his definitive biography, *John Steinbeck, Writer*,[1] Jackson J. Benson records the interaction between Steinbeck and Joseph Campbell, now a leading authority on mythology. In 1932 Campbell had moved next door to Ed Ricketts, and the three men often met at Ricketts's lab for freewheeling discussions ranging from "the new physics" to Oswald Spengler's *Decline of the West* to Edward Gibbons's *Decline and Fall of the Roman Empire*. To add to the mental stimulation provided by the conversations among the writer, the scientist, and the mythologist, they were joined on occasion by Evelyn Ott, a Jungian psychoanalyst; Francis Whitaker, a metal sculptor; and other writers and artists. The friendship between Ricketts and Steinbeck became especially close as they shared ideas, music, literature, and the camaraderie of these friends. Campbell later maintained that the image of the Madonna in *In*

Dubious Battle was probably inspired by these discussions in Ed Ricketts's lab. In all likelihood, they also influenced Steinbeck's adaptation of this image in the end of *Grapes*.

Like the ancient Greek philosopher Aristotle, Steinbeck believed fiction depicting the human drama to be of a higher order than history recording mere facts about human events. For Steinbeck, fiction had to be true to the human condition. Therefore, in preparing to write his novels, he was both a scholar and a researcher. In addition to reading widely and deeply, he insisted on field experience that would provide firsthand information to enable him to capture a sense of immediacy. Although there are echoes of the American tradition in *Grapes*—particularly Thomas Jefferson, Ralph Waldo Emerson, Henry David Thoreau, and Walt Whitman—on the basis of Steinbeck's reading, Benson believes that the Greek concept of the bond between human beings and nature was a primary influence on Steinbeck's worldview (Benson 233–34).

It is likely also that he was influenced by some of the eighteenth-century British and Scottish novelists, poets, and essayists—especially James Thompson and Robert Burns, whose preromantic view of the bond between human beings and nature was quite similar to that of the Greek writers. Certainly the impact of this view on *Grapes* may be observed in chapter three of *Grapes*, which offers an empathic portrayal of a turtle's progress in crossing a road. This turtle becomes, of course, a symbol for the persistence with which the Joads will move toward what for them becomes an elusive and ever-receding goal. But Steinbeck uses the personal pronoun "he" for the turtle rather than "it," with the effect that it becomes much more than a symbol. To illustrate, the turtle is personified as having "fierce, humorous eyes, under brows like fingernails," and his struggle is dignified by close, sympathetic description. Steinbeck is in company here with a mystical view of the oneness and brotherhood of all things as well as with the close, empirical observations of scientists—any distinctions between the two are blurred.

Approaching this chapter from an anagogical point of view that goes beyond experience provided by the five senses, Warren French finds in this chapter a depiction of the "life-force, . . . the creative principle that exists not just within time, but beyond time."[2] Such a view is in accord as well with Saint Francis of Assisi's admonition: "Tread softly. The rocks, too, are thy brothers." A similar affinity with nature may be observed in Steinbeck's response to Robert O. Ballou's June 1932 request for a biographical sketch for *The Pastures of Heaven* in which Steinbeck maintains that the most important things to him would have little meaning for anyone else. Like Wordsworth, the events associated with nature hold the most import: his memories of sparrows, his conscience that was awakened by the sound of a bell, the teddy bear that a fire truck ran over, and the terrible morning when he discovered his pony was sick (Benson 255). Such close observations seem at times to lead to what Ed Ricketts called "a breaking through," a seeing and experiencing that goes beyond the realm of the physical. Such observations strive to capture the emotional and empathic impact of seeing the kinship between the world and one's self—a poet's way of looking at the world.

Just as Steinbeck desires to capture these human connections to the natural world, he also wants to make connections with his reader, his audience. In considering the genesis of *Grapes*, it is instructive to observe an evolving methodology of writing that intentionally keeps the reader in the center of the process from the very beginning. This evolution of method took place in the years immediately preceding the publication of *Grapes*. While listening to a Bach obbligato and writing *To a God Unknown*,[3] published in 1933, Steinbeck focused on one particular person, not on a general audience—a practice he continued from that point on.[4] Steinbeck's audience of one for *To a God Unknown* was Carlton A. Sheffield, a friend from his days at Stanford University, to whom he later gave the ledger containing the original, handwritten copy of the novel; journal notes; and musings on its composition. This technique of addressing one person, a known and trusted friend, in part at least accounts for the sense of immediacy that will later draw the reader of *Grapes* into a close, participatory role.

The notes accompanying the text of *To a God Unknown* document not only Steinbeck's interest in creating a bond among human beings, the natural world, and his reader, but also the strong metaphysical, or philosophical, intentions that underlie all of his longer works: "The new eye is being opened here in the west—the new seeing. . . . The story is a parable, . . . the story of a race, growth and death. Each figure is a population, and the stones, the trees, the muscled mountains are the world *and* man—the one inseparable unit man plus his environment" (Benson 260).

Defining story as parable in *To a God Unknown* supports Howard Levant's later observation in his 1974 *The Novels of John Steinbeck* that the final one-third of *The Grapes of Wrath* "descends into allegory." Rather than a descent, however, it is its allegorical, or parabolic, moorings that take *Grapes* beyond realism to a mythic depiction of the human experience—particularly of the American identity in relationship to a land considered to be a new Eden. Steinbeck, then, is less a realist who portrays what *is* and more of a poet-philosopher who depicts what *might be* and what *ought to be*. In an August 9, 1933, letter to Carl Wilhelmson, Steinbeck states explicitly that he does not intend to write fiction in the realist tradition (*SLL* 87). He has left realism behind, he states, because he has no faith in it; it is itself a way of fantasizing.

Furthermore, Steinbeck also reveals an early interest in the interior landscape of the mind and in reader response that draws him more closely to postmodernism than to realism. Working on *The Red Pony* in his family home in Salinas during intervals between caring for his mother, who was seriously ill in the hospital, in a 1933 letter to George Albee he writes: "The whole thing is as simply told as though it came out of the boy's mind although there is no going into the boy's mind. It is an attempt to make the reader create the boy's mind for himself" (Benson 262). Leaving the story thus—squarely in the hands of the reader—is a postmodern technique that Steinbeck uses also in the ending of *Grapes*. Here the Joads, like the hero in a Greek drama, have reached the nadir—the very lowest point—of their California experience. But at the same time they have also reached a pinnacle of human awareness, and out of their own dire need, they attend to the needs of others. This transcendence, rising above their circumstances, gives their story mythic import. Out of their own coldness, wetness, sickness, grief over a stillborn child, hunger, homelessness, joblessness, and fear for the future, they give what they have to sustain another. But readers are left to draw these implications for themselves; Steinbeck does not do it for them but rather leaves them with a dramatic and intense panorama intended to work upon their nerves and heart.

Steinbeck formulated his theory of the phalanx during this same period while he was tending his mother. In a June 21, 1933, letter to Carlton A. Sheffield he recorded his close observations of his mother's paralysis, trying to understand what was happening to her, seeing her body as whole but with cells that were working against each other so that she could not function normally (*SLL* 76). This realization led to his thesis of the phalanx—that the whole is greater than the sum of its parts. And this whole in turn becomes a newly created individual with feelings and goals. Benson points out that this thesis is a key to the novels written over the next fifteen years (Benson 265, 268–70). In *Grapes*, then, the movement of the migrants, brought about by dire necessity, becomes a kind of phalanx into which individuals and families are caught up and become more than what they are alone.

Drawing on the sources and materials gathered in preparation for writing *In Dubious Battle*, in the spring of 1934 Steinbeck wrote "The Raid," a short story to be included later in *The Long Valley*.[5] His first work dealing with the problems of labor, this story offers a precursor to Casy's death scene in *Grapes*. Wounded by raiders sent to break up an organizational meeting of strikers, Dick and Root lie in a hospital prison cell, and the young

Root—as Casy will later do in *Grapes*—comments, "You remember in the Bible, Dick, how it says something like 'Forgive them because they don't know what they're doing'? . . . I felt like saying that. It was just kind of the way I felt" (*The Long Valley* 105). "Breakfast," also one of *The Long Valley*'s short stories, is likewise a forerunner of a similar scene in *Grapes* in which the hospitable Wallaces share both breakfast and work with Tom Joad.

Steinbeck's preparation for writing *In Dubious Battle*, as it will be for *Grapes*—only with a more intensive personal involvement—included firsthand discussions with strike organizers who kept him apprised of conditions in the agricultural fields. In January 1935 he wrote to Albee, telling him this book is multilayered into the surface story, the psychological underpinnings of the group, and philosophical conclusions (Benson 311). Later, regarding *Grapes*, he wrote to Pascal Covici to tell him that this novel has "five layers" but that he will not label them, maintaining that readers may find only as many as they have in themselves.

In journals, notes, and letters, Steinbeck thus leaves trails that show his intentions, concerns, and methods. For a further example, while writing "something that happened," later titled *Of Mice and Men*, he reveals concerns for "beauty," "matter" (i.e., content), "picture making," and his "experiment" with the "unexpected" that characterizes the lives of "real people" (Benson 331). All of these concerns carry over into *Grapes*—synthesized in the elegance of its intricate structure, in images that have so informed the nation's imagination that the Joads' journey on Route 66 is an integral part of its mythic identity, and in characters who encounter catastrophe with a predictable and noble generosity of spirit.

In August 1936, preparing to write on migrant farmworkers for the *San Francisco News*, Steinbeck equipped a bakery truck for use as a camper and set off with Eric H. Thompson. A former preacher who was director of the migrant camp program in the Central Valley, Thompson accompanied Steinbeck on a visit to migrants living in Hoovervilles. After this journey Steinbeck had no doubt about the subject for his "big book." Having seen migrants who were destitute, on the verge of starvation, so close to total defeat that they lacked the will to keep going, he was determined to write their story. At Arvin Sanitary Camp, or "Weedpatch Camp," he meets Tom Collins, to whom he will later dedicate *Grapes*, with the inscription "To TOM who lived it." Steinbeck spent some time observing the camp under Collins's direction, and Collins gave him access to meticulously thorough reports that included such diverse material as stories in dialect, collections of music, and records of the migrants who stayed there. Steinbeck used these materials both in the articles for the *San Francisco News* and later in *Grapes*, especially in the chapters on Weedpatch Camp.

In September 1936 *The Nation* published Steinbeck's brief overview of California's migrant workers. And between October 5 and 11, the *News* ran a series of seven of his articles, entitled "The Harvest Gypsies," based on the trip with Thompson and covering topics ranging from the origins of migrant labor in California, to the economic plight and living conditions of the present migrants who had fled the dust bowl region, to future concerns (Benson 347–48). During this same period, a strike among lettuce workers in Salinas led to an explosive situation, which Steinbeck described in a letter to Albee as explosive, with rioting and death in his hometown—the beginnings of a general revolution (*SLL* 132). Troubled and angry by the oppression that he had witnessed, Steinbeck first wrote a satire about these events, "The Great Pig Sticking," and then began on what he intended to be his "big book," "L'Affaire Lettuceberg"—both of which he later destroyed. Both served a cathartic purpose, however, for he could not have written *Grapes* without them.

In February 1938 at the request of the Farm Security Association, he accompanied Tom Collins to Visalia, revealing a sense of urgency and mission in a letter to Elizabeth Otis as he went to help those who were flooded out and starving (*SLL* 368). He made two trips, helping wherever he could. Although *Life* magazine underwrote the cost of the second trip, the editors agreed to run Horace Bristol's photographs but not Steinbeck's article, reissuing the photographs and a short article on *Grapes* after its publication and again after the production and release of the movie. In April, however, the *Monterey Trader* published the article originally written for *Life*, "Starvation Under the Orange Trees."[6] Later, when Helen Hosmer republished the seven articles written for the *News* as a pamphlet entitled *Their Blood Is Strong*, she also included "Starvation Under the Orange Trees," along with her own preface and cover photographs by Dorothea Lange.[7] The proceeds went to help the migrants.

On May 2, 1938, Steinbeck wrote to Elizabeth to tell her that he had finished a first draft of "L'Affaire Lettuceberg" but that it was not well written because of his own anger; he suggested that it should probably be burned and forgotten (*SLL* 163). A sense of mission underlay Steinbeck's desire to tell the migrants' story, as evidenced in the urgency shown in the letter to Otis, indicating that he had to go to Visalia. Although writing "L'Affaire Lettuceberg" gave Steinbeck opportunity to vent his spleen, it did not, finally, serve his purpose. In order to be heard, such stories must be told in such a way as to enable the reader both to understand and to participate empathically in the migrant experience. Such an angry book, he realized, would not fulfill this goal; he destroyed the manuscript.

Using the same material from his field experience with the migrants, Steinbeck began *Grapes*, working this time not only from a sense of mission, but also with a clear aesthetic vision and a commitment to maintain the emotional distance essential to artistic integrity. Still, the same urgency to tell the migrants' story in such a way as to reflect their anguish and suffering so that readers are engaged in their experience underlies *Grapes*.

He completed the novel in one hundred days. The journal that he kept while writing it reveals a methodically envisioned work,[8] with the narrative and interchapters plotted out in preparation for the next day's writing session and with a sense of the ending and the whole from the outset. The propelling, compelling verb "must" occurs frequently in these journals, mapping out both the author's psyche during composition and his method of writing:

> My people *must* be more than people. They *must* be an over-essence of people. . . . Today comes the funeral in the night of Grampa. . . . It *must* be good and full of fullness and completions. And that feeling must go into it. *Must.* I seem to use the word *must* more than any other. It's a good word though. . . . In 16 more days I'll be half through. And I *must* get my people to California by then [emphasis added]. (WD 39–41, 44)

These journals thus reveal an iron-hard discipline, a peopled imagination, and a deep love both for his craft and his creation. To illustrate, on July 6, 1938, Steinbeck wrote, "Work is the only good thing. Tomorrow is." The incomplete sentence with which he concluded this entry is typical, pointing toward tomorrow's work, which he prefaced with "Now it's Thursday." Then he again mapped out the interior landscape of his own psyche, the ordinary domestic demands of the day, and the direction of the book taking shape in the ledger before him.

These journals reveal as well Steinbeck's reverence for the text that he was creating. In the August 3, 1938, entry, he hoped to be worthy of his work, and he ended the day's writing with gratitude (*WD* 51). Occasionally, as he was caught up in the ambiance surrounding his work and the book taking shape beneath his pen, there is an echo of the account of the Creation in Genesis in which God sees each day's accomplishments as "good." To illustrate, halfway through the novel, Steinbeck looked ahead, contemplating the enormity of the symbolism in its conclusion, after which he wrote, "And that was a good thing" (*WD* 36). Often, though, plagued with doubts, he fervently hopes that his writing is "good"—"I hope to God it's good"—with the hope as both aspiration and prayer (*WD* 93).

Even as he struggles with self-doubt, however, Steinbeck's aesthetic vision saw the novel whole. It moved him inexorably toward that dry barn on the hill where an unidentified boy, whose unnamed father is starving nearby, gives a dirty comforter to the Joads for Rose of Sharon—who is sick, feverish, exhausted from childbirth, shivering in rain-drenched clothes. And she, in turn, breast-feeds the starving man. In entry #28 of his journal, written on June 30, 1938, he contemplated the magnitude of this ending and was humbled by his own story: "I grew again to love the story which is so much greater than I am. To love and admire the people who are so much stronger and purer and braver than I am" (*WD* 36). At this point Steinbeck's sense of mission and his aesthetic vision coalesce.

This closing scene, then, evidently is in his mind from the outset. And it is both a climax and a conclusion, occurring simultaneously, with no resolution following. There are no answers for the remaining questions concerning the final outcome of the Joad saga: Where is there left to go after this barn? Does anyone get a job? It is implied that Pa may have stolen the ten potatoes that he himself peeled and cooked for their meal in the railroad car. Will he, then, be one of those shot, to fall wounded in the mud? Did Ma Joad ever get that little white house her heart is set on? And so on.

Although this final scene created an uproar of protest, with even his publishers initially calling for its removal, Steinbeck was steadfast, writing to Pascal Covici on January 16, 1939, before the book's publication that this ending has to occur accidentally and quickly. He asserted that its meaning would be warped if the stranger were integrated more fully. The emphasis is on the very fact that the starving man is a total stranger, and breast feeding has no more sentiment than giving bread. This ending, Steinbeck maintained, is intentional and purposeful—essential to the novel's meaning, structure, and balance (*SLL* 178). With artistic integrity, he closed this novel at the point at which the Joads reach their lowest point—caught in California's rainy winter season with no money, no food, no work. Paradoxically, as in a Greek drama, coinciding with this lowest point, they reach their highest awareness of the needs of others around them and of their own responsibility for others, experiencing what Warren French has called an "education of the heart."[9]

In *Grapes* Steinbeck's mission, his aesthetic vision, and his artistic integrity, then, are all cut from the same cloth. Further, readers are an integral part of his plan, invited to enter into any gaps or unfinished business as participants in the actual experience of these migrants. He transformed the journalistic accounts in "The Harvest Gypsies" and "Starvation Under the Orange Trees"—later republished in Hosmer's pamphlet, *Their Blood Is Strong*. With the fire of his anger subsumed in writing the destroyed manuscripts of "The Great Pig Sticking" and "L'Affaire Lettuceberg," he achieved in *Grapes* his passionate desire to write a book with enduring aesthetic merit.

Needless to say, his accomplishment in writing *Grapes* was one not to be repeated. Steinbeck did not intend to write another book after the same mold or even on the same or similar topic. His love for the craft of writing was such that it propelled him forward into new experiments. Although *East of Eden* and *The Winter of Our Discontent* carry on a prophetic vision of America and Americans—to echo a later nonfiction publication by that title—they differ strikingly in structure, characterization, and style. Still, taken as a whole, *Grapes*, *Eden*, and *Winter* form an epic sequence, and all have a nation's greed and exploitation as primary themes.

Like a Greek tragedy, *Grapes* begins amidst the Oklahoma Dust Bowl and the Great Depression; *Eden* moves backward to the beginnings of settlement in California; and *Winter* depicts a nation in the present that seems to be on the brink of moral bankruptcy. All three novels offer what Robert DeMott calls "a gossamer thread of hope," with *Winter* looking forward to a future in which a nation's great strength joins together with a sense of responsibility to others. Perhaps Steinbeck's trilogy symbolically provides the balance that Viktor E. Frankl in *Man's Search for Meaning* boldly maintains the United States so sorely needs:

> Freedom . . . is not the last word. Freedom is only part of the story and half of the truth. Freedom is but the negative aspect of the whole phenomenon whose positive aspect is responsibleness. In fact, freedom is in danger of degenerating into mere arbitrariness unless it is lived in terms of responsibleness. That is why I recommend that the Statue of Liberty on the East Coast be supplemented by a Statue of Responsibility on the West Coast. (134)

A number-one national best-seller, *Grapes* first earned for Steinbeck election into the National Institute of Arts and Letters and later, in 1940, the Pulitzer Prize. But the award that would matter the most to him is that of the continuing ability of his story to ring true and to gain a reader's empathy. In Studs Terkel's title introduction to Viking's 1989 deluxe edition of *Grapes*, he maintains that "we still see their faces." Further ingraining this story on our national psyche, Route 66 from Oklahoma to California has become a part of our folklore. And, as Americans, we bear an affinity for both the Joads and for their oppressors. In our national character there is vast capacity for great nobility, sacrifice, bravery in the face of oppression, and love for the downtrodden. But there is also a deep-seated, look-out-for-number-one, me-first greediness so ingrained that it sometimes seems that that there are no limits to how far we will go to turn a profit. *Grapes* has the power to hold the mirror for us to see which of the faces of our national identity we are wearing at the moment. It still fulfills Steinbeck's intention to "rip a reader's nerves to rags" (*SLL* 178).

NOTES

1. Jackson J. Benson, *John Steinbeck, Writer* (New York: Penguin Books, 1984). Hereafter quotations from this work will be cited parenthetically within the text, identified by the author's last name with pertinent page numbers.

2. Warren French, "*The Grapes of Wrath*," in *A Study Guide to Steinbeck: A Handbook to His Major Works*, ed. Tetsumaro Hayashi (Metuchen, NJ: Scarecrow Press, 1974), 41.

3. Robert DeMott, *Steinbeck's Typewriter: Essays on His Art* (Troy, New York: The Whitston Publishing Company, 1996), 126.

4. Elaine Steinbeck and Robert Wallsten, *Steinbeck: A Life in Letters* (New York: Viking Penguin Inc., 1975), 64. Hereafter quotations from this work will be cited parenthetically within the text, identified as *SLL* with pertinent page numbers.

5. John Steinbeck, *The Long Valley* (New York: Viking Penguin Inc., 1938, reprinted by Penguin Books, 1986).

6. John Steinbeck, "Starvation Under the Orange Trees," *Monterey Trader*, 15 April 1938, pp. 1, 4.

7. John Steinbeck, *Their Blood Is Strong* (San Francisco: Simon J. Lubin Society of California, 1938).

8. John Steinbeck, *Working Days: The Journals of "The Grapes of Wrath,"* ed. Robert DeMott (New York: Penguin Books, 1989). Hereafter quotations from this work will be cited parenthetically within the text, identified as *WD* with pertinent page numbers.

9. Warren French, "The Education of the Heart," *John Steinbeck's Fiction Revisited* (New York: Twayne Publishers, 1994), 75–84.

4   Contexts

Written against the backdrop of human disasters of monstrous proportions, Steinbeck's *Grapes* stands as a monument to the power of the human spirit to transcend the immediate catastrophe, to rise to meet the challenge of the moment even when everything seems hopeless. The Great Depression had begun with the stock market crash of 1929, and by 1933 the market had dropped to its lowest point—with almost two million men thrown out of work. And the trickle-down economic policies of the time did little to relieve the situation. Subsidized by his father's fifty-dollars a month check, Steinbeck himself was struggling to publish something that would support him and his wife, Carol, at a time when publishers were also facing hard times. Publishers McIntosh & Otis and Robert Ballou had both rejected *Tortilla Flat* when Pascal Covici, of the Covici-Friede publishing house, offered to purchase it, along with publishing rights to all of Steinbeck's work both past and future.

Occurring during the thirties, the Oklahoma Dust Bowl included Texas, New Mexico, Colorado, and Kansas as well as Oklahoma. While its devastation contributed to the general misfortune and misery of the Great Depression, it was but a part of that era of general misfortune and financial ruin. Precipitated by human exploitation of the environment as well as by drought and fierce winds, the dust bowl was catastrophic. One of the undercurrents that runs like a requiem throughout *Grapes* is a lament for the erosion of land that had been overworked, misused, abused, and exploited for ready profit—knowingly "cottoned-out" as Steinbeck describes it in the novel. Previously used for grazing but now plowed under, with even the most rudimentary of rules for agriculture ignored, the land lay vulnerable to drought, wind, and flood. Always low in rainfall—less than twenty inches a year—in the early thirties the misused and overused land lost its topsoil to strong winds and drought, creating dust storms that on occasion became "black blizzards" that obscured the sun and piled up enormous drifts of dirt.

Warren French's 1963 *A Companion to "The Grapes of Wrath"* documents the press's coverage of the dust bowl phenomenon from November 1933 to 1939.[1] In November 1933 a dust cloud formed a triangle that extended from Texas to South Dakota, with its peak in Milwaukee, Wisconsin. At first considered a singular, isolated occurrence, it became obvious by 1935 that this dust—that had obscured the sun in six states, that had suffocated a child in Kansas, and that had forced Texas senators to wear gas masks during their April 10 and 11 sessions—was widespread (3–4). Along with this overview of press coverage, French includes excerpts from three documentaries on the subject—two scientific and one personal. Brief summaries of these articles elucidate the causes, effects, and human suffering of the dust storms.

French's first excerpt, a scientific documentary, is Ivan Ray Tannehill's "Dusters and Black Blizzards," from his 1948 book, *Drought: Its Causes and Effects*. Tannehill traces the nation's experience with drought in the plains over a period of sixty years when the land use changed from pasture and grazing to agriculture. Alternating periods of adequate rainfall and severe drought made life difficult for farmers, many of whom gave up farming and moved away to find other means of support. Occurring intermittently over a period of years, the dust from these storms choked out pastures so that livestock starved or suffocated; stopped trains, cars, and planes; darkened the sun at noon; and caused suspension of business (French 7). Tannehill further describes muddy balls of snow and plagues of grasshoppers, which thrived in the heat and dryness (French 7–8).

The second excerpt, another scientific documentary, is M.M. Leighton's "Geology of Soil Drifting on the Great Plains," from the July 1938 *The Scientific Monthly* and traces "soil drifting" from prehistoric to modern times, succinctly and clearly finding human exploitation of the land to be the direct cause of the dust bowl in the thirties. He traces this exploitation from the white man's arrival, resulting in widespread destruction of the balance of nature—direct cause of the dust storms. Human beings, Leighton maintains, have the power to cause such ravaging soil-drifting nationwide (French 14–15).

French's third excerpt, a personal documentary, is Caroline A. Henderson's "Letters from the Dust Bowl" from the May 1936 *Atlantic Monthly*, adds a personal, experiential note to the studies of the geologists Three letters to "My Dear Evelyn"—June 30, 1935, January 28, 1936, and March 8, 1936—show the personal toll taken by the dust bowl. Closely observant and articulate, Henderson describes her family's continuing struggle to survive and keep the farm in which they have invested twenty-seven years of hard work and planning. In these letters she worries about the monocropping of wheat in her area and about adjacent farms where contour plowing and terracing to conserve moisture and prevent erosion are not put into practice. Most poignantly she longs for the green, growing plants and flowers of Kansas that are in sharp contrast to her family's Oklahoma farm, which she describes as "the dust-covered desolation of No Man's Land" where nothing grows, not even weeds.

Moreover, there are ominous personal notes that underscore the toll taken by the dust-bowl catastrophe, as she observes that twenty-six families are leaving her area, that dust-precipitated pneumonia is a constant threat, giving her husband bronchitis and killing two people. But both continue working, and one letter concludes that she must now go out to get the work done before the arrival of "a great reddish-brown dust cloud . . . rising now from the southeast" (French 16–21).

Henderson's actual experience, fearsome as it was, did not include the dispossession that the Joads experienced in *Grapes*—eviction from the land, forced out on the road to survive as best they can as they search for a new home and work. Such legal expulsion, however, was the fate of thousands. As a result of debt accrued year after year in order to farm the land, some farmers had become tenants on land they had once owned. These tenants and others, who were barely surviving, were forced off their farms by large landholders who could now work the land more efficiently with tractors. One driver could now take the place of ten tenant farmers, assuring a profit for the owner's investment. Jobless and homeless, these displaced tenant farmers and their families were forced to go on the road, thus joining the ranks of the Great Depression, when homeless men already wandered the streets of America's cities, seeking work, standing in breadlines for food.

This human disaster triggered by the 1929 stock market crash and the Oklahoma Dust Bowl was to be alleviated only by a far greater, more momentous tragedy: the German invasion of Poland in September 1939 and the onset of World War II. *Working Days: The Journals of "The Grapes of Wrath"* documents Steinbeck's awareness of the impending war as he was writing the novel.[2] In the journal entries written between Thursday, September 15, and Thursday, September 29, 1938, "yet" is the telling, worrying word that shows Steinbeck's mindset: the war had not started *yet*; he cannot tell as *yet* what is going to happen; and, concerning Czechoslovakia, he thought that it was not "the end *yet*" (79). He also records Chamberlain's visit to Hitler; England's, France's, and Poland's attempts to stay out of war even as tensions heightened; and the Munich petition to divide Czechoslovakia (*WD* 71–79). Although in the September 27, 1938, entry Steinbeck hoped that Hitler might have backed away from the forces gathered against him, by October 11 he regretfully faced the inevitable tragedy of the continued Nazi growth that would lead finally to war (78, 85–86).

In a November 13, 1939, letter to Carlton A. Sheffield after the publication of *Grapes*, Steinbeck grieved for a sick world and maintained that the natural world of the tide pool was more understandable than the political world of humans. Then, typically, he announced that he was looking in more reliable places—among them, undoubtedly, the tide pool—for an alternate pattern of behavior. Typically, too, he maintained the optimistic belief that something new was already developing, ready to replace the old patterns.[3]

Attesting to the accuracy of Steinbeck's prophecy of a new world, between the years of 1939 and 1945 World War II brought an unprecedented economic boom to the United States. Published in October 1939—on the heels of the Great Depression and the dust bowl and at the onset of World War II—*Grapes* deals with two facets of a nation's poverty—the impoverished spirit of its privileged and the impoverished economic outlook of its migrants. And this novel still points resolutely toward the possibility of transcendence over hatred, greed, and self-absorption even as it ends with a fragile hope for humanity in the face of economic depression, natural disaster, and world war.

While T.S. Eliot's image of "hollow men" epitomizes the modern world's exiting and dying "not with a bang but a whimper," Steinbeck's Joads face impending disaster with courage, hope, and love. Even now they set a poignant example for the nation's privileged, those with spirits dwarfed and diminished by greed and devotion to a ready profit. The face of an impoverished, exhausted Madonna still looks "up and across the barn" and out of this novel at the reader with her mysterious smile. In her lies the only panacea for a nation's hatred, greed, and self-absorption: love. And in her also lies a source of the discomfort of so many critics who have tried to dismiss this ending as sentimental, overwrought, or unrealistic. Rather, in this ending Steinbeck has taken his story into the realm of mystery—and myth. *Grapes* is a novel very much *of* its times, but it is also a novel *for* all times.

The literary and cultural context during the two decades preceding the publication of *Grapes* includes Eliot's 1922 *The Waste Land*, a monument to the vacuity and sterility of modern life; Sinclair Lewis's 1920 *Main Street*, on the provincialism of small-town life in America; and Theodore Dreiser's dark naturalism in his 1925 *An American Tragedy*, based on a New York murder case. F. Scott Fitzgerald's 1926 *The Great Gatsby* and Ernest Hemingway's 1926 *The Sun Also Rises* are accounts of the futility of the modern world, both novels echoing *The Waste Land*. Hemingway's 1929 *A Farewell to Arms* tells a tragic love story ending in desolation William Faulkner's 1929 *The Sound and the Fury*, set in Jefferson, Mississippi, provides a four-part stream-of-consciousness story of the Compton family in which love, incest, feeblemindedness, and drunkenness are prominent features. Like these novels, *Grapes* deals with human tragedy and weakness; unlike them, it offers hope for transcendence.

Playwright Eugene O'Neill's 1920 *The Emperor Jones*, an example of symbolic expressionism; his 1921 *Anna Christie*, a story of a fallen woman's regeneration; and his 1924 *Desire Under the Elms*, a story of love, moral degeneration, and murder, earned him an international reputation. And between 1919 and 1940 Harlem's literary renaissance produced writers such as Langston Hughes, Zora Neale Hurston, Sterling Brown, and Countee Cullen. In 1939 Adolf Hitler's *Mein Kampf* (in an English translation), James Joyce's *Finnegan's Wake*, and Richard Llewellyn's *How Green Was My Valley* were published along with *Grapes*, which won the Pulitzer Prize perhaps because it captured the soul of a nation and the essence of America both then and now.

In architecture, film, music, and theater Americans had achieved a degree of artistic grandeur. Skyscrapers became a prominent part of the cityscape and Frank Lloyd Wright was in his heyday as an architect. Hollywood produced films such as *The Wizard of Oz* and *Gone with the Wind*—films to escape from the period's catastrophes, just as Astaire and Rogers's on-screen characters were. Benny Goodman's jazz orchestra of racially mixed musicians played in New York City's Carnegie Hall. During the time when he was writing *Grapes*, Steinbeck's *Of Mice and Men* would enjoy a successful run in Pittsburgh.

The founding of New York's Museum of Modern Art in 1929 had brought together experimental art in the abstract or surreal, often with the artist creating forms and images defying explication or explanation. Many of these drawings and paintings were sometimes indecipherable even with a title suggesting what the artist intended. For example, neither Hans Arp's *Arrangement According to Laws of Chance (Collage with Squares)*, a random assortment of irregular, square squiggles of assorted sizes, nor Georgia

O'Keeffe's *Evening Star, III*, a snail-like shape with a dot in the center atop two horizontal lines connected at one end, resembles either its title or an empirical reality. Anna M. Robertson, "Gramma Moses," and Pablo Picasso, however, were also painting during this era—one a primitivist, another a surrealist. Although the aesthetic of *Grapes* has little in common with Arp and O'Keeffe, it does take a grotesque twist on Robertson's idealized farmscapes, and Steinbeck's use of the grotesque also bears a surrealistic mark, as, for example, in the color red that runs throughout the novel, culminating in the petals of a scraggly red geranium that Ruthie tears apart.

Similar to John Milton, who fits neither with the seventeenth-century Cavalier poets nor with the metaphysical poets, but stands alone, Steinbeck's achievement in writing *Grapes* is singular, standing out from other writers and artists of his time. Like the romantics, he found glory in the commonplace, elevating an impoverished migrant family to heroic stature. Unlike most writers of his time, his worldview was not, finally, a wasteland, nor were human endeavors ultimately futile. For in spite of their dispossession and proximity to desperation, the Joads experience love, enlightenment, the bonds of brotherhood and sisterhood with some of those whom they meet, determination, and a will to keep on going even into what seems to be unending darkness. They always seem to find the resilience to rise above despair. Although Steinbeck always walked *with* his times, with a journalist's eye for story and detail, there is a very real sense in which he was not *of* his times—molded by a deep inner life that was nurtured as much by his reading as it was by outward events and circumstances. He is a curious mix of romance and realism—a modernist, but not a modernist.

In a November 13, 1939, letter to Carlton A. Sheffield written after the publication of *Grapes*, Steinbeck stated that he needed to begin all over again as a writer because he had taken the novel as far as he could. Although he did not know what shape the format replacing the novel might take, he believed that it would be suitable for the emerging thought of a new era (*SLL* 194). In a journal entry for October 16, 1939, a year after the completion of *Grapes*, as he was searching for this new format, he had a poetic, synaesthetic vision—one that transforms observation into music, seeing into song, science into poetry. He writes about the music of microscopes, glass tubes, and X-rays, finding in them the poetry that he wanted to write, the rebirth for which he was seeking (107). Although Steinbeck eventually abandoned the projected drama "The God in the Pipes," this poetic vision of writing remains as a strain that runs in lyrical passages throughout his ensuing works—from *Sea of Cortez: A Leisurely Journal of Travel and Research, Cannery Row, Sweet Thursday,* and *East of*

Eden, to *The Winter of Our Discontent*, *Travels with Charley in Search of America*, and *America and Americans*.

All these works affirm Jackson J. Benson's observation that, underneath it all—under the journalistic stance, the empirical observation, the scientific theory, the humane and humanitarian devotion to the ordinary person—Steinbeck was a poet. He sought to see the wholeness and the holiness of all things. Like William Blake and Jim Casy, he believed that all life is holy—a belief that can be held neither by the modern naturalists nor the modern realists. Steinbeck's worldview, however, does encompass their waste-land abyss of futility, sterility, and emptiness—but only to go beyond it, out of it, breaking through it to the other side to some hope and joy, even though they may be seen only dimly.

In 1938 the United States Supreme Court ruled that the University of Missouri Law School had to admit African Americans because there was no comparable school in the area, and Harvard University granted an honorary doctorate to African American opera singer Marian Anderson. In the world of music, Benny Goodman's band played jazz as it had not been played before—helping to establish this music form as quintessentially American, with its roots deep in the nation's heritage from blues and slavery. Richard Wright published *Uncle Tom's Children*, parodying *Uncle Tom's Cabin*. Racial equality had not arrived, but there was hope. It is no wonder that years later, in his 1966 *America and Americans*, Steinbeck wrote, "Any attempt to describe the America of today must take into account the issue of racial equality, around which much of our thinking and our present-day attitudes turn. We will not have overcome the trauma that slavery has left on our society, North and South, until we cannot remember whether the man we just spoke to in the street was Negro or white" (66). Changes in the philosophy of education were likewise imminent, for also in 1938 John Dewey published *Logic: The Theory of Inquiry* and *Experience in Education*, advocating a hands-on, more student-centered approach to learning that is still influential.

In *Working Days*, Steinbeck recorded both his personal involvement with the social and domestic world around him and his intense devotion to the creative, fictional world taking shape in his novel. Around him there was a circle of events impinging upon the embryonic creation that was more vital and real to him than the larger reality of his immediate surroundings, the ordinary business of life, and even an impending world war.

Documenting convivial dinner parties either at the Steinbeck home or at a friend's house, a cavalcade of personalities marches through these journals—among them Louis Adamic, author of *Dynamite*; Miguel Covarrubias, artist, illustrator, and caricaturist for *Vanity Fair*; Charlie

Chaplin, actor; Martin Ray, vintner; and Pascal Covici, his publisher. These journals also record domestic irritations, such as the sound of the washing machine and the construction noises next door to their Los Gatos home, annoyances that Steinbeck determined were not going to deter him from the writing task at hand. Carol's influence on the writing of *Grapes* ranged from typing the manuscript, making suggestions, providing moral support that kept Steinbeck writing during times of discouragement, and, as he himself states in the dedication, willing the novel into being. Without her, it may never have been completed.

The purchase of the Biddle ranch and the subsequent building of a new house of necessity occupied some of his time, demanding attention to the construction. Once he and Carol move in, however, he writes on October 5, 1938, that the silence is "absolutely delicious" and his "story is coming better" (82–83). Still, in the October 7, 1938, journal entry, he complains of "a goatish sexuality" coming over him, the "furnace men coming this afternoon," and "one fly" that he cannot find (84). In addition to these social, domestic, and personal events and distractions, the journals, too, frequently reveal Steinbeck's tiredness, sickness, or discouragement as he tried to maintain focus on the novel—the true center of his life at this time. Like an often-repeated refrain, the word "must" occurs again and again as he compels himself to write his story with plenty of movement but to keep it at a slow, steady pace and to keep up his drive by taking one day's writing at a time. Between October 13 and October 25, 1938, he wrote of a "blind weariness," a "tiredness" and nervousness that upset his stomach, a shaky hand, and "plain terror" as he approached the ending of the novel even though he had "every single move mapped out" (87–92). The October 25 journal entry ends with an often-repeated hope that in reality is more like a prayer: "I only hope it is good" (92).

But just as the journals document tiredness, sickness, and discouragement, they also record the centrality of what Steinbeck calls his people and his story as he enters the world of his creation. As Robert DeMott points out in *Steinbeck's Typewriter: Essays on His Art*, on at least one occasion, recorded in his October 20, 1938, journal entry, Steinbeck

> imagined that Tom Joad actually entered the novelist's work space, the private chamber of his room. . . . With that breakthrough . . . Steinbeck arrived at the intersection of novel and journal, that luminous vector, that fifth layer of involvement where writer and text not only merge but interpenetrate. He entered fully the architecture of his own novel and, however briefly, lived in its fictive space, its scene of writing. (186)

Here the fictive reality became for him more real than the actual—a mystical mingling of writer, character, and text.

During the writing of *Grapes*, then, Steinbeck's life became like a series of concentric circles—with the creative endeavor at the very center, the middle, the heart. Excited about his story, he realizes that finishing it is going to make him sad. Almost prayerfully he hopes that the book will be good, but he is uncertain (86–88). For months he has outlined and planned, brooded and labored, agonized and rejoiced over the writing of this book. With its gestation period approaching an end and the publication date nearing, sadness mingles with excitement, for he must now relinquish his brainchild to the public and the critics and find another center for himself.

In *"The Grapes of Wrath": Trouble in the Promised Land*,[4] Louis Owens maintains that Steinbeck was "influenced by John Dos Passos's narrative experimentation in the novel *U.S.A.*," from which "evolved the structural strategy of two kinds of alternating chapters" (28). Similarly, in "Steinbeck's Debt to Dos Passos,"[5] Barry G. Maine writes that "in setting out to write a novel about farm labor conditions in the American West, Steinbeck borrowed conceptually from *U.S.A.* in planning the structure of his novel, borrowed technical procedures from *U.S.A.* in developing the interchapters, and benefited from whatever stock of American speech Dos Passos had floated into literary currency. That is the full extent of the debt" (160).

Maine finds that such borrowings would enable Steinbeck to broaden the focus of his novel to include the widespread suffering beyond the Joads' personal tribulations, to include another voice in the interchapter to speak on current political and economic issues, and to capture "American voices" that cover a wide spectrum—including the privileged as well as the downtrodden.

But he believes that

> in every other way the two novels are quite different because they are based on opposite conceptions of human experience. The tone, direction, thematic implications, politics, and vision of *The Grapes of Wrath* owe nothing to *U.S.A.* They are uniquely Steinbeck's. The tone is compassionate, the direction forward-looking, the politics collectivist, and the vision one of guarded hope in building a new community. In *U.S.A.* the tone is satiric, the direction backward-looking to a "storybook democracy," the politics disillusioned, and the vision of community bankrupt. *The Grapes of Wrath* is a testament to the power of the human spirit to endure and prevail over his-

tory, whereas *U.S.A.* is a testament to the power of history to triumph over Man. . . . As much as it is form it is vision that separates and distinguishes these two writers of the Depression era. (160)

Authenticating these observations, in *Steinbeck's Reading: A Catalogue of Books Owned and Borrowed*,[6] Robert DeMott cites a letter Steinbeck wrote to Joseph Henry Jackson, book critic for the *San Francisco Chronicle*, in which Steinbeck states that he may have been influenced by Dos Passos only to an extent (142). As Maine points out, however, such influence was transformed by Steinbeck's differing style, emanating from a more positive worldview and vision.

One less obvious influence may have been Henry Fielding's *Tom Jones*, written in 1715, also with interchapters with commentary on the times. In *Steinbeck's Reading*, DeMott cites four direct references to this early novel over a time period from 1930 to 1951. In the first, he writes Amasa Miller that he has been rereading Fielding. Two of these references mention Fielding's use of humor, with one drawing *The Wayward Bus*, which Steinbeck was writing at the time, into connection to three other very early novels: *Tom Jones, Tristram Shandy*, and *Don Quixote*. The final entry on *Eden* maintains that this novel's pace has more in common with Fielding than with Hemingway (41).

With his typical dogmatic asperity when discussing the works of Steinbeck, Harold Bloom, asserts that "the shadow of Hemingway hovers over every descriptive passage in *The Grapes of Wrath*. . . . The prose filters the King James Bible's rhetoric through Hemingway's mode of writing about the object-world."[7] Even more disparagingly, Bloom claims that "Steinbeck's naturalistic humanism itself seems confused," worries that he "cannot keep so clear a vision [as Hemingway] as to whether the human will is significantly free or not," insists that he is "Hemingway's involuntary disciple" (6). While it is true that Steinbeck admired Hemingway's ability, he was not a disciple. In such strident assertions and evident distaste for this monumental literary work that he paradoxically cannot dismiss outright, Bloom himself seems confused, offering no real substantiation for his claims. He wants to have it both ways—to claim that *Grapes* is at once classic and inferior. Trapped inside the box of his own theory of a writer's ties to other writers, in this case he finds influence where it cannot be demonstrated clearly.

Bloom is quite right in citing the Bible as an influence on *Grapes*. For Steinbeck grew up with the Bible and lived with it so that it informed his thinking, infiltrating into everything he wrote—especially *Grapes*. As DeMott notes in *Steinbeck's Reading*, "Though he was not orthodoxly religious, JS responded powerfully, with an artist's temperament, to the Bible's spirituality, poetical rhythms, symbolism, characterizations and moral dimensions, perhaps never more fully than in GOW" (134).

Biblical themes, symbols, motifs, structures, language, spirit, and tone are pervasive in *Grapes*. Its title is an obvious reference to Julia Ward Howe's "Battle Hymn of the Republic" and its allusion to Revelation 14:19 with its description of "the great winepress of the wrath of God." As Peter Lisca has pointed out, the three divisions of the novel correspond to the Israelites' exodus from Egypt.[8] The Oklahoma section and the drought parallel the Israelites' oppression and the resulting plagues in Egypt, the journey corresponds to the Exodus, and the hostility in California corresponds to the opposing tribes in Canaan. Lisca also discusses biblical symbolism in the grape image, Rose of Sharon's name, and the concluding scene in which Rose of Sharon is a Madonna-like figure. And, importantly, he illustrates Steinbeck's use of a biblical, Old Testament style of writing—parallel structure and meaning, simple diction, vivid detail, repetition—a style that gives cumulative weight and significance to this story (572–88).

But, as Lisca points out, *Grapes* is a veritable compendium of styles, ranging from chapter 7's clipped staccato voices of the salesmen, to chapter 9's requiem of the tenant women for the treasured belongings they must leave behind, to chapter 23's poetic, rhythmic description of the young Texan man and Cherokee woman's dance, and more (582–83).

This variation of styles is partly absorbed and produced from Steinbeck's reading, partly from his acute ear for the authentic American voice, partly from the rhythms of music. It grows out of the researcher, the journalist, the lover of good music, the lover of people and flows into an authentic, genuine voice capable of speaking to the heart as well as to the mind.

NOTES

1. Warren French, *A Companion to "The Grapes of Wrath"* (New York: Viking Penguin, 1963; Penguin Books, 1989). References to this work are cited parenthetically in the text.

2. John Steinbeck, *Working Days: The Journals of "The Grapes of Wrath,"* ed. Robert DeMott (New York, Penguin Books, 1989). References to this work are cited parenthetically within the text, identified as *WD* with pertinent page numbers.

3. Elaine Steinbeck and Robert Wallsten, eds., *Steinbeck: A Life in Letters* (New York: The Viking Press, 1975). References to this work are cited parenthetically within the text, identified as *SLL* with pertinent page numbers.

4. Louis Owens, *"The Grapes of Wrath": Trouble in the Promised Land*, Twayne's Masterwork Studies, no. 27 (Boston: Twayne Publishers, 1989). References to this work are cited parenthetically in the text.

5. Barry G. Maine, "Steinbeck's Debt to Dos Passos," *Steinbeck Quarterly* 23 no. 1–2 (1990), 17–27; reprinted in *The Critical Response to John Steinbeck's "The Grapes of Wrath,"* ed. Barbara A. Heavilin (Westport, Conn.: Greenwood Press, 2000). References to this work are cited parenthetically in the text.

6. Robert DeMott, *Steinbeck's Reading: A Catalogue of Books Owned and Borrowed*, Garland Reference Library of the Humanities, vol. 246 (New York: Garland Press, 1984). References to this work are cited parenthetically in the text.

7. Harold Bloom, *John Steinbeck's "The Grapes of Wrath,"* Bloom's Notes Series, ed. Harold Bloom (Pennsylvania: Chelsea House Publishers, 1996), 5–6. References to this work are cited parenthetically in the text.

8. Peter Lisca, ed., with Kevin Hearle, *"The Grapes of Wrath": Text and Criticism* (New York: Penguin Books, 1997). References to this work are cited parenthetically within the text, identified as *Grapes* with pertinent page numberss.

5 Ideas

GREED: THE PROBLEM OF HUNGER IN A NATION OF PLENTY

Just as the King of Brobdingnag in Jonathan Swift's *Gulliver's Travels* praised great scientific minds that could increase agricultural yields, thus benefiting humankind, so Steinbeck in *The Grapes of Wrath* praises the scientific minds behind agricultural progress in California. But he is outraged because people starve in this land of plenty.[1] There is a prophetic fierceness in what some critics have called his "jeremiad"—his warning against greed, injustice, and inhumanity that hardens hearts and tightens purse strings so that the bottom line becomes profit. In bardic tones he describes the destruction of food—oranges, potatoes, pigs—with hungry people watching, helplessly. While this rotting food assures a profit, children die from malnutrition. These crimes, sorrows, and failures, Steinbeck states, eventually transform into wrath, echoing the novel's title, and showing the chaotic result of a nation's greed (*Grapes* 346–49).

In intercalary chapter 14 of *Grapes*, the narrator portrays a million migrants moving westward in search of a home and food for their families and addresses directly in the second person "you" the landholders "who own the things people must have" (152). The result is a nervousness and restiveness not only on the part of the migrants, but also in the Western States that fear the changes to come as a result of their hunger and need. The only solution, this narrator advocates, is for these owners to think of the needs of others as well as themselves. The Golden Rule—"Do unto others as you would have them do unto you"—comes to mind here, a seemingly simplistic Sunday-school lesson. But the real-life application Steinbeck recommends is far from simple: it is, rather, ameliorative and curative. What other reasonable and humane answer could there possibly be?

In *Rachel and Her Children: Homeless Families in America*, Jonathan Kozol similarly describes today's homeless people and, like Steinbeck, focuses on the deprivation of their children.[2] Both writers depict the sheer terror of homelessness and joblessness. Both show the lack of food, shelter, schooling, nurture, and stability in the lives of children; both place the blame for their deprivation squarely on the shoulders of the society that tolerates it. Whereas society, for the most part, advocates a "look out for number one" philosophy, Steinbeck and Kozol picture the harsh reality of dispossession. And, by their focus on children, they bring home the responsibility that their plight places on society at large.

Today the silence of those who drop into the abyss of our society's homeless would no doubt grieve Steinbeck. He had an indomitable faith in America's democracy of the people, by the people, and for the people—and he believed that their voices could and would be heard. For our own times—when the marketplace, vacation cruises, and Walmart-size dwellings take priority over the homeless, helpless, and dispossessed in the midst—such certainties seem wistful.

HOSPITALITY: THE STRANGER IN THE MIDST

> The best that we had was brought out for our guests and the tables were loaded with food. . . . Hospitality was a built-in duty every man owed to every wayfarer. . . . A family always offered the best and most valued possessions to a passing stranger.
>
> —John Steinbeck, *America and Americans*, 1966 (132)

A related theme to that of greed and hunger is hospitality, with an especial emphasis on kindness to strangers. This theme is as ancient as literature itself. From Zeus's decree that strangers have a right to hospitality, to the Psalms' statement that "the Lord preserveth the strangers," to the admonition in Hebrews 13:2 that we should not be "forgetful to entertain strangers: for thereby some have entertained angels unawares," this theme appears in Homer's *Odyssey*, Virgil's *Aeneid*, and the Hebraic-Christian tradition. This time-honored theme is at the heart of the very structure of *Grapes*, culminating in the final scene in which the son of a starving man gives their "comfort" to the wet, cold, feverish Rose of Sharon, who is exhausted from childbirth, and she, in turn, nurses the starving father. "Comfort" is undoubtedly intended in a double sense here, as both the specific blanket and also the abstract concept of a spirit of caring and concern. In this hospitable exchange, each family gives out of its own destitution to help another.

By strong implication, Steinbeck thus maintains that a common humanity demands kindness to strangers. The Joads treat others whom they encounter throughout the novel with kindness and hospitality, and other characters as well serve to delineate this theme, creating a thread of hospitable actions and kindness to strangers. Still other characters, inhospitable and unkind, however, portray the opposite. Chapter 2 begins the Joad narrative with an early statement of theme. Paroled and on his way home from the penitentiary where he has been incarcerated for manslaughter, Tom Joad asks a truck driver for a ride. In response to the driver's inquiry whether he had seen the No Riders sticker on his windshield, Tom replies that he has seen it, but good guys do not permit a rich boss to control them (*Grapes* 11). Although he may act out of guilt, by giving Tom a ride and wishing him luck when they part, this trucker thereby takes his place with the novel's good guys, those kindly people who are willing to help a stranger.

Symbolic of the hospitable and inhospitable forces that the Joads and other migrants will encounter, in chapter 3 a woman risks her life in swerving to avoid hitting a turtle as it crosses the road while a man swerves to hit it. Symbolic of strong people like the Joads, although the man's car clips the turtle, it rolls off the highway and goes on.

Chapter 4 provides the philosophical undergirding for the hospitality theme, a philosophy more romantic than realistic—a view as mystical as Dante's final vision of the harmony of all things in "Paradise" or Emerson's oversoul. Here Tom meets Jim Casy, a former preacher who has known Tom since he was a boy. Sharing a bottle of liquor with him, Tom listens to his Emersonian ramblings about the Holy Spirit and the human spirit all mingled with the people one loves and of the one soul of which everyone is a part (*Grapes* 27). This philosophy undergirds the entire novel, removing it from realism and placing it among romantic or visionary works. Complementing one another, chapters 5 and 6 both show the desecration and the preservation of this one soul. Chapter 5 provides general images of inhospitality: the monstrous bank that drives the people from their homes and the nameless tenant man, his wife, and quiet children staring after the tractor that has crumbled their home. Chapter 6 provides specific images as Muley Graves tells of his own family's dispossession and of the Joads who have gone to Uncle John's, preparing to join the hosts of tenant farmers heading for California.

Chapter 5 further depicts the desecration of the human spirit in images of ragged children who eat fried dough as they watch a tractor driver eat his Spam sandwich with pickles and cheese and a piece of store-bought pie (*Grapes* 40). Chapter 6, however, provides a contrasting view, showing the human capacity for transcending circumstances and for generosity. When Casy asks Muley Graves whether he is going to share the rabbits he has caught for his own supper, Muley replies that he really has to share because he could not go off and eat by himself, leaving them hungry. He has no home, no table, no chairs; with only the rabbits that he is carrying to share, he is still hospitable, sharing from his meager store. Observing, Casy proclaims that Muley has insight into something that is bigger than himself, something neither he nor Casy can fully comprehend.

Against the backdrop of used-car salesmen who dupe the people in chapter 7—a foreshadowing of problems to come both with the Joad's truck and with those who take advantage of strangers in their desperation—in chapter 8 Tom and Casy arrive at Uncle John's where the Joad family is preparing to leave for California. Of two hundred dollars earned by chopping cotton and selling household and farm goods, they have spent seventy-five dollars on a used truck. Although Tom and Casy have talked about Ma Joad as they journey, she appears for the first time in this chapter—from the very beginning portrayed as the epitome of graciousness and magnanimity. Wanting Tom's return to be a surprise, Pa asks her whether they have enough food for some fellows who have just dropped by. Willing to offer a place at her table even to strangers, she tells him to bring them in because there is plenty, with bread fresh out of the oven (*Grapes* 73).

Providing a complementary backdrop for the activities of the Joads, in chapter 9 unnamed tenants sift through their belongings, preparing to leave home. Like the used-car salesmen, buyers take advantage of them. The narrator bitterly points out that they are not buying trash, but rather people's trashed lives (*Grapes* 88). As the Joads prepare to leave Oklahoma in chapter 10, they meet around the old Hudson automobile, the new center for family life. In this chapter occurs a key passage on the hospitality theme. In reply to Pa's question whether they have room and food to take Casy to California with them, Ma unhesitatingly says: "I never heerd tell of no Joads or no Hazletts, neither, ever refusin' food and shelter or a lift on the road to anybody that asked. They's been mean Joads, but never that mean" (*Grapes* 104).

Chapter 11 closes the Oklahoma section of the novel with a short treatise that defines and underscores the worth of land and of human beings.

Steinbeck maintains that the earth cannot be defined by its chemical composition—its nitrates and phosphates—nor can human beings be so defined. Both are far more than the chemicals of which they are made, and neither can finally be reduced to analysis. This interchapter closes sadly with the image of a deserted house, inhabited by the wind, cats, mice, and bats—an image highlighting the tragedy underlying the desolate land and the dispossessed people, whose worth is incalculable.

Chapter 12 introduces the journey to California on Highway 66. The hospitality/inhospitality theme continues in two vignettes. In the first, automobile repairmen try to overcharge a migrant for a damaged tire, and the migrant complains bitterly that stealing a tire makes a person a thief, but overcharging for a damaged tire is good business. In the second, a dispossessed family of twelve with no car pile possessions into a homemade trailer and wait beside Highway 66 until a man in a sedan comes along, gives them a ride, provides for their needs on the long journey, and pulls their trailer along behind. This generous man shows in action Casy's vision of unity, of the enormous soul of which everybody is a part.

In chapter 13 as the Joads' journey begins, Ma's insistence on taking Casy along with them echoes this story of the man in the sedan. Al questions whether the truck can carry the load, wondering whether they should have brought Casy along. Ma assures him that they were right to bring the preacher, that they'll be glad he is with them before the journey is over. Reminiscent of chapter 12's plaintive refrain of the little boy, Danny, who wants a drink of water, Ma takes a tin cup full of water to Granma and Grampa who are riding on top of the load. Like the man in the sedan who provides for a family of twelve strangers, so the Wilsons offer their tent to shelter Grampa when he becomes too ill to go further—even though they have not known the Joads before—and Sairy Wilson gives them a quilt for his burial. Strangers before meeting on this journey, the Wilsons and Joads decide to travel together, helping one another along the way.

Chapter 14 defines human beings as those who are unlike anything else, who are greater than the work they do, who rise by their concepts, and come out ahead of their successes. Related to Casy's vision of the unity of the Holy Spirit and the human spirit, combining with all those whom we love, the abstract concept of human aspirations and accomplishments comes to life in a series of vignettes. Dispossessed migrants grow increasingly desperate in their efforts to survive and begin to unite and share what little they have. But the Western States nervously watch the changes taking place.

As Mary Ellen Caldwell points out, chapter 15 is "unique and central to the story, an epitome of the whole work." [3] As the fifteenth chapter in a thirty-chapter novel, it is central both structurally and thematically. It opens with a vignette of the hamburger stands on Highway 66, the stopping places where hospitality is for sale; moves to the waitress's and cook's displays of generosity; and closes with a portrait of the people whizzing by in big cars. From the generic description of hamburger stands, the image shifts to one stand in particular, with Mae as waitress and Al as cook. With all customers except truck drivers, Mae's hospitality is artificial, her smile forced as she looks past them. For the truck drivers, however, she is genuinely friendly, smiling. Al is quiet, all business as he tends the grill. Both, however, are kind to a migrant stranger with limited funds who comes in to buy ten-cents worth of a fifteen-cent loaf of bread. Al insists that Mae give him the entire loaf for a dime. Entering into the spirit of the occasion, Mae sells his two boys five-cent candy at two for a penny, and the truckers leave her generous tips as a reward for her charity.

The people in the bigger, expensive cars, however, show no such generosity either in tips or politeness and furnish as foils for Al, Mae, and the truck drivers. The women in these cars are listless, bothered by the heat, and carrying with them clothes, medications, makeup, and devices for birth control—an image of sterility, barren as the land. Still, they are discontent, sullen, and resentful whereas Ma Joad concerns herself with good nutrition, cleanliness, education for her children, and the broader world of humanity. Mae calls the people in the big cars "shitheels," her name for those whose narrow world encompasses only themselves. Chapter 16 will answer a question posed by chapter 15: Mae wonders what the migrants will find in California.

In chapter 16 the Joads encounter a man returning from California who answers Mae's question and provides a bleak forecast of what they and the other migrants can expect when they arrive: work for pay so low that it will not provide food or shelter and, for some, death by starvation or malnutrition. True to the man's prediction, they find California not only inhospitable but also hostile.

Against the backdrop of chapter 17's general description of the migrants as sociable, hospitable, law-abiding people, in chapter 18 Ma faces a darkly tanned policeman who orders her family out of his territory within twenty-four hours because they do not want "Okies" settling in California (*Grapes* 291). Structurally this is the end of the journey, and from now on the Joads are a displaced people in a hostile land.

Chapter 19 provides a brief overview of exploitation in California: the Americans who took the land from the Mexicans, the squatters who became owners and imported cheap laborers—Chinese, Japanese, Mexicans, Filipinos—and the businessmen who took over farms that grew larger as smaller farmers lost their lands. Now the dispossessed are coming, insisting that they are not foreigners but Americans of European descent who have been in this country for seven generations. Instead of jobs and homes in a rich, fertile land, these dispossessed Americans find hatred, hunger, and inhospitality, and they are forced to live in Hoovervilles by rivers on the edges of town. In the final vignette of this interchapter, a child dies of malnutrition.

Against this ominous panorama, in chapter 20 the Joads encounter their first Hooverville. As Ma starts to prepare their evening meal, a circle of quiet, hungry children stand watching, coming so close to her that she brushes against them as she works (*Grapes* 350). Sending her family into the tent to eat their own meager servings, Ma leaves a portion in the pot for the children, feeling that she has taken from her own family to feed the children of strangers and realizing that it is not enough to do them any good.

Chapter 21's description of the plight of migrant men who are desperate for jobs highlights the introduction of Timothy and Wilkie Wallace, who, in the midst of their own great need, bring Tom Joad to their boss and share work that will soon run out. Although the Wallaces are almost starved to death after the previous year's floods, they invite Tom to breakfast, thus sharing both their food and their work with a stranger in need. In the midst of images of starving, sick children, men desperate for work, and the fermenting anger of hungry people who are strangers in a hostile land, the Wallaces live by Casy's philosophy of love and unity, showing the possibilities of magnanimity inherent in the human spirit.

Unfortunately, people are capable of niggardliness and destruction as well, as the following chapters attest. Chapter 23's description of the migrants' innocent desire for amusements—ranging from jokes, storytelling, and music to square dancing and preaching—sets the stage for chapter 24's story of a Saturday night dance at Weedpatch Camp, at which deputies try to instigate a riot in an effort to drive these migrant strangers out of their territory and to close the government camp. And chapter 25's images of the fruitfulness of California and the scientific expertise invested in seed cultivation and insecticide shift to bitter images of loss and wastefulness. Small farmers lose their land because of debt, and children must die of pellagra because the orange crop is destroyed to keep prices up (*Grapes* 477).

Against this bleak scene, the plight of the Joad family worsens as the novel progresses. Forced to leave the security of the Weedpatch Camp to search for work, they find employment picking peaches at the Hooper ranch for wages inadequate to buy sufficient food. Even here, though, the cycle of human kindness continues as the manager of the ranch store charitably puts ten cents from his own pocket into the cash register so that Ma can buy sugar for Tom's coffee to go with their slight evening meal. From here on, the Joad's situation deteriorates rapidly. Interchapter 29 foreshadows the concluding chapter, describing first the winter rains and then turning to the plight of the migrants who face three months with no work, money, or food. No one will help them—neither the local residents safe in their own homes nor the doctors. Inhospitably, they turn their backs on the hungry and the desperate—even on pregnant migrant women, sick with pneumonia, who bear their babies in abandoned, leaky barns (*Grapes* 592). In narrative chapter 30 as winter rains pour torrentially, Rose of Sharon, sick with fever, gives birth to a stillborn child. Fleeing the flooded boxcar in which they have been living, the Joad family seeks refuge in a barn where they find a young boy and his starving father. In contrast to those who ignore the needs of others, each destitute family offers something to alleviate the need of the other. The boy provides "a dirty comfort" so that Rose of Sharon can get out of her wet clothes. To save the adult stranger from dying, Rose of Sharon breast-feeds him.

The hospitality theme that measures people by their treatment of their fellow human beings thus comes full circle. Casy's vision of unity involves a law of hospitality requiring kindness to strangers. From the beginning the Joads have observed this law as a code to live by. In the conclusion of the novel, then, they simply act in character, at the same time providing a fitting thematic finale. As Steinbeck has observed, the novel is structurally and thematically balanced. In the Aristotelian sense, the ending has followed of necessity from what has preceded it. For the Joads have been heading toward this ending from the beginning. In ever worsening circumstances, they have always acted with hospitality and humanity. What is finally important in this novel, therefore, is not their circumstances at all. It is the Joads' own attitude and behavior. Even when they are destitute, they will behave like Joads, with a kindness in the final scene that by now is endowed with nobility.

CHILDREN: "THE LEAST OF THESE"

And the King will answer, "I tell you solemnly, in so far as you did this to one of *the least of these*, . . . you did it to me" [emphasis added].
—Matthew 25:40, (Jerusalem Bible)

Although children are a part of thematic sections on hunger and hospitality, their presence is so pervasive in *Grapes* that it deserves to be brought into closer focus. Sometimes unnaturally quiet and still, sometimes typically playful, whining, argumentative, engaged in sibling rivalry or tattling, they are present in both interchapters and narrative chapters, from the beginning of the novel to the end. Steinbeck is attentive to them and insistently, persistently brings to the reader's attention their innocence and vulnerability—and by implication at least, a civilized society's responsibility for their well being. But even beyond this emphasis is Steinbeck's ability to enable the reader to know what it *feels* like to be a child of dispossessed parents with no home and no work. In general chapter 1, the children are still and silent, oppressed by their fathers' burden of worry and perplexity. When these men begin to hope that they have found a new beginning point for continuing with their lives, the children resume their play very tentatively, attuned to the inner turmoil of the grownups if not to their mental grappling with what to do next, where to go, how to live.

To illustrate further, in interchapter 14, two men squat down before a fire over which a stew is simmering to discuss their plight, their quiet women standing behind them with the children, who listen "with their souls to words their minds do not understand." Because the welfare of children is a shared community responsibility, in the same chapter, to provide warmth for a sick baby, a stranger gives away a cherished family blanket that had belonged to a mother who was either left behind or dead (*Grapes* 152). Similarly, in narrative chapter 20, Ma Joad exemplifies the only appropriate response to children in need. If they are hungry, they must be fed—even though what one has to share is insufficient.

In contrast to Ma's act of neighborly kindness, in interchapter 25's fierce "jeremiad," food is destroyed to keep prices and profits high. Tersely, the narrator concludes that in the midst of all of the rotting food, children have to die in order to keep food prices and profits high. Like Kozol's examination of the current effects of homelessness on children,[4] Steinbeck thus focuses sharply on the migrants' children. Whereas some might consider helping the migrants themselves an act of charity, the well being of children is everyone's responsibility. Their prevailing presence in *Grapes*, then, in the persons of Winfield and Ruthie Joad and the unnamed children throughout speaks volumes even when they are quiet and still. For, through Steinbeck's participatory aesthetic, they are *our* children and must be cared for. Even Rose of Sharon's stillborn child bears this message. In the floodwaters Uncle John sets the child afloat in a box, with the admonition to go down and rot in the streets: a picture of neglect, loss, destitution, and society's failure to care for its own.

RACIAL INJUSTICE: THE NATIVE AMERICAN IN THE MIDST

Related to the theme of hospitality and the stranger is that of the migrants' own unjust treatment of the Native American, who is for them an exotic stranger who must be eradicated just as they try to eradicate snakes and other varmints that may interfere with their homesteading. Although the Joad family, especially Ma Joad, has been, for the most part, exemplary in its treatment of the stranger in the midst, this phase of the migrants' history is shameful. Steinbeck portrays the Native American as poignantly and empathetically as the story of the migrants themselves. Typically moving from the narrator's general observation in interchapter 5, "Grampa killed Indians," to the storyteller's particular tale of shooting an Indian brave in interchapter 23, Steinbeck tells us what the men who shot him experienced afterwards. These men felt that they had spoiled something better than themselves and spoiled something in themselves as well—never to be repaired. Thus, the migrants are themselves culpable because of the way the Indian has been treated—just as the large landholders and banks are culpable for their disregard for and exploitation of the tenant farmer.

ECOLOGY AND THE ENVIRONMENT: HUMAN EXPLOITATION OF THE LAND

In accord with the mystic tradition of Saint Francis of Assisi, who admonished humankind to "tread softly; the rocks, too, are thy brothers," Steinbeck lovingly establishes the land itself as a primary entity in *Grapes*. The earth becomes one of the characters in its own right—humanity's benefactor, capable of bountiful production, but also humanity's prey and subject to exploitation, capable of great suffering. In the opening general chapter of *Grapes*, Steinbeck describes the onset of drought and the effects of erosion on the land. In the opening paragraph he creates images of a land that is sick—suffering not only from drought but also from abuse and misuse. The "scarred earth" cannot soak up the much-needed rain. With no regard for the conservation practice of contouring, the plows cross and recross land that is already lying injured and abused. The sun is relentless in its fiery heat; the land crusts over like a festering boil; and, finally, the earth pales and is deathly sick. The second paragraph follows with a continuing image of a sick and dying land, with the penetrating rays of the sun striking it like a weapon over and over again, relentlessly.

Steinbeck tells the human story behind the takeover of farmland in order to establish an agribusiness—tracing the evolution from a family-owned homestead, to a bank-owned farm on which the former owners are tenants to an agribusiness. He tells this story straightforwardly, showing the human culpability of each "owner" of the land—the grandfathers killing and driving out the Indians, the fathers borrowing money from the bank and exhausting the land with cotton, and the banks cashing in on unpaid mortgages, becoming the owners.

Purposefully, Steinbeck shows that both as landowners and as tenant farmers, the migrants have contributed to an environmental catastrophe. Tom Joad tells Casy that for as long as he can remember, his family was sure that a good crop was coming, but it never materialized. Underlying Tom's comment is an indictment of agricultural misuse of land, continually taking out until it is exhausted. After five good crops, the nutrients in the earth were depleted, but they kept on plowing, planting, and hoping for a good harvest from worn-out land. Muley Graves also admits that the land where his family lived was good only for grazing and should never have been broken up for farming. And now continual cotton crops have left the land depleted. The tenants know well that they should practice crop rotation in order to replenish the soil. But although such rotation is a primary principle of responsible agriculture, they have pragmatically and short-sightedly ignored it, preferring to raise cotton, the primary money crop of their times. This practice contributed to the disaster of the Oklahoma Dust Bowl.

Interchapter 5 portrays the land's condition under the large landholders when good husbandry is still disregarded. A robotlike mechanized tractor driver plows in straight rows, no matter how the land lies, without regard for its well being. Wearing protective clothing and a face mask to protect against the dust, he is cut off from the land—he does not see it, smell it, feel it, walk on it. It does not matter to him what happens to the seeds he plants or to the seedlings that grow to be withered by drought or drowned in a flood. Like the bank, he does not love the land.

In this interchapter Steinbeck also describes the farming of his times as it evolved from privately owned or tenant farms into a megabusiness in its own right. He would no doubt be even more appalled by today's financial pressures that again force even these farming megabusinesses to sell out, so that much of America's prime farmland is being stripped of its topsoil and asphalted over for strip malls, apartment complexes, and subdivisions. The owners describe a takeover by a monstrous agribusiness—a profits-and-interest-breathing entity—stronger than a bank or even a company.

In this interchapter landholders bring eviction notices, explaining to the tenants what they already know all too well—that the land is depleted. They fully realize that rotating crops replenishes the land, but, because of financial pressures and the need for a quick profit, they have not practiced good agricultural husbandry. Facing eviction, these tenants are themselves ruthless in their outlook, for they are willing to continue to exhaust the land by monocropping cotton if the price is right, even hoping for a war to drive the prices up.

The large landholders are more ruthless. In ugly images of robbery, blood-sucking leeches, and a monster that breathes and eats profits, this interchapter describes both the tenants' abuse and overuse of a victimized land and the landowners' subsequent abuse of the tenants and determination to continue raising cotton until the land is totally unfit. As with today's developers, who first cut down every living thing on a plot of land and then scrape off the topsoil to sell before they begin building, these owners plan to exhaust the land completely and then to sell it as real estate to people in the East.

Steinbeck depicts as monstrous the banks and companies that drive the tenant farmers off the land, and he describes their machinery, the tractors that take the place of the tenants' draft horses, as "snub-nosed monsters," an animal-like image of destruction. As incredibly strong as insects, these tractors come, move, lay, roll, pick up, putter, thunder, settle down, raise dust, and strike with snoutlike noses. They run on roadbeds that they have created by going straight through "hills and gulches, water courses, fences, houses" (*Grapes* 38).

Steinbeck is ahead of his times here in describing the detrimental effects of deep plowing, which he calls "surgery." Recognizing the impact of dead panning (packing the soil down so that it hardens) and the loss of topsoil caused by such plowing, many Midwestern farmers have now turned to no-till farming. In one of the ugliest but most effect scenes in literature, Steinbeck portrays the rape of the land as the tractor rolls over it with steel blades that cut, push aside, cut, push aside, slice, and comb "with iron teeth" until it lies "smooth." "Behind the harrows, the long seeders—twelve curved iron penes erected in the foundry, orgasms set by gears, raping methodically, raping without passion" (*Grapes* 39). The images are all hard, even the one of the driver sitting on an "iron seat" who feels no affection for this machine that he neither owns nor loves but whose powerfulness he relishes. The final image is one of rape and rapine: "The land bore under iron, and under iron gradually died; for it was not loved or hated, it had no prayers or curses" (*Grapes* 49). In this image of great pain and unimaginable suffering, the land is personified as soft and vulnerable—like a woman taken by force in wartime, bearing offspring, and dying "under iron."

The image of land that is dying from misuse and overuse runs through the first third of the novel, set in Oklahoma, and the tenant farmers are not spared their share of the blame for the atrocious abuse of the land. It is interesting to note that Rachel Carson's *Silent Spring* was first published in 1962, about the same time as the publication of Steinbeck's *Travels with Charley in Search of America*, and that the scientist and the novelist shared similar concerns about the environment. In *Grapes*, as has been noted, the land itself is as much a character as are the Joads or their oppressors; it is depicted as an integral part of the whole. There is both sadness and horror in Steinbeck's description of the desecration and rape of the land.

GOOD AND EVIL: KINDNESS TO "THE LEAST OF THESE"

Despite some critics' views to the contrary, Steinbeck has a strong sense of evil. In *Grapes* Casy describes the current evil behind the mass dispossession of tenant families as something worse than "the devil [that] got hold a the country" (*Grapes* 129–30). Casy metaphorically compares this evil to a large poisonous lizard, a Gila monster, that bites, holds on, and drips poison into the wound until its head is pried off.

But Steinbeck's view of evil is much more subtle than this image, horrible as it is. It is more in line with Christ's portrayal of evil as a negative action, leading to a loss of the kingdom of heaven: "I was hungry and you never gave me food; I was thirsty and you never gave me anything to drink; I was a stranger and you never made me welcome, naked and you never clothed me, sick and in prison and you never visited me. . . . I tell you solemnly, in so far as you neglected to do this to one of *the least of these*, you neglected to do it to me" [emphasis added] (Matthew 25:42–46, Jerusalem Bible).

The picture is clear here as it is in *Grapes* with its primary theme of hospitality and kindness to the stranger in the midst—or its opposite, a lack of hospitality and kindness. It is all so very simple. For Steinbeck, like Christ, love and attention are the panaceas for the world's ills. That is why the details in *Grapes* matter so much, why they come like a barrage, demanding attention: Danny, the little boy sitting in the backseat, wants a cup of water. Winfield is malnourished because of the Joad family's meager diet. Rose of Sharon needs milk for her unborn child. The Joads and other migrants need shelter from California's winter rains and the flood. Exhausted from giving birth and heartbroken because the child is stillborn,

Rose of Sharon is feverish and needs dry clothes. And, finally, the starving father in the leaky barn needs milk.

It is no wonder that some readers grow uncomfortable. For, like Toni Morrison's *Beloved* in the novel by that title, the Joads do not really go away once the book is closed. As *Beloved* reminds us of the horrors of the Middle Passage and slavery, so the Joads remind us of the homeless, underprivileged, sad, and alienated of our own times. *Grapes* is now an inescapable part of the American myth, of the American Dream gone awry. Hubert Humphrey once said that a nation's greatness may be measured by how it treats the young, the old, and those who are physically or mentally ill. And it is exactly at this point that Steinbeck portrays the great evil in simply ignoring the needs of "the least of these."

A MATRIARCHAL HERO: THE COMPASSIONATE WISDOM OF MA JOAD

Poverty-stricken, middle-aged, with sparse gray hair pinned in a granny knot on top of her head, her body heavy from bearing children and working, and her hands worn from washing clothes—Ma Joad is hardly the typical image of a hero. But Steinbeck declares her to be the family's "citadel"; from her comes guidance and strength. A figure of imposing stature in lineage as well as in physical, intellectual, and spiritual prowess, she is proud and self-sufficient, reminding her family members that Joads do not have to look up to anyone. She does not let them forget that their forebears fought in the Revolutionary War and that their family had been landowners until overtaken by bad years and debt.

Like the ancient Greek hero, she is magnanimous and hospitable—giving food, shelter, or a ride to those in need. And her battles, like theirs, are decisively won. She subdues an argumentative tin peddler by beating him with a live chicken; she challenges the men in her family with a jackhandle when they want to divide into two groups rather than to continue traveling as a unit; and she threatens a policeman with a skillet when he vows to arrest her family if they do not leave by the next day.

She understands and exemplifies Casy's new gospel of love. Determined that her family will get across the desert to California under cover of night, she conceals Granma's death from them and holds the dead body in her arms all night. Later, facing her own family's poverty and hunger, she shares a meager stew with fifteen starving children. And it is she who encourages Rose of Sharon to feed a starving man from breasts swollen with milk for her dead child.

Beyond these brave and sacrificial acts, she is also an ideal of woman-hood. Her concern for cleanliness, courtesy, decency, good food, and hospi-tality, together with her display of strength, wisdom, magnanimity, and love provide a standard by which other characters in the novel may be mea-sured. For example, her godlike love for her fellow human beings stands in stark contrast to the silliness of Granma's religious ecstasy in which she si-multaneously speaks in tongues and nearly rips off one of Grampa's but-tocks with a shotgun blast. Moreover, her simplicity of dress and lifestyle contrasts sharply with the women in the big cars whizzing by on Highway 66 on their way to a California vacation. Whereas they are self-absorbed, she is concerned with her family's well being.

Significantly, the character of Ma Joad is historically important because she participates in the breakdown of the gender roles that typically separate men and women. This breakdown occurs early in the novel in an inter-change between Ma Joad and Casy. Ma is busy salting pork in preparation for their journey. Knowing that she is carrying a heavy load of responsibility and has numerous tasks to perform to get ready to leave, Casy offers to take over the job of salting the meat. She stops working, hardly believing what she is hearing and finally tells him that this is not man's work, but woman's. Casy tells her that it is just work, and there is no time for dividing it up ac-cording to gender, insisting that she leave this task to him. Reluctantly, she consents but stays to watch long enough to be assured that he is doing it right.

Later, Pa laments this reversal of roles that Casy accepts so easily, per-haps because he fears that Ma has challenged his role as head of the family. He sarcastically observes that whereas men used to have the final word, it seems that women are taking over now. By the end of the novel, however, Pa's sarcasm has softened into acceptance, but he does not lose his own strength in acknowledging Ma's. Rather, Ma and Pa Joad gain strength and depth of character from each other.

The reversal in gender roles appears also in passages that present parallel vignettes. In an interchapter early in the novel, tenant women stand beside the men, looking at them cautiously, trying to *feel* whether or not they were going to hold up under the strain. These women feel safe once they can as-sure themselves that the men are angry, figuring a way to resist the disaster upon them. Two later interchapters repeat this scene in which the women watch the men's faces, relieved when they *feel* that anger replaces fear—knowing that the men can face the unknown as long as they are not paralyzed by fear. In a parallel vignette, but a reversal of gender roles, when Pa is out of work and the family must leave the security of the Weedpatch

Camp, he *feels* Ma's sadness and studies her face. *Feeling*, at first recognized without question as the province of the female, becomes Pa's in this scene.

Later, when they are living in an abandoned boxcar, Pa and Ma Joad discuss men's and women's roles. Pa tells her that he does not even care that she is taking over the role of leader in the family. She reassures him with the observation that women adjust better to change than men do because they lift life's burdens with their arms whereas men carry them with their intellect. Close after this scene, however, these gender attributes are reversed. Throughout the novel Ma has prepared food for her family, but as they huddle on platforms in the boxcar to escape rising floodwaters, Ma watches sullenly as Pa goes after potatoes and cooks them for supper. The next morning she vehemently insists that they leave the boxcar for higher ground, telling Pa that he can come or not, but she is taking Rose of Sharon and the children out of the flooded boxcar to higher ground. Like men, who plan things out, she has thought about their problem and has made her decision. She has taken the man's prerogative, but Pa follows her lead without protest, only, with some sarcasm, reminding her later that she has not told them *where* they are going. There is no doubt that he will follow her.

And in one of the most poignant scenes in the novel, Pa again takes the reverse role of the woman whose arms carry life's burdens. Taking his daughter, Rose of Sharon, in his arms, Pa holds her as high as he can and wades through the floodwaters carefully, setting her on her feet and holding on to her when he gets to the highway. Like a woman, he has sheltered his daughter from the flood, carrying her in his arms and lovingly supporting her when he puts her down on dry ground. As Casy points out early in the novel, there is no time for gender roles: work is work.

Working together at whatever comes to hand, men and women find that specific gender roles no longer seem important. True, Ma Joad is a matriarchal hero, but by the end of the novel, Pa Joad himself takes on the very attributes of courageous love that make her so heroic. He is not diminished by her, then, but augmented and built up so that he participates more fully in the life of the family. In the final scene, Ma waits by his side outside in the toolshed while Rose of Sharon breast-feeds the dying stranger. Together, it is implied, as they have in the past, they will find strength and direction.

COMMUNITY: GATHERING STRENGTH FROM ONE ANOTHER

Steinbeck not only portrays the strength of character that both Ma and Pa gain by transcending gender roles, he also shows that cooperation, collaboration, and caring are greater than the sum of their parts. It is this cooperative and caring pathway that he recommends as a solution to the problems of the migrant workers. Human beings gain strength from one another: two people working together overcome their perplexity and loneliness; a family sharing meager supplies with a family that has no food gains kinship and goodwill. Together they are stronger than alone. For example, although we do not observe the outcome in *Grapes*, Tom's moving away from *I* to *we* shows the first step toward overcoming catastrophe.

Dispossessed of their homes and livelihood in the midst of a land of plenty, over and over again the migrants demonstrate a sense of community, sharing in another's hardship and grief. A child at one of the overnight camps dies of malnutrition, and his family does not have enough money to bury him. Sharing out of very limited resources, the migrant campers leave a small pile of coins in front of the grieving family's tent. Ironically, these hardships and the hostility of the local residents and law officials serve also to unite the migrants and to weld them together.

NOTES

1. Peter Lisca, with Kevin Hearle, eds. *"John Steinbeck, The Grapes of Wrath": Text and Criticism* (New York: Penguin Books, 1997), 1. Hereafter references to this work will be cited parenthetically within the text, identified as *Grapes* with pertinent page numbers.

2. Jonathan Kozol, *Rachel and Her Children: Homeless Families in America* (New York: Fawcett Columbine, 1988).

3. Mary Ellen Caldwell, "A New Consideration of the Intercalary Chapters in *The Grapes of Wrath*," *Markham Review* (May 1973), 116.

4. See note 2.

6 Narrative Art

> I think a book should be itself, complete and in print. What went into
> the writing of it is no business of the reader. I disapprove of having my
> crabbed hand exposed.
> —Letter to Pascal Covici, February 23, 1939, Elaine Steinbeck
> and Robert Wallsten, *Steinbeck: A Life in Letters* (1975), 180–81

PROCESS AND PRODUCT

Steinbeck insisted that his novel should stand on its own—an artifact complete in itself—that how it came to be written was none of the reader's business and that he did not want to make his writing process open to public view. Such insistence is delightfully ironic, for he has left behind him a journal and letters that contain a meticulous account of the context in which his novel was written and of a disciplined writing process that produced over six hundred pages in one hundred days. These letters and the journal that accompany *Grapes* show us a writer who was not only extraordinarily aware of the art of writing, but who was also determined to document his process in writing. That is, he not only gives us a monumental work of art, but often he also shows us in elaborate detail how it came into being.

The symbiosis of process and product here could be compared to the modern technique of ultrasound whereby parents may observe the embryo of their developing child, discover its gender, and watch him or her move and grow over time. As the embryo becomes a recognizable baby, so the mapped-out plan of the writer is transformed into recognizable, complementary forms—one a novel and the other a documentary of its making. Steinbeck's observations about the process and experience of writing *Grapes* may be found in letters and in the journal entries written between May and October 1938, published in 1989 as *Working Days: The Journals of "The Grapes of Wrath,"*[1] edited by Robert DeMott. A rhetorical analysis of his observations on writing alongside the novel itself elucidates the relationship between process and product by making transparent Steinbeck's thoughts on writing, his persona in the novel, and his intentions—including the relationship among writer, text, and reader—writing strategies, stylistic techniques, and character creation.

THE DAILY TASK

The journal entries tell us much about Steinbeck's writerly concerns and his occasional doubts over whether or not he is fit for the task at hand. In detail they set forth his writing experience and process, together with the domestic scene, the noise, and the interruptions of his everyday life at the time. He was always intensely aware of his physical surroundings; in the Los Gatos house he was frequently bothered by the noise of the neighbors' constantly blaring radio (*WD* 28). Often, too, the sound of the washing machine annoyed him. Still, because he is going beyond the creation of an image for readers to the creation of an experience in which they can feel and participate, he determines that he must keep working at a slow, steady pace if his novel is to be good. He believed, too, that he had to maintain discipline over himself, the material of his novel, and the language of the story for it to be couched in the most fitting words, in the most fitting places (*WD* 26). This acute awareness of his physical surroundings, this insistence that his writing pace must be disciplined and slow in order to evoke an experience for the reader, and this concern for decorum in his use of language are prevalent throughout the journal and evident throughout the novel itself.

On July 25, 1938, he is especially concerned with himself and his physical surroundings, with the minutia of life: he has an upset stomach from eating melon; he has endured a restless, scary, windy night with Carol away from home; and the flies in the house are disturbing him. When he shifts his focus away from the immediate domestic circumstances to his work, however, he immediately turns a devoted attention to the materials of his writing—a daily journal and a writing pen. He begins his writing task on this day, as always, with the journal, first stating that "this diary is really valuable" and next turning his attention to his pen. Appreciatively, he observes that if he holds it up straighter, it "writes thinner. . . . This has been a good pen to me so far. Never had such a good one" (*WD* 49).

Later, after he and Carol are settled at the Biddle ranch and after the publication of *Grapes*, in the journal entry for July 26, 1940, Steinbeck describes an idyllic scene in which the writing task, the tools of writing, and his surroundings are in accord. Again he writes of the physical aspects of writing: how he keeps his fingers from getting sticky in hot weather by rubbing them with alcohol and how important it is to him for the pen to feel "slick" in his hand. He luxuriates in the sensuousness of his surroundings as well as of the pen in his hand and the "fine paper" on the desk before him:

> There's something very good about this kind of affair. My room is cool and lovely. Outside a blinding sun and I at a roll top desk—I've always wanted one and they are perfect. . . . And a swivel chair that comes to the perfect height. I can see the greenhouse from here, and the perfect pen and the perfect paper and me working on work that pleases me. . . . And it is fun. Well the time is now to go to work and I have a good feeling about it. It is nice to be this way. (*WD* 118)

Such joy comes only rarely in the human experience, and here it results from his anticipation of writing in this place. Here Steinbeck is the bardic artist and creator at work. "Good" is a word he has repeated over and over again in these journals—hoping and praying that his work will be good. But here it is the process of the work itself that is good. Childlike, he revels in the "fun" of writing and creating. There is pure satisfaction, contentment, and self-abandonment in this scene as he surveys the prospect of beginning to work again at a task that he loves. True, an ominous note intrudes even now, for he remembers that critics await his next brainchild as they have the others, and, for the moment, he questions whether he will even submit it for publication. Of course, this thought is a rationalization—for him, writing can be such a frightening thing. Superstitiously he concludes that he is a bit fearful when things go right for him, knowing that the experience cannot last.

In the journal entry for September 30, 1938, Steinbeck had given the other side of the picture, a time when he had to be constantly on guard against intrusions, when he is confused by the pressures of everyday life on top of the book that must somehow get written: "I must get down to it now and prove to myself that I can still concentrate no matter how badly. . . . Get to it and fight it through" (*WD* 80). But later in the July 29, 1940, entry, speaking from experience, he tells how he managed to survive the ordinary, everyday grind. In order to complete a writing task, he muses, one has to be a person of habit, determined to get a set number of words down on paper day after day: "In writing, habit seems to be a much stronger force than either willpower or inspiration" (*WD* 118). And on August 23, he determines to continue writing slowly and deliberately, believing this pace to be appropriate for him (*WD* 119). Later, in *Travels with Charley in Search of America*,[2] he affirms the importance of achieving such a perspective and distance so that people can have time to absorb the material: "Man has to have feelings and then words before he can come close to thought," a process that takes "a long time" (*Travels* 33).

Steinbeck's observations concerning the necessity of achieving a deliberately slow pace so that the feelings can be translated into thought are reminiscent of the Romantic writers Jean-Jacques Rousseau and William Wordsworth. In his *Confessions*, Rousseau proclaims, "I felt before I thought: this is the common lot of humanity."[3] Similarly, in his 1802 *Preface to Lyrical Ballads, with Pastoral and Other Poems*, Wordsworth defines poetry as "the spontaneous overflow of powerful feelings: it takes its origin from emotion recollected in tranquillity."[4] All three writers thus suggest a progression from the subjective to the objective in the translation of human emotions, or "feelings," into words and thoughts—requiring an observation of the self and its experiences from a distance. Thus, given an ever-widening, distancing focus, "powerful feelings" become modified and diffused as time and reflection alter perspective. The slow pace that Steinbeck determines to follow, then, provides both him and his reader time for translating emotions, or feelings, into thought. The question arises here, however, of just how Steinbeck achieves such an objective.

ACHIEVING A SLOW PACE

How, then, does Steinbeck achieve a suitably slow pace so that readers can go through the process of translating emotions into thought? Through his creation of a narrative persona and statement of intentions, he answers this question. Steinbeck wanted the narrator to be an authentic voice, to be transparently honest in giving background, in setting a scene, in depicting the contrasting lives of the tenant/migrants and the large landowners/companies. His intention, therefore, was to capture the diction, rhythm, and flow of language to decorously fit the topic, the occasion, and the characters. Such use of language often owes as much to music and poetry as it does to straight exposition. In journal entry #6 for June 4, 1938, Steinbeck stated his intentions to capture in interchapter 5 what he considers to be a most important tone and overtone—the sounds and the smell of the tractors and the tractor drivers. For this is the tone that accompanies the eviction of the tenants and the reason for their departure from the land (*WD* 22–23).

This interchaper portrays the banks and large land companies as they are "tractoring off" the tenant farmers who were once owners of the land. In this entry he states that this chapter "must have a *symphonic* overtone, . . . must make *music* again [emphasis added]" (*WD* 22). The key words here are "symphonic" and "music," and interchapter 5 draws on the sonata in both structure and material. A perusal of the sonata form of exposition, development, recapitulation—the latter used especially for the first movement—and the structure of interchapter 5 illustrates how Steinbeck used the ponderous complexity and variety of a symphony as a structural device. In this chapter the narrator's persona performs similarly to an orchestra conductor, with the intention of giving great dignity, weight, and momentum to the tragic dispossession of the tenant families, hence Steinbeck's continual concern with the pace of his writing. The exposition occurs in the first paragraph when the landowners come out to the farms and meet with the tenant men. The development occurs in scenes.

The development begins in the first scene in a discussion between the owners and the tenants centering around a monstrous bank that must continually consume profits in order to live.[5] For this reason the tenants are to be evicted, their houses leveled, the land tractor plowed into straight rows to grow cotton, a good money crop (*Grapes* 34–38). When the land is exhausted from the cotton, it will be sold for real estate to people out East. To no avail the tenants protest that the land had been theirs, or their fathers', or their grandfathers' before debt forced them to borrow from the bank. With a lingering focus on the anxiety, pain, and terror of the tenant families, the scene closes and a spacebreak is created on the page.

Following this spacebreak, the second scene continues the development by focusing on the coming of the tractors, described as "snub-nosed monsters" snouting around in the dust, plowing straight lines that go right on through the fences, yards, and even ditches (*Grapes* 38). The driver of the tractor, more robot than man, neither cares for nor understands the land. Hence, he guides the plow down the straight, straight rows with no regard for the well being of the land's contours and its need for the variety of rotating crops so that it can replenish itself. Instead, these tractors plow in preparation for monocropping cotton that will leech out nutrients essential to its life. This scene closes with hideous images of rapine of the land with the image of the tractor's seeders metaphorically compared to twelve penises that rape "methodically, . . . without passion. . . . The land bore under iron, and under iron gradually died; it was not loved or hated, it had no prayers or curses" (*Grapes* 39). Scene two closes the separation between the land and human beings, leaving both alienated and cut off from the other.

After another spacebreak on the page, scene three in this symphonic development depicts a single tenant's house, in front of which parents and curious children, who are eating fried dough, watch as a tractor driver eats a Spam sandwich with pickle and cheese, followed by a piece of store-bought pie. Then, explaining that he must do his job and keep his rows straight, the driver, who is a neighbor's son, bumps over the family's house with the tractor. The tenant man, his frightened wife and children beside him, just stands, staring after the tractor, gun in hand (*Grapes* 39–42).

The end of scene three is also a recapitulation, an echo of the opening scene with the tenant men and their wives and children, who are looking out of their doorways at the landowners in their "closed cars" (*Grapes* 34). But there is a final variation from scene one's third person plural portrayal of tenant men, women, and children. For the final scene telescopes in on one particular tenant family—a man with his wife and children—as they look out over the plowed land and the straight rows after the departing tractor driver. The movement of the music and the story have come full circle, a return to the beginning but here with a sharp, particular focus that enables the reader to understand the broader, fuller implications of their story.

As Steinbeck had determined in his journal, this chapter has "a symphonic overtone" in pace as well—a slow, ponderous movement that gives readers the time to develop their feelings and emotions into thoughts (*WD* 22). He achieves this symphonic pace in interchapter 5 by employing several musical, poetic devices: repetition and variation of words and phrases; epithets, parallel structure, and "and-and"construction; and dialogue in first and second person alternating with an omniscient, omnipresent narrator's voice who speaks in the third person. The voice of this narrator is that of the Old Testament prophet. Whereas the voices of the landowners and the tenants are often laden with dramatic irony and reveal more than the speaker realizes or intends, the narrator speaks in the authentic voice of one who has seen all and knows all.

Repetition and variation of words and phrases are the first devices by which Steinbeck slows the pace of his prose. Like an echoing, reverberating motif, the words "you know" and "God knows" are repeated in close juxtaposition, sometimes with variation, in paragraphs three, four, five, and six of interchapter 5:

Paragraph three: "*You know* the land is poor. . . . *God knows.*"

Paragraph four: "*They knew, God knows.*"

Paragraph five: "*You know. . . . You know.*"

Paragraph six: "*They knew, God knew*" [emphasis added] (*Grapes* 34–35).

This repetition and variation give the text a biblical, somber tone, a sad antiphonal echo that alternates between the dialogue in second person and the narrator in third person. With a similar effect, juxtaposed in six paragraphs, the words "three dollars a day" occur nine times and "three dollars" once. Other words repeated for emphasis and tone include "straight," "raping," "no man," and "under iron," among others (*Grapes* 38–40).

Paragraphs three, four, five, and six of interchapter 5, quoted above, demonstrate also the alternation between the first-person and second-person dialogue and the narrator's third-person exposition. So close is the narrator to the tenant men and the owner men in this dialogue, it is as though he were also a participant with them in this drama leading up to the tenant men's dispossession and eviction. He knows their thoughts and their feelings and records them in the third person, interspersed in the dialogue: "The squatting tenant men . . . knew, God knows. If the dust only wouldn't fly. If the top would only stay on the soil, it might not be so bad. . . . If they could only rotate the crops they might pump blood back into the land" (*Grapes* 34–35).

The narrator experiences the pathos of this dramatic enactment of the tenant men's desperation, their frustrated hopes and futile dreams. But they all know that when the owner men show up in their sealed cars to do an analysis, all is lost. For such men never appreciate all of the factors involved, always ignoring the exhausted land and the evicted people.

Although the people in this interchapter are not named, each bears an identifying epithet that takes the place of a specific name. Steinbeck's use of epithets is similar in effect to repetition but with a more specific purpose. A Homeric epic device, the epithet serves as an identifying characteristic. For example, "owner men," varied once in this interchapter as "the fifty-thousand-acre owner," and "tenant men," varied once as "the squatting men," at once identify and characterize, defining the relationship between the two groups of men.

Also, parallel structure is similar in effect to repetition and is often used in conjunction with it, as shown below. Steinbeck's use of parallel structure is a poetic as well as a rhetorical device, and all that some of these passages require to make them poetry is to be set off in lines, illustrated in the format below. Thus, setting off words, phrases, or clauses in parallel grammatical structure serves to make the impact of this structure greater than the sum of its individual parts—each part gains weight by being juxtaposed in parallels. For example, note the following description of the monster bank's goggling and muzzling the tractor driver—formatted to highlight the parallels. The "monster" has

> "*goggled* . . . and *muzzled* him—
>
> *goggled his mind*, *muzzled his speech*,
>
> *goggled his perception*, *muzzled his protest*" [emphasis added] (*Grapes* 38).

Like a hammer blow, the repetition of the words and the parallel grammatical structure of the verbs and direct objects depict the tractor driver's powerlessness and helplessness, with blinders on his eyes so that he cannot see, a muzzle on his tongue and mouth so that he cannot speak or protest. Throughout this interchapter there are similar poetic reverberations, ponderously affecting meaning as well as tone. The parallels describing the condition of the land after the dispossession of the tenants and the takeover by the large landowners are especially poignant:

> "It was not *loved or hated*,
>
> it had no *prayers or curses*" [emphasis added] (*Grapes* 39).

These parallel words—first parallel verbs and then parallel objects of the verb—reinforce one another. Human beings are passionate about land with which they have a connection—land they have crumbled in their hands, smelled, stood upon, felt—loving or hating it in turn, depending on the year or the yield. With the coming of the tractors, however, the connection and the passion are gone, and in their place is simply indifference.

Steinbeck similarly uses "and-and" construction to create the tenant experience for the reader. The use of "and-and" construction is another rhetorical means of giving a passage weight, intentionally drawing out the meaning rather than condensing it. The passage quoted and specially formatted below, for example, could be condensed to read, "They came in closed cars, felt the dry earth with their fingers, and sometimes drove big earth augers into the ground for soil tests." Such a sentence has precision, but not weight, not taking the reader step by painful step into the horror and nightmare of the tenant families who are watching this scene. Steinbeck's use of "and-and" construction is reminiscent of the Bible and of Walt Whitman's *Leaves of Grass*. It is cumulative, building and connecting until a picture or a concept takes form. And, on occasion, the opposite word, "but," gives a contrasting viewpoint.

In paragraphs one through nine of interchapter 5, which is a little more than eleven pages, there are nine compound sentences joined with "and"; three opening transitional uses of "and"; six compound verbs joined by "and"; and three compound nouns joined by "and." In paragraph nine the opposite, or "but," is used as an opening transitional word, providing a contrast rather than a connection. There are a total of twenty "ands" in eight paragraphs, with a "but" introducing the ninth paragraph. An example in the second sentence of this interchapter shows this seemingly simple construction that nevertheless builds with detail after detail—details that are often cumulative actions. The format is altered here to show the connections graphically:

They came in closed cars, *and*

they felt the dry earth with their fingers, *and*

sometimes they drove big earth augers into the ground for soil tests
[emphasis added] (*Grapes* 34).

Here "and" connects a string of related independent clauses in a compound sentence. Sealed off from the tenants and the land in their cars, the land-owners come to analyze and test the land just as they would analyze and test a machine in a factory. For them, the land is "soil," a growing medium for an agricultural factory, from which they will take all that they can get, with no regard for its well being. Throughout the novel this "and" construction has a similar weighty, cumulative, connecting effect.

Paragraph nine begins with a contrasting connector, "but." The tenants have asked that they be considered when the banks make their decisions about the land—at least to the extent that they be paid enough to cover taxes owed on the land and food for their families. Their humble request is countered with a sentence beginning with "but." They cannot possibly be considered because banks must have more and more profits to breathe, to eat, to consume—an ugly image of an entity that is constantly consuming and demanding more.

Although the author's narrative persona in this most carefully created symphonic interchapter is omniscient and omnipresent, he also cares, grieves, and walks with the migrant men and their families—knowing and feeling their thoughts and emotions. Steinbeck has made his intentions clear. That is, by drawing this dramatic scene with such obvious empathy, enhanced by its musical overtones, he has intended also to draw readers into the picture as well, so that they are taken beyond the memorable image into a participation, an experience. In letters and in journals he has made his designs on readers clear. He wants to make them understand both cognitively and empathetically what it is like to be among the dispossessed, lonely, and alienated in the midst of a land of plenty. He accomplished his task—as readers read this story, they become one with the novel.

WRITER, TEXT, AND READER

The relationship among writer, text, and reader was of the utmost importance to Steinbeck. Devoted and dedicated to his work, he concerned himself with a continuing analysis of all aspects that touched on his writing, with the ultimate end—illustrated above—of involving readers in the experience of his story. In the journal entry for August 4, 1938, Steinbeck confirms his belief that both keeping the journal and writing his novel are worthwhile even when he is not in a frame of mind to work (*WD* 52). In a journal pep talk to himself, he maintains that he has to continue writing and that he must not think about anything else. In part at least, the reason for his dedication to the task of writing is that the novel has its own reality for him. There is a very real sense in which he himself actually enters into the world of the Joads and participates in it. In *Steinbeck's Typewriter: Essays on His Art*,[6] DeMott states: "His act of composing was also an act of validation and self-creation, a way of fulfilling his emotional and psychological dream of belonging, by being 'at home,' by living in the architectural spaces he created. In fact, this creative, interior, or architextual level of engagement is the elusive and heretofore unacknowledged fifth layer of Steinbeck's novel."

Such an "architextual level" of involvement with the text may be observed in Steinbeck's journals in which he writes about the Joads as "my family" and maps out where he must take them during the day's work: "Now today I must move my family fast" (*WD* 52). The closeness of his involvement with his created family may be seen most clearly in the journal entry for October 20, 1938. Ill and on the verge of exhaustion, he evidently has a vision of Tom Joad's actually coming into his work space: "'Tom! Tom! Tom!' I know. It wasn't him. Yes, I think I can go on now. In fact, I feel stronger. Much stronger. Funny where the energy comes from. Now to work only now it isn't work any more" (*WD* 91). Here, as DeMott points out, "Steinbeck arrived at the intersection of the novel and journal, that luminous vector, that fifth layer of involvement where writer and text not only merge but interpenetrate" (*Steinbeck's Typewriter* 186).

Just as there is an intersection at which Steinbeck and the Joads merge and he enters into his text as a participant, even so there is a level at which he expects the reader to enter into a similar relationship with the text. He is concerned to write this book with "honesty," and, in an epigrammatic statement in his journal entry for June 18, 1938, he makes clear his purpose: "Never temper a word to a reader's prejudice, but bend it like putty for his understanding" (*WD* 30). He is not writing a novel to please his readers, but he is writing one into which they can enter with empathy, as he himself has done. For Steinbeck there is no other path by which human beings may arrive at understanding. As C.S. Lewis has so graphically illustrated in *The Abolition of Man*, human beings "without chests," or hearts, are not human beings at all. With the heart as well as with the head, human beings can understand—but never with just the head alone. Steinbeck, then, does not appeal to the mind alone when he seeks understanding, but to the emotions, the soul, and the spirit. Although his purpose is to make the reader know through experience, he is then criticized for sentimentality.

STYLISTIC DECORUM

By what stylistic techniques does Steinbeck create a book that becomes a series of experiences for the reader? Perhaps most importantly he loved language and had a concern for linguistic decorum—choosing just the right word for use in just the right place. Drawing on this sense of decorum, Steinbeck created in *Grapes* a veritable compendium of styles—each suited to the occasion, the speaker, the audience, the times. With biblical and Whitmanesque overtones—parallel structure, "and-and" constructions, repetition of key words—chapter 1 sets a mood of impending disaster. Interchapter 3's symbolic account of the turtle's crossing the road is in the voice of a storyteller. In interchapter 5 the symphonic account of the coming of the tractors and eviction of the tenants is in the voice of the poet bard who lends the pathos of poetry and music to the tragic tale. Throughout *Grapes* each voice of the narrative persona is likewise fitted to the occasion and the purpose.

Concerned for decorum in diction as well as in tone and voice, Steinbeck sought just the right word to create for the reader what he called "the actuality" of the migrant experience. One of the most striking of Steinbeck's stylistic characteristics in diction is his use of verbs, with one well-chosen verb bringing an action to life so that it defines character. To illustrate, in narrative chapter 8 after Tom's release from prison for second-degree murder in self-defense, as he and Casy arrive at Uncle John's house, they observe Pa Joad's transforming a Hudson Super-Six sedan into a truck. His hammer *thunders* the nail into a board (*Grapes* 73). Immediately the reader knows that Pa is a man of great strength and decisive resolution, that he knows what has to be done and does it with vigor—from thundering nails into a board to any other chore that comes to his hand.

Later, near the end of the novel, this thundering quality of Pa's character will stand in contrast when he will respond "weakly" to Ma's insistence that they must leave the flooded boxcar. He will tell her that they cannot leave—knowing that they have no where to go, no money, and no work. Although he believes that the man should be the head of the household, the one who makes the decisions, he will finally acquiesce and follow her lead (*Grapes* 450). With this one verb, "thunder," then, Steinbeck has depicted one of Pa's primary characteristics, one that Ma will take on at the novel's end.

Chapter 8 opens with another felicitous choice of verb. Morning is approaching, and Steinbeck signals this approach, stating that "the sky *grayed* among the stars" [emphasis added], capturing the essence of that first lightening of the darkness that comes before the dawn (*Grapes* 69). In the same scene, as Tom and Casy look down on the morning light shining on Uncle John's house, they see that "the sun *flashed* on the windows of the house," and "two red chickens on the ground *flamed* with reflected light" [emphasis added] (*Grapes* 72). With the specificity and intensity of poetry, the verbs *flashed* and *flamed* vividly reinforce one another here, both in the impact of their capturing exactly what the early morning sun does and in the alliteration of their initial letters.

Also, the sun is an active, dynamic entity in its own right in *Grapes*, its relative glare or dimness documenting the drought or an approaching dust storm. In general chapter 1, for instance, while the dust is hanging in the air "like fog, . . . the sun was as ripe as ripe new blood" (*Grapes* 7). The metaphorical comparison of dust to fog and the sun to "ripe new blood" is reminiscent of the Old Testament prophet Joel's description of the "Day of the Lord," or the end of times: "I will show wonders in the heavens and on the earth, blood and fire and billows of smoke. The sun will be turned to darkness and the moon to blood before the coming of the great and dreadful day of the Lord" (Joel 2:30–31, *The Jerusalem Bible*). And it was just this sense of apocalypse and catastrophe that characterizes these times of natural disaster and human displacement. Steinbeck thus fittingly describes the natural setting in which the tragedy of the dust bowl took place.

The sentence style and diction that Steinbeck employs for the opening paragraph of general chapter 1 is likewise suited to its description of the scenic backdrop for the parallel stories of the dust bowl tenant farmers turned migrants and the Joad family. It is instructive at this point to consider the view of a critic who does not view this passage—or *Grapes* itself for that matter—favorably. In his 1988 *John Steinbeck's "The Grapes of Wrath,"* [7] Harold Bloom has challenged the artistry of *Grapes* in general and of this opening in particular, claiming that "the wavering strength" of this opening "is located in a curious American transformation of biblical substance and style that worked splendidly in Whitman and Hemingway, but seems to work only fitfully in Steinbeck" (Bloom 1).

Bloom asserts further that "Steinbeck suffers from too close a comparison with Hemingway, whose shadow always hovered too near" (1). To substantiate this assertion, Bloom chooses the opening of *Grapes* and a passage from *The Sun Also Rises* to illustrate his point, claiming unconvincingly and without substantial evidence that Steinbeck's opening "is not so much biblical style as mediated by Ernest Hemingway as it is Hemingway assimilated to Steinbeck's sense of biblical style" (Bloom 2). Not bothering to analyze it or give examples, he just makes a sweeping claim.

The criteria by which Bloom evaluates style are left in doubt here, for even a cursory perusal of the Hemingway and Steinbeck passages reveals more differences than similarities between the styles of the two writers. To illustrate, Hemingway uses more periodic and balanced sentences—varied with a cumulative sentence, three "there was" or "there were" constructions, and two subject-verb inversions. He uses a form of the verb "to be" fifteen times. Steinbeck, on the other hand, uses almost as many loose sentences as periodic, sometimes beginning them with a prepositional phrase. He uses no subject-verb inversions, no cumulative sentences, no "there was" or "there were" constructions. He uses a form of "to be" only twice, preferring strong, descriptive verbs: "flared," "crusted," "dusted," "frayed," "edged," "struck," "widened," "moved," and "paled."

The two authors use similar colors: Hemingway uses white, dusty green, brown, dark gray, and red, whereas Steinbeck uses red, gray, dark red, pale green, white, and brown. But Hemingway describes a journey leading to a peopled landscape with "red roofs," "white houses," and "the gray metal-sheathed roof of the monastery of Roncevales," whereas Steinbeck provides not just a landscape but ironic images of death: the sky and the land on which all earthly life depends are growing "pale" and "brown," seemingly dying.

Bloom praises "Hemingway's Basque landscapes" in which "the contrast between rich soil and barren ground, between wooded hills and heat-baked mountains, is a figure for the lost potency of Jake Barnes, but also for a larger sense of the lost possibilities of life" (Bloom 3). But he negates Steinbeck's achievement: "Steinbeck, following after Hemingway, cannot learn the lesson. He gives us a vision of the Oklahoma Dust Bowl, and it is effective enough, but it is merely a landscape where a process of entropy has been enacted" (Bloom 3).

By invoking his own theory of the literary relationships between the great writers and their predecessors, Bloom misses the point here.

Steinbeck's "vision of the Oklahoma Dust Bowl" is not "merely a landscape," but an ominous, threatening image of the death of the land itself, a fitting backdrop for the struggles of human beings dependent upon the land. For his further assertions that Steinbeck "lacks skill in plot, and power in the nemesis of character," Bloom offers no explanation or evidence (Bloom 4).

Steinbeck's consummate artistry in this opening paragraph speaks for itself. Even the opening sentence sets a scene with a sense of something badly awry with the earth itself: "To the red country and part of the gray country of Oklahoma, the last rains came gently, and they did not cut the scarred earth" (*Grapes* 5). There is a specificity of place here—"Oklahoma"—that gives the scene an immediacy, a closeness. The adjective "last" is ominous and even apocalyptic, leaving the reader with a sense of foreboding that there will be no felicitous outcome to this tale of natural disaster. The adverb "gently" tells us that the hard-packed earth cannot soak up the rain. And the verb "cut" invokes images of surgery or infliction of pain on an earth already "scarred" and sorely wounded. This sentence speaks with great beauty and decorum. Yale University's Sterling Professor Bloom, for all of his many talents, simply does not read Steinbeck well—or does not want to read Steinbeck well.

ARTISTRY IN DRAWING CHARACTER

As noted above, as well as asserting that "Steinbeck's aesthetic problem was Hemingway, whose shadow always hovered too near," Bloom also states that Steinbeck "lacks ... power in the nemesis of character" without offering any explanation or evidence (4). Actually, focusing on one short scene—the funeral of Grampa in narrative chapter 13—and on the accompanying journal entries demonstrates an artistry in drawing character that is uniquely Steinbeck's own. In the journal entry for July 11, 1938, Steinbeck stated that his writing topic for the day would be Grampa's funeral. Planning to complete it in one day, he only gets half of the scene done, however, finishing it on the following day. In his journal he writes that he intends for this section to be "*good* and *full* of *fullness* and *completions*. And *that feeling* must go into it. .... *The force of folk ceremonial*" [emphasis added] (*WD* 41).

This section captures the essence of the Joad family in their connections to one another, to the Wilsons, and to the universe itself. For Steinbeck's characters are defined by their actions, their gestures, their interactions with others—by their deeds as well as by their appearance and their words. After Grampa dies in the Wilsons' tent, charitably loaned to them,

Steinbeck writes that "the family became a unit," with the men in the typical council position, squatting down on the ground together to discuss the situation, and Ma, Ruthie, and Winfield standing behind (*Grapes* 140). Granma is sitting "proudly" and "coldly" as long as the family is watching, stoically bearing up under grief as her people always do, but when they turn their attention away from her, she lies down and covers her face (*Grapes* 140).

It is evening, and the reddening sunset lights up their faces as the sunrise had reddened the windows of Uncle John's house when they drove away in the loaded down truck, leaving home behind them. The sky is reflected in their eyes, connecting them to the enormity of the universe—a connection they will not leave behind. The evening itself is personified in this scene, for it is limited as the Joads and Wilsons are—like them prohibited from the resplendent shining of reflected glory in the windows of a house—and is reduced, like them, to picking up "light where it could" (*Grapes* 140). So it shines in the eyes of the people.

These people are defined by their actions and gestures. The Wilsons have proved themselves hospitable by lending their tent, where Grampa died. Sairy Wilson shows her sympathy by sitting with Granma, but respectfully avoiding touching her because such a gesture might make her break down—unacceptable behavior for her kind of people. The Joads all agree that they are "beholden" to the Wilsons for their kindness in lending the tent. Although the Wilsons maintain that when someone is dying, there are no debts owed for helping out, Al volunteers to repair their car, with Tom's help. And, reinforcing the family unit again, Al is especially pleased to be the one in the family who can return the Wilsons' favor. The lengthy debate over how to have a funeral and burial for Grampa reveals an honest, law-abiding, decent family. And their decision to go against the law, to bury him themselves as their forebears had done and leave a note explaining he had died of natural causes, attests to their humane and responsible reasonableness in doing what must be done (*Grapes* 140 ff.).

Ma's insistence that the burial note have some scripture verse written on it shows her concern for the spirit as well as the body, as does the family's gratitude in having Casy, a former preacher, to preside over the service. Casy's presence comforts and assures the Joads even though he keeps telling them he is no longer a preacher—evidence of his leadership ability and his sincere concern for their family. Although she is still a fatuous, adolescent girl, Rose of Sharon's worry over her unborn child reveals her potential to be a devoted, responsible mother—another citadel around which a family may be established—as Ma Joad has been to her. Ma's own laborious task of washing and preparing Grampa's body for burial, lovingly performed, shows a woman of great strength and boundless love for her family. Ruthie and Winfield's unnatural solemnity, their horror at putting Grampa underground, and Winfield's pitiful, lonely crying portray the bewilderment of children in the presence of death and loss. And the Wilsons and the Joads prove themselves to be kindred spirits, hospitably caring for another, lifting loads, and sharing responsibilities. Later, the reader is reluctant and sorry to see the Wilsons, of necessity, left behind as the Joads continue their journey.

In his journal entry Steinbeck had wanted this scene to be "good." Further, he defines what he means by "good": (1) "full of fullness and completions," (2) with "that feeling" in it, and (3) with "the force of folk ceremonial." The echoing of "*full*" and "*fullness*" indicates the richness and totality that he intends for this scene. This "fullness" is there in the defining gestures: in Granma's proud coldness as she sits in the family gathering, knowing that this is her moment, her time to be on show, her time to hold up on the outside even when the inside may be crumbling; in the details of Ma's laying out the body; in Sairy Wilson's helping Rose of Sharon prepare the evening meal; in the kindness of both families during a time of loss and sorrow. The "completions" are there in the unity of the family and their friendship with the Wilsons, and the "completions" are there in another sense in that Grampa's life is completed at this time. For his body is prepared for burial by Ma; his obituary is written by his grandson, Tom; and he is buried by his sons. As Tom will later point out, even if Grampa made the journey to California, his spirit would never have left Oklahoma. His life, then, is completed before the journey is well begun.

"That feeling" is most certainly there as well in the care with which Tom and Ma plan the contents of the note to be buried with Grampa, agree that it is suitable for Tom as a kinsman to write the note, and place it carefully in a glass jar, with its lid tightly screwed. It is also there in Pa, Uncle John, Noah, and Al's carrying the dead body to the grave site and Pa's leaping into it, holding up his arms to receive his father's body in his hands and lower it gently to the ground. The feeling is there, too, in the firelit scene of the family gathered around for Casy's brief funeral service, for they did not dare bury him during the day because of the law. In Ruthie's solemn proclamation to Winfield that their Grampa is under that pile of dirt; in their concealment of the grave, despite Pa's protests—in all of these actions and gestures comes "that feeling" of pathos for the human condition. For Steinbeck has created the feeling and the experience for the reader by what he called "the force of folk ceremonial," but also by the loving participation of the writer as he mingles among his people in that fifth, elusive layer of meaning in this novel. Ideally, at its best, as here in the burial ceremony for

Grampa Joad, the text, its writer, and the reader participate in an experience that is fully engaging, one that demands the exercise of the will and the heart, as well as the mind—as Steinbeck intended.

Steinbeck's desired "completion" and "feeling" are evident in scenes throughout the novel, defining character as well as developing theme and plot. And here as in Grampa's funeral, gesture and action, as well as description, define character. Readers remember Ma, jack handle in hand, amazing Pa by her defiance, insisting that the family stay together rather than leave Tom and Casy behind to repair the Wilsons' car. They remember, too, Ma's preparing a meager stew for her family, with a circle of hungry children watching—close enough to brush against her as she works—and her leaving some stew for them in the bottom of the pot. These actions capture the essence of Ma Joad. She and Rose of Sharon are likewise characterized by the scene in which Ma pierces her ears and gives her daughter a pair of earrings—a most cherished possession, one of the few personal items she has brought with her. Along with the earrings, she is passing along a heritage of strong, noble, loving women. Not surprisingly, Rose of Sharon will act in character in the novel's end, giving to a stranger out of her own need.

Other characters are similarly defined in motion, gesture, and action. The first major character in the novel is introduced in chapter 2, in which Tom Joad is on his way home after serving four years of a seven-year sentence for manslaughter in self-defense. Although he is Ma's right-hand man, on whom she depends and in whom she confides her hopes and fears, the reader is aware throughout the novel of his potential for violent retaliation. Leaving Hooverville, Ma sits beside him as he drives, warning him to keep calm when they are stopped at a roadblock, enabling him to play the humiliating role of a subservient when he is questioned, and praising him for playing the part well. Tom later behaves in character, then, when he strikes out at the man who kills Casy.

Tom Joad Sr. is a hardworking family man, and, for all of his chatter about taking a stick to Ma when she defies his leadership, he often defers to her, valuing her wisdom and trusting her judgment. In the end he is defined most poignantly as he takes on some of Ma's responsibilities and attributes. For instance, he peels and cooks potatoes (that he has probably stolen) for the family's supper and carries Rose of Sharon in his arms through floodwaters from the boxcar to the highway and then up a hill to a deserted barn where he sets her down gently. His brother, Uncle John, is always sad, walking under a dark cloud because he holds himself responsible for his wife's death from appendicitis; as a result he goes on occasional drinking sprees, quite literally to drown his sorrows.

Al Joad is at once typically adolescent—in his constant search for girls—and mature in his knowledge of cars, proving himself dependable at least in this arena. Ruthie and Winfield are typical children. They argue, whine, play, sneakily hide so that they can watch Rose of Sharon give birth—falling asleep, however, and missing out. Granma and Grampa are portrayed as feisty old people, needing extra rest and attention. For example, Granma's religiosity is prominent—in her favorite phrase, praising God for victory, and in her delight in having the preacher Casy say grace or pray for Grampa when he becomes ill. In his constant cursing and fumbling with his pants buttons, which he can never get quite right, Grampa is portrayed as notably cantankerous and senile. His grandson Tom laughingly tells Ma that even if he lives for a hundred years, Grampa will never be housebroken, a most appropriate description.

Noah Joad, the oldest son, was injured in childbirth, leaving him with no apparent emotions or even a sexual drive. A reliable worker, helping his family get ready for the trip and traveling as far as the river at Needles, he nevertheless leaves them at this point to travel downstream alongside the river, fishing for a living. Although he tells Tom that he is sad to be leaving them, this lonely figure parts from Tom with no handshake, no gesture of affection. Noah is mostly remembered, then, for what is *not* present in his character, rather than what is. Jim Casy, a former preacher, still has a deep love for people and goes along with the Joads as the thirteenth person on their journey to California. As Tom describes him, he is a "talker," a gregarious, outgoing, caring person who sacrificially offers himself as the guilty culprit who has attacked a deputy in a confrontation at Hooverville and who also sacrificially dies during a strike at the peach orchards of the Hooper ranch.

Connie Rivers, Rose of Sharon's husband, may be seen as more of a lover and a dreamer than a husband. The couple seems happy enough for the first half of the journey. As young lovers they retire to the fields to sleep apart from the family, they giggle together at their own private jokes as they make fun of passersby, and they make love on the back of the truck during the night journey across the desert—the night that Granma dies and Ma holds the body in her arms all night. But Connie is finally characterized by his cowardly desertion of his young wife and unborn child when the Joad family falls on desperate times.

Muley Graves's name is an epithet that defines his character. Stubborn, like a mule, he has remained behind when his family fled to California in search of work when they were evicted from their home. He refuses to leave, even though he is very lonely and obviously would like to accept the Joads' offer to take him along with them as a fourteenth person on an already overloaded sedan-turned-truck. Casy cannot foresee a good ending for Muley, because he taunts authorities who want to pick him up for trespassing on land that used to belong to his family. Nor does his last name of "Graves" give much hope of a felicitous outcome for him. Muley describes himself as an old, graveyard ghost, and he is likely to be shot and killed in a confrontation with the law.

Ivy and Sairy Wilson are hospitable people whom the Joads meet at a camping site. Although Sairy is herself very ill, she offers her tent as a shelter for Grampa, who is very ill. When he dies, she gives the Joads a beloved family quilt to wrap around him for burial. Although the two families start out from this camp to travel to California together, the Wilsons finally must stay behind because of her illness. The Wainwright family, also friendly and hospitable, occupies the opposite side of the Joads' boxcar near the novel's end, after the Hooper ranch experience. Mrs. Wainwright assists at the birth of Rose of Sharon's stillborn child. Al and Aggie Wainwright plan to get married.

All of these people, no matter how minor, are developed so that their actions give a sense of the fullness of "completion" of character. But the people are not the only living entities that have character and fullness in *Grapes*. The turtle in interchapter 3 emerges as a character in its own right, and it, too, is defined by its memorable actions as it struggles up an embankment to the highway, encounters a four-inch concrete wall, scrambles over it with difficulty, and waggles onto the highway. A woman swerves to avoid hitting it, but a man swerves to try to run over it, just glancing it and sending it off the highway to land upside down on the opposite embankment. A symbol of the Joads and the other migrants, the turtle's actions here depict its perseverance. No matter what the obstacle, it keeps on going. And it has brought with it from the other side a spearhead of wild oats that drops into the trench made as the turtle goes along, to be covered with dirt dragged over it by its shell.

Although this turtle symbolizes the migrants in their strength and perseverance in tribulation, even traveling in a southwesterly direction as they do, it is more than a symbol. It also serves as a foil for the tractors with their iron seeders, compared to penises that rape the land. First, whereas the tractors go in straight lines, the turtle's direction is not straight south or straight west, but slanted toward the Southwest. Second, like the tractors, the turtle also plants, but its furrows, unlike the straight, deeply plowed lines of tractors, are wavy and shallow, contoured to the embankment. By implication, in contrast to this turtle, the tractors are working against the laws of nature. There is something of the natural wisdom of the ages, then, residing in this old turtle with its eyes full of both ferocity and the saving grace of humor. Third, its plodding pace is Steinbeck's chosen tempo for *Grapes*, slow—but with dignity, decorum, determination, and grace—carrying with it the seed of new life.

Another living entity other than the human characters in *Grapes* is the land itself, for the novel's plot is carried out against a backdrop of land that is suffering acutely under drought and abuse. The land, however, is not defined by actions of its own. It is a victim of human actions that are destroying it by planting cotton over and over again because cotton is a good cash crop, thereby leeching the land of its nutrients and over time killing it. Irresponsibly, the landowners and tenant farmers ignore practices that would restore the land, such as crop rotating, contour plowing, and terracing.

The scene for the Oklahoma Dust Bowl is established in general chapter 1, in which the land is experiencing the throes of death. It is scarred, marked, crusted over, cut, and pale, with the red earth now turned pink and the gray earth now white. Its topsoil has turned to dust and runs like water in little streams when the wind blows. And it gets paler as each day passes. In interchapter 5 in which the migrants are tractored off of land now mortgaged to the bank, the land is dying bit by bit under the harsh iron tractors that rape it, forcing crops from it without replenishing it by rotation. Treated as a slave and deprived of care by men who no longer have connections to it and who do not love it, the land dies gradually. The pathos of the land, then, is presented fully, with a sense of both completion and compassion.

Steinbeck's desired "completion" and "feeling" are thus replete throughout the novel, even in scenes in which minor characters play a role. For example, in a scene following the one of Ma Joad wielding a jack handle, Tom and Al go to a wrecking yard to find a part for the Wilsons' car. With great care and meticulous detail Steinbeck introduces and develops the caretaker of the junkyard. He is given no name, but simply an epithet, a characterizing phrase: he is "one eye" or "the one-eyed man." This man is skinny, and both his person and his clothes are filthy, covered with the grease and oil of his trade, his empty eye socket uncovered. But his actions and gestures are even more telling. He pouts, with his lower lip hanging out "sullenly"; he blows his nose in his hand, wiping the discharge on his pants. He shambles or shuffles when he walks, indicating a lazy disposition. He pants with fury, and his only eye flares with anger at his boss, his lost eye, his loneliness (*Grapes* 178–82).

Although he complains that people "edge" away from him, he seems to welcome Tom and Al's company as they do business. He helps them find the automobile parts they need, provides tools essential for the repair, holds a flashlight so that they can see, and sells them the parts, the flashlight, and a battery for it at a reasonable price. When they leave, he goes to a rundown building behind the junkyard business, lies down on a "mattress on the floor," and cries as he listens to the cars going by on the highway, cut off from the world in his loneliness (*Grapes* 180–82). Why does Steinbeck go to such lengths to give breadth and depth to an unnamed, minor character?

There are at least four possible reasons for such a broad portrait of this one-eyed man. One is that Carol, his wife and most trusted critic, reminded him of the importance of details. Second is his own devotion, even to "the little details," as he writes in his October 6, 1938, journal entry (*WD* 83). Third is his concern to maintain a slow tempo and movement in his novel—to give it the ponderous weight of a symphony. The latter reason is connected also to his desire to create an experience for readers, one involving an empathic understanding. And fourth is that everything (even the one-eyed man) contributes to the overarching theme of human compassion. Such a portrait enables the reader to know what it was like to be at this junkyard on a particular evening and to be assisted by a stranger who is at once repulsive and helpful. Even though the one-eyed man is a minor character, then, his portrait is complete and full. Such is Steinbeck's devotion to his narrative art.

NOTES

1. John Steinbeck, *Working Days: The Journals of "The Grapes of Wrath,"* ed. Robert DeMott (New York: Penguin Books, 1989). Hereafter references to this work will be cited parenthetically within the text, identified as *WD* with pertinent page numbers.

2. John Steinbeck, *Travels with Charley in Search of America* (New York: Penguin Books, 1962). Hereafter references to this work will be cited parenthetically within the text, identified as *Travels* with pertinent page numbers.

3. Jean-Jacques Rousseau, *Confessions,* in *The Norton Anthology of World Masterpieces,* 5th ed., Maynard Mack, ed. (New York: W.W. Norton and Company, 1987), 1630.

4. William Wordsworth, *Preface to Lyrical Ballads, with Pastoral and Other Poems* (1802), in *The Norton Anthology of English Literature: The Major Authors,* 7th ed., M.H. Abrams, ed. (New York: W.W. Norton and Company, 2001), 1447.

5. Peter Lisca, with Kevin Hearle, *"The Grapes of Wrath": Text and Criticism* (New York: Penguin Books, 1997), 1. Hereafter references to this work will be cited parenthetically within the text, identified as *Grapes* with pertinent page numbers.

6. Robert DeMott, *Steinbeck's Typewriter: Essays on His Art* (New York: The Whitston Publishing Company, 1996), 183. Hereafter references to this work will be cited parenthetically within the text, identified as *Steinbeck's Typewriter* with pertinent page numbers.

7. Harold Bloom, ed., *John Steinbeck's "The Grapes of Wrath,"* Modern Critical Interpretations Series (New York: Chelsea House Publishers, 1988). Hereafter references to this work will be cited parenthetically within the text, identified as Bloom with pertinent page numbers.

7 Reception

In March 1989, there was a Steinbeck conference in San Jose, California; and the keynote speaker was the celebrated critic of American literature Leslie Fiedler, who managed, by finishing his address with a "grace note" acknowledging the right of *Grapes* to continue to be read, to earn himself (all unknowing) the year's Harold Bloom award for graceless patronization.

—John Ditsky, *Steinbeck and the Critics* 2000 (99)

MISREADINGS

Harold Bloom's 2000 *John Steinbeck: Comprehensive Research and Study Guide*, identified as one of a series entitled Bloom's Major Novelists and published by Chelsea House, is a prime example of this established critic's misreading of (or not reading carefully) Steinbeck's *Grapes*, one of the novels discussed in this text.[1] Why should he? He evidently does not have to read a book with care in order to edit what his publisher touts as "a definitive guide for independent study and a single source for footnoting essays and research papers." And we might add, at this point, it is likewise a source for footnoting without having to plow through an entire essay on your own—these are predigested and considerably shortened. The series title, with Bloom's name, by the way, is in larger, bolder print than the title of the text itself, with Steinbeck's name receiving a lesser emphasis—a telling point in itself.

But why the assertion that Bloom either has misread or has not carefully read *Grapes*? First, he does not get the facts straight. He gets the genesis of Steinbeck's interchapters wrong in his summary of the plot, stating that "as Steinbeck moved through the Joads' story, he found that the narrative alone did not cover the entire picture he hoped to create. In order to include the material he felt was needed, he inserted chapters that summarize the Joads' general situation, rather than showing us their specific actions" (Bloom 13).

These general chapters were not an afterthought, inserted after the narrative had been written. As Steinbeck's journals on *Grapes* show, the interchapters were an integral part of his plan, evidently mapped out in his head ahead of time. But Bloom's gravest error is in his depiction of the novel's ending, also in the plot summary, in which he leaves Pa Joad out of the final scene altogether: "Ma, unable to accept her family's complacent air of defeat, takes it upon herself to lead Rose of Sharon, Ruthie, and Winfield away from the drowning camp to seek shelter on higher ground" (Bloom16). By missing Pa's acquiescence to Ma's taking on the role of leader of the family, Bloom misses a vital part of the heart of this ending—a demonstration of Pa's gentle strength.

In this scene the floodwaters have entered the boxcar in which the Joads have been living. When Ma insists that they leave for higher ground, Pa picks Rose of Sharon up, steps down into the deep floodwaters, and carries her in his arms, holding her up as far above the water as he can. When they get to the highway, he sets her down, steadying her so that she does not fall. Rose of Sharon walks between her parents for a while. But when she can go no further, her father again carries her in his arms up the hill and into the deserted barn, where he sets her down gently on a box.[2] Pa's actions here serve to define his character and that of his family as well, for these gestures speak of the nobility of their love and kindness. Pa gains stature by them, as does the Joad family as a whole. By omitting such a demonstration of love, tenderness, and concern, Bloom does *Grapes*, Steinbeck, students, and scholars a great disservice. An honest assessment of an author's work demands accuracy and truth to the text at the very least.

In addition to these egregious errors in simple plot summary, Bloom asserts that "*The Grapes of Wrath*, *whatever its aesthetic flaws*, remains the authentic American novel of the now-vanishing Twentieth Century" [emphasis added] (9). His reputation as a critic well established and his position as Sterling Professor at Yale University assured, Bloom evidently does not have to offer substantiation for the implication that *The Grapes of Wrath* has grave aesthetic flaws of which the reader and student must be forewarned. Both the unspoken rules of worthy scholarship and the demands of professional courtesy, however, demand such substantiation. Lacking such evidence, Bloom's assessment is assertive rather than analytical.

These recent, blatant examples of a critic's misreading of *Grapes* and bringing into question its aesthetic merit without evidence illustrate a negative reception that has accompanied this well-wrought 453-page novel from the earliest reviews to the present. Part of the problem perhaps lies in its very length, and another part perhaps resides in Steinbeck's determination that its tempo and movement must be slow to give the reader ample time to enter into the experience of its story. It is not easy for a reader to hold all of the various facets of such a long novel in the mind simultaneously. Some of it is bound to drift out of the borders of the reader's ken or range of view and perception. At the same time, however, in order to appreciate the artistry of *Grapes* fully, a sense of the whole is vital. Attentive readers do feel the novel's impact, but perhaps subconsciously, a cumulative effect.

QUESTIONS OF ARTISTRY

Questions concerning the artistry of *Grapes*, however, arose even before it was published and released in 1939. Steinbeck's publishers worried that some of its diction would be unacceptable to the general public and that the ending was too abrupt and startling. Steinbeck acquiesced to the change of some of the wording, but on the ending he was adamant. He would make no changes because he had balanced the whole novel around the New Testament concept of kindness to the stranger in the midst, on hospitality, generosity, magnanimity. In keeping with this theme of kindness to strangers, in this grotesque, mysterious ending there is a reenactment of the Nativity in the Gospels. Rose of Sharon—a true Joad—gives of herself when there is nothing left to give. The scene is grotesque in the sense that Rose of Sharon, like all the rest of humanity, is broken. She is crushed by the loss of her runaway husband and stillborn child, but she nurses at her breast one of God's "little ones," one of those bruised and battered by economic forces that have left him helpless and dying. The scene is mysterious because it enters the realm of myth, and the story needs no ending other than this one to show what it means to be truly human.

But this writerly, postmodern assessment of the ending of *Grapes* comes from the early twenty-first century—not from the early twentieth century. In 1939, reviewers and critics sometimes struggled to discover exactly what Steinbeck had achieved in *Grapes*. After all, Steinbeck is not another Ernest Hemingway or William Faulkner—although he is forever linked with them by chronology and critical comparison. Nor is he a John Dos Passos, although *Grapes* does bear some resemblance to the *U.S.A.* trilogy. Also, as some critics have pointed out, he does not fit well either with the proletarian or the modernist traditions. Some critics argue that to an extent at least, he is a romantic, and, therefore, removed from his times. To an extent, too, he is postmodern, and, as such, both ahead of his times and far removed from them. It is no wonder that critics and reviewers in 1939 struggled to evaluate and classify *Grapes*.

EARLY REVIEWS

The early reviewers, then, like Steinbeck's publishers, also grappled with this long, complex novel with its mythic ending, many of them responding to it in emotive terms of their own experience in reading it rather than in terms of an analysis of its aesthetic merit. A sampling of five of these early reviews shows some of the struggle in analyzing and appreciating *Grapes* in all of its length and complexity. In the April 1939 *Partisan Review*, Philip Rahv's article, "A Variety of Fiction,"[3] reviews seven works of European and American fiction, among them Steinbeck's *Grapes*, finding that "the difference between the literature of the old world and the new amounts to the difference between manifest and latent horror" (106). "Latent horror" would be the description Rahv assigns to *Grapes*, for Europe at the time was facing World War II—a "manifest" horror indeed. Like Bloom, Rahv has little good to say of Steinbeck and his work in general, and, again like Bloom, he either damns with faint praise or vehemently denies the aesthetic merit of his fiction: "From Mr. John Steinbeck—whose *inspired* pulp-story, *Of Mice and Men*, swept the nation like a *plague*—one expected nothing. It is therefore gratifying to report that in *The Grapes of Wrath* he appears in a more sympathetic light than in his previous work, not excluding *In Dubious Battle*. This writer, it can now be seen, is really fired with a passionate faith in the common man" [emphasis added] (111). Rahv's response is more puzzling than informative, for the words "inspired" and "plague" used in the same sentence to evaluate *Of Mice and Men* leave the reader in limbo from the beginning.

His description of *Grapes* as an "authentic and formidable example of the novel of social protest" likewise sends a mixed message—"authentic" is a good trait; "formidable" probably is not intended as a good trait. One does not have to read far, however, to discover why Rahv calls it formidable.

The book is at the same time a *detailed* exposure of dreadful economic conditions and *a long declaration* of love to the masses. It is *an epic* of misery—a *prodigious, relentless,* and *often excruciating* account of agrar-

ian suffering. . . . Mr. Steinbeck *spares us not* a single scene, not a single sensation, that could help to *implicate us emotionally.* . . . The novel
is far too *didactic* and *long-winded.* . . . Its *unconscionable length* is *out of
all proportion* to its *substance* [emphasis added]. (111)

Rahv is puzzling in his implication that the human suffering depicted in
Grapes lacks "substance." Also, his exasperated description of *Grapes* could
be translated simply as "this is a very, very, very long book; and it made me
feel sad."

He complains further about Steinbeck's characterization, maintaining
that the author follows his characters everywhere and perseveres in copy-
ing "down everything they say and everything they do" (112). If he were
here, we could hear Steinbeck's laughter in the background, for Rahv complains because the novel achieves exactly what the author intended all
along. That is, as Steinbeck intended, it moves at a slow tempo, and it
draws the reader into its experience. More serious than his exasperation
with its "unconscionable length" is Rahv's assertion that *Grapes* "fails on
the test of craftsmanship," particularly in characterization and what he
calls an "*'ornery' dialect spoken by its farmers*" (112). But these assertions are
not nearly so well substantiated as his complaints about the novel's length.

Other early reviewers puzzled over the classification of *Grapes*, among
them Louis Kronenberger in his "Hungry Caravan,"[4] published in the
April 15, 1939, *Nation*, in which he declares that "'The Grapes of Wrath' is
a superb tract because it exposes something terrible and true with enormous vigor. It is a superb tract, moreover, by virtue of being thoroughly ani-
mated fiction, by virtue of living scenes and living characters (like Ma),
not by virtue of discursive homilies and dead characters (like the socialistic
preacher). *One comes away moved, indignant, protesting, pitying*" [emphasis
added] (441). This review, like Rahv's, takes away as much as it gives in
weighing the aesthetic merit of *Grapes*. Kronenberger's description of
Grapes as "a superb tract" is an oxymoron. A tract is a pamphlet or leaf-
let—small in size, small in intent, small in impact. A thing that is "superb"
is splendid, rich, sumptuous, supremely excellent. Although the tension
created by an oxymoron can be rich with meaning, here there is no tension,
simply an absurdity. Placing *Grapes*, for example, alongside a Salvation
Army pamphlet is an exercise in the ridiculous. Further, Kronenberger
finds "Steinbeck's sentimentalism . . . bad when it blurs his insight" (441).
Critics from 1939 to the present often revert to the term "sentimentalism"
when they want to dismiss Steinbeck's fiction as lacking aesthetic merit.
Kronenberger argues also that in the interchapters, Steinbeck brings his

story to a halt while he editorializes—another dismissive assessment, implying that the interchapters in *Grapes* are propaganda, not art.

For all of this critic's negative and mixed final assessment, he nevertheless makes two observations that are remarkably insightful. In the first, he acknowledges problems with trying to rank Steinbeck in comparison to his contemporaries: " '*The Grapes of Wrath*' . . . is, from any point of view, Steinbeck's best novel, but it does not make one wonder whether, on the basis of it, Steinbeck is now a better novelist than Hemingway or Farrell or Dos Passos; it does not invoke comparisons" (440). Kronenberger is astute in not attempting to make Steinbeck anyone's follower or disciple and in not trying to evaluate *Grapes* alongside other works of its day, with which it does not fit well, if at all. In the second statement, he declares that " '*The Grapes of Wrath*' . . . simply makes one feel that Steinbeck is, in some way all his own, a force" (440). Significantly, Kronenberger here recognizes that Steinbeck is an artist to be reckoned with in his own right. The source of this "force" he finds in the theme of *Grapes*—a theme that "is large and tragic and, on the whole, is largely and tragically felt" (440). Such initial assessments do not fit well with Kronenberger's conclusion that this novel is "a superb tract" and that its author is guilty of sentimentalizing his topic and editorializing in the interchapters.

From the vantage point of the twenty-first century, James M. Vaughan's July 1939 review in *The Commonweal*[5] seems quaint in its squeamish repudiation of Steinbeck's "realism"—which he finds at times "vulgar to a revolting degree"—and appears grasping in its attempt to understand *Grapes* well enough to categorize it: "Besides being a novel, *Grapes of Wrath* is a *monograph* on rural sociology, a *manual of practical wisdom* in times of enormous stress, *an assault on individualism*, an *essay* in behalf of a rather vague form of pantheism, and *a bitter, ironical attack* on that emotional evangelistic religion which seems to thrive in the more impoverished rural districts of this vast country" [emphasis added] (341–42). While Vaughan finds "the impact of this book . . . very powerful," he evidently did not have time for its total impact to be felt. No reader, for example, who surveys Ma Joad very carefully will assert that Steinbeck is launching "a bitter, ironical attack on . . . emotional evangelistic religion" (342). She is the very model of the New Testament ideal of entertaining strangers as though the children of God, as Steinbeck strongly implies that they are. He is, rather, telling an honest story about people, some of whom are religious fanatics. Nor would the careful reader advocate *Grapes* as a how-to-manage-your-stress manual.

In an attempt to rank novels according to merit (without providing the criteria by which he measures), Malcolm Cowley's "American Tragedy"[6] in the May 1939 *New Republic* states that *Grapes* does not "rank with the best of Hemingway or Dos Passos. But it belongs very high in the category of the great angry books like 'Uncle Tom's Cabin' that have roused a people to fight against intolerable wrongs" (383). Here Cowley fails to see that *Uncle Tom's Cabin*, while powerful, is melodrama; *Grapes* is life. Although Cowley does not rank *Grapes* highly aesthetically, he does give a surprisingly accurate glimpse of Steinbeck's sustained writing process, his method in creating characters, and his intention to involve readers. For his characters, Cowley writes, Steinbeck has

> a deep fellow feeling that makes him notice everything that sets them apart from the rest of the world and sets one migrant apart from all the others. In the Joad family, everyone from Grampa—"Full a' piss an' vinegar," as he says of himself—down to the two brats, Ruthie and Winfield, is a distinct and living person. And the story is living too—it has the force of the headlong anger that drives ahead from the first chapter to the last, as if the whole six hundred pages were written without stopping. The author and the reader are swept along together. (382–83)

"Headlong" and "driving ahead" are most appropriate terms for describing a writing process that led to the completion of what in its first publication was a six-hundred-plus page novel in one-hundred days. And in his journals Steinbeck had written that he was determined to make these characters—whom he considered to be his people—come to life. He determined as well to so involve readers with the story that they became participants in it. Cowley was most perceptive in his writing analysis, but less so in his ranking, which lacks criteria and substantiation.

Christopher Isherwood's 1939 "Tragedy of Eldorado" in *The Kenyon Review*[7] asks a question that is still being raised by a few Ivy League critics, "Why isn't *The Grapes of Wrath* entirely satisfying as a work of art?" and a related question, "Can propaganda produce good art?" He begins his discussion from a thoughtful, carefully wrought premise with which no critic would disagree. But when he applies this premise to *Grapes*, his application does not quite fit. With discernment, Isherwood observes that

> it is a mark of the greatest poets, novelists and dramatists that they all demand a high degree of cooperation from their audience. The . . . latent content of a masterpiece will not be perceived without a certain imaginative and emotional effort. In this sense the great artist makes every one of his readers into a philosopher and poet, . . . according to

that reader's powers. The novelist of genius, by presenting the particular instance, indicates the general truth. . . . The final verdict, the ultimate synthesis, must be left to the reader. . . . In this way, masterpieces, throughout the ages, actually undergo a sort of organic growth. (452)

Acknowledging that in a sense "all art is propaganda," Isherwood states that in *Grapes* Steinbeck oversteps his boundaries and intrudes on the reader, making "the 'propaganda' overt," thereby limiting and frustrating his reader and diminishing his novel's aesthetic appeal. Quite cogently he argues that "overt political propaganda . . . must always defeat its own artistic ends: the politico-sociological case is general, the artistic instance is particular" (452–53).

Yet again, the critic falters in his judgment because of the interchapters in *Grapes*, now generally accepted as an integral part of its structure and theme, giving the reader a means by which to focus on the Joad narrative against a backdrop of its context. Further, these interchapters move *Grapes* beyond propaganda by establishing a tone, foreshadowing what is to follow in the narrative, and prophetically speaking of the end results of a nation's greedy disregard for and consumption of its own land and people in the name of profit.

CRITICAL TRENDS

In "The Pattern of Criticism" in the 1972 and 1997 editions of *"The Grapes of Wrath": Text and Criticism*, Peter Lisca classifies these early reviews with other critical assessments of *Grapes* up to 1955. During this fifteen-year period between 1939 and 1954, criticism tended to be assertive rather than analytical; after that period it tended more toward the analytical. David Wyatt's 1990 *New Essays on "The Grapes of Wrath"* argues for "a third phase of response to the novel," culminating with his own text.[8] Following Lisca's lead, he characterizes the

three phases of response, each of about fifteen years, . . . as the Histrionic, the Formal, and the Contextual. In the first the novel is subjected to a correspondent theory of truth that measures it against some putative social reality and the commentator against his or her political credentials. In the second, the novel provokes attention as a work of art that fulfills literary conventions and expectations. In the third, the novel is framed by its biographical and regional fields of force. The three-fold pattern can be cast another way: Pretext (1940–1955), Text (1955–1973); and Context (1973–1989). (4)

Wyatt states that Lisca covers phases one and two, or pretext and text, and that his text surveys the third, context.

While these categories of criticism are highly useful in considering the overall body of criticism on *Grapes*, they do overlap to an extent; for some of the more assertive reviewers and critics may have significant insights while some who appear to be more analytic may wax assertive. As we have seen, some of the early reviewers are on occasion perceptive even though they arrive at negative conclusions. Kronenberger, for example, realized that Steinbeck's artistry in *Grapes* should not be compared with his contemporaries because it is different in kind, and he recognized, too, that Steinbeck possessed a "force" unique to himself. On the other hand, some current criticism, purporting to be analytical, may be strongly assertive;Bloom's 2000 critique, for example, views *Grapes* primarily as an aesthetically flawed sociopolitical novel—as did some 1939 reviewers—while again, like early reviewers, providing no evidence. Steinbeck's own tongue-in-cheek summation of critics and their work helps to put them and their criticism in a true perspective. His observations on critics in "Critics—From a Writer's Viewpoint,"[9] first printed in the August 27, 1955, *Saturday Review* and reprinted in E.W. Tedlock and C.V. Wicker's 1957 *Steinbeck and His Critics: A Record of Twenty-Five Years*, should certainly have a bearing on a discussion of the reception of *Grapes* and its critical analyses. He points out that critics often cancel out one another, that "the critic is primarily a writer himself and that his first interest lies in his own career." "A man's writing is himself," Steinbeck states, reflecting his own kindness, or meanness, or wisdom, or illness. He suggests that "it would be very interesting for a good and intelligent critic to exercise his craft on a body of work of his fellow critics. If this should happen I think it would be found that the product of a reviewer is not objective at all, but subject to all the virtues and vices of other writers in other fields. . . . Poor things, nobody reviews them" (49–51).

But, like magpies, reviewing one another is precisely what most critics do. For example, as Warren French points out in *Sixteen Modern American Authors*, Harry Thornton Moore's 1939 *The Novels of John Steinbeck: A First Study* falls in line with the critical biases of his times in upbraiding Steinbeck for not modeling his writing after D.H. Lawrence (372).[10] Still, Moore realizes that there is more to *Grapes* than he can articulate: He suggests that "there are new beginnings which may lead to future developments."[11] Bloom admits this difficulty, too—that there is something beyond him. And, like Steinbeck's definitive biographer, Jackson J. Benson, Moore recognizes the poetic element in his works, concluding that he is becoming "the poet of our dispossessed" (70, 72). That Moore later revises this book with a more negative estimate of the Steinbeck aesthetic matters not at all, for he is simply once more following the critical trends.

FOCUS ON THE TEXT

Peter Lisca's chapter on *Grapes* in his 1958 *The Wide World of John Steinbeck*,[12] the second book-length critical study on Steinbeck, is representative of the critical reception of *Grapes* devoted to the text itself. In this chapter Lisca provides an analysis and commentary that bring to Steinbeck studies a close reading as meticulously observant of art as that of the new criticism. For through the eyes and criticism of Lisca, *Grapes* emerges as though it were a magnificently long, intricately woven epic poem. His discussion of the novel's first paragraph illustrates his approach to Steinbeck's prose style. "The opening paragraph is as carefully worked out as an overture to an opera. The themes of red, gray, green, and earth are announced and given parallel developments: red to pink, gray to white, green to brown, and ploughed earth to thin hard crust. The pervading structural rhythm of each sentence is echoed in the paragraph as a whole, a paragraph promising a story of epic sweep and dignity" (161).

Lisca further shows the variety of styles used in the interchapters—ranging from biblical, to "staccato," to "hectic," to rhymthic, to Whitmanesque, and more. Finally, in studying Steinbeck's style, Lisca demonstrates the intricacy with which the interchapters are interwoven into the very fabric of *Grapes*, concluding that "they have enough individuality of subject matter, prose style, and technique to keep the novel from falling into two parts, and to keep the reader from feeling that he is now reading 'the other part'" (165).

Lisca's reading and commentary also cover the novel's thematic structure and methods of characterization, concluding that Steinbeck succeeded in creating a "'well-made' and emotionally compelling novel" even though he minimized both his plot and his characters (177). Concerning the ending, Lisca maintains that Steinbeck did achieve a sense of closure by the creation of the nativity symbol and paradox. Rose of Sharon, herself destitute, gives to the stranger her life-giving milk. And the Joads, in the nadir of despair, reach a summit of faith (176–77).

Also first published in 1957 and including several articles that center on the text itself, E.W. Tedlock, Jr. and C.V. Wicker's *Steinbeck and His Critics: A Record of Twenty-Five Years*, brings together what the authors considered to be "all important attitudes toward Steinbeck and his writing" (vi). A fourth printing of this text was published by Tedlock in 1969, attesting to the need for such a compilation and study, which its authors describe as "almost as much a panorama of critical approaches as a survey of Steinbeck's works" (xi). In their introduction, "Perspectives in Steinbeck Criticism," they survey this panorama of approaches—from Maxwell Geismar's 1942 *Writers in Crisis*, with a sociopolitical approach of doubtful value that evaluates *Grapes* as Steinbeck's longest novel, but not his best; to Frederick Ives Carpenter's 1941 "John Steinbeck: American Dreamer," which discusses the novel's overtones of "the American Dream" and 1941 "The Philosophical Joads," which places *Grapes* squarely in the American social and philosophical tradition. In the latter article Carpenter discusses connections between *Grapes* and Ralph Waldo Emerson's oversoul and self-reliance, Walt Whitman's love for people and allegiance to democracy, and William James's ideal of the active life. Although Carpenter's articles are early, note that both are concerned with text, sources, and context.

Included in Tedlock and Wicker and centered on the text are Martin Staples Shockley's "Christian Symbolism in *The Grapes of Wrath*" and "The Reception of *The Grapes of Wrath* in Oklahoma." In the first of these essays, Shockley proposes "an interpretation of *The Grapes of Wrath* in which Casy represents a contemporary adaptation of the Christ image and in which the meaning of the book is revealed through a sequence of Christian symbols" (266).

Shockley locates these symbols in the novel's language with its biblical overtones, in the Joad family's similarities to the Israelites seeking the Promised Land, in Casy as a Christlike figure, in the final scene as Holy Communion: "This is my body. Take and eat." He concludes that he finds these Christian symbols throughout *Grapes* in character, plot, and theme, creating a "conscious and consistent Christian allegory" (271). In his second essay, as its title implies, Shockley traces the primarily provincial, we-aren't-like-Steinbeck's-Okies, antimeddling-outsiders reaction of native Oklahomans to *Grapes*. From Oklahoma's senators on Capitol Hill, to a high-school English teacher, to a county agricultural agent, to newspaper editors, and citizens—all joined in the fray over the factual accuracy of *Grapes*. While "outrage" would probably have been a more apropos word choice in the title than "reception," Shockley provides an interesting study of regional attitudes toward contemporary problems as they are presented in *Grapes*.

Also in Tedlock and Wicker, Chester E. Eisinger's "Jeffersonian Agrarianism in *The Grapes of Wrath*" adds Jeffersonian agrarianism to the American roots of *Grapes*, joining Carpenter's observations on the novel's origins in the American Dream, Emerson, Whitman, and James. Moving away from these essays seeking sources, Joseph Warren Beach's "John Steinbeck: Art and Propaganda" defends Steinbeck's aesthetic in *Grapes*, classifying it as a proletarian novel that deals "primarily with the life of the working classes or with any social or industrial problem from the point of view of labor" (250). He admires *Grapes* for its humanity; its simple, uncomplicated story; the "technical variations and combinations" that make the interchapters function integrally as a part of the whole; and the aesthetic mastery with which he brings characters to life (258–64). Beach concludes that the Joads have now taken "their place with Don Quixote, Dr. Faustus, with Galsworthy's Forsytes and Lewis' Babbitt, in the world's gallery of symbolic characters, the representative tapestry of the creative imagination" (265). He wonders, however, whether Steinbeck's "colors" will hold, whether his characters will be as enduring as those with whom he lists them. But in 1941 Beach does not have the vantage point and perspective that only the passing of time can give. Later readers and critics have decided this question of the enduring art of *Grapes*: the Joads are epic and enduring.

SCHOLARSHIP AND DEBATE

Attesting to the enduring art of Steinbeck is the ever-growing list of recent works that assist the Steinbeck scholar: an excellent definitive biography,[13] a second biography that is also an appreciation and a reassessment,[14] a catalogue of books that Steinbeck either owned or borrowed,[15] a book of essays devoted to his literary art,[16] a new study guide,[17] an updated bibliography,[18] a forthcoming Steinbeck encyclopedia,[19] a guide to dissertation abstracts,[20] and more. In addition, there are several book-length studies on *Grapes* itself.[21] It is interesting to note at this point that the first of these book-length studies was published in 1963; the second, in 1968; and the third was not published until 1982—fourteen years later. Since 1989, however, seven book-length studies have been devoted to *Grapes*—certainly indicating the sustained critical dialogue that Lisca maintains is essential to its standing as a work of art.

The most valuable asset to the study of *Grapes* itself is without question Robert DeMott's 1984 publication of *Working Days: The Journals of "The Grapes of Wrath."* Two authentic voices pervade this book: the voice of Steinbeck, the creator recording the process and progress of his writing, and the voice of DeMott, the scholar seeking to recreate and recapture the essence of an artist at work on a masterpiece. Steinbeck's journal entries occupy 75 pages—less than half of the book. The preface, introduction, commentary, and "Notes and Annotations: A Bibliographical Preface," together with 8 pages of photographs, occupy the remaining 105 pages. In effect, these two voices often constitute an antiphony—with Steinbeck's providing his personal view of the writing task that he has envisioned and of the events and people impinging on this task and with DeMott's elucidating, broadening, and commenting on the topic at hand.

Attesting to the enduring critical battle over the question of the aesthetic merit of *Grapes* is Harold Bloom's 1988 *John Steinbeck's "The Grapes of Wrath,"* a part of the Modern Critical Interpretations Series.[22] So extensive has been this critic's influence that in *John Steinbeck's Fiction Revisited*, Warren French, a renowned Steinbeck scholar and advocate, has focused his reassessment of Steinbeck and *Grapes* in light of Bloom's criticism.[23] Thus, French ponders the question of Steinbeck's

permanent place ... in twentieth-century American literature, particularly in view of his remaining one of the most widely read American authors of this century despite the reservations of many critics, especially those influential ones associated with what has been called the Eastern Ivy League Establishment.

Just as I was beginning this project, one of the most ambitious of these critics, Harold Bloom, provided a narrow focus for it by including in his Modern Critical Views series ... a volume devoted to Steinbeck, introducing it with the sweeping statement that Steinbeck's "best novels came early in his career: *In Dubious Battle*, ... *Of Mice and Men*, ... *The Grapes of Wrath*. ... Nothing after that, including *East of Eden* ... bears rereading." Concluding that "Steinbeck is not one of the inescapable American novelists of our century," Bloom adds, "yet there are no canonical standards worthy of human respect that could exclude *The Grapes of Wrath* from a serious reader's esteem." (x)

Acquiescing to Bloom's judgment that "Steinbeck is not one of the inescapable American novelists of our century," French joins him in contemplating "why one is yet compelled to 'be grateful' for *The Grapes of Wrath*"—a question neither writer answers specifically.

Acquiescing also to Bloom's dismissal of Steinbeck's advocates and supporters as "liberal middlebrows, both in his own country and abroad" French himself takes up this reductive term for the Steinbeck audience in a brief discussion of *Grapes* as an example of survival literature. Placing it in this Procrustean Bed, French assigns it a place alongside Stephen Crane's *The Red Badge of Courage* and Joseph Conrad's *Heart of Darkness*—strange company indeed for a woman of Ma Joad's stature and for the epic and poetic grandeur that characterizes *Grapes* as a whole.

Bloom finds *Grapes* "a very problematic work, and very difficult to judge." He does not hesitate to judge, however, and very harshly—asserting that Steinbeck "aspired beyond his aesthetic means" and that "he fell into bathos in everything he wrote" (4). French finds the Ivy League critics problematic, and now acquiesces to their lead in his reassessment of *Grapes*. At this point we have about come full circle from the first full-length study of Steinbeck in 1939 in which Moore follows the critical trend of his day in berating Steinbeck because he did not follow the lead of D.H. Lawrence. The assertive, histrionic voices of the early period of Steinbeck criticism are still present as, without adequate substantiation, Bloom insists that Steinbeck's "problem" is Hemingway and as French complains that Steinbeck does not "recognize his kinship with the beat generation" and Allen Ginsberg. In considering *Grapes* within the context of our own times, critics do not have to fall into such assertive fallacies.

AN "INESCAPABLE" NOVEL

Interchapter 23 of *Grapes*, a fittingly poetic prelude to the dance at Weedpatch Camp in the narrative chapter following, depicts the simple pleasures in which the migrants engage—storytelling, music, dancing, and even baptisms. The bardic narrator in this interchapter states that the migrants "climbed up their lives with jokes, . . . and their participation made the stories great" (325). This description of a synthesis of storyteller, story, and audience working together to make a story "great" fits well with Steinbeck's intention in creating *Grapes* as a story in which readers participate in the actuality of the migrant experience. And it is, in part at least, this synthesis of author, text, and reader that endows this novel with its status as a classic of world literature—not just of American literature—because readers worldwide can place this novel within the context of their own times, their own places, and their own conditions.

Against an introductory background of stories and storytellers, Eugene R. August's 1995 "Our Stories/Our Selves: The American Dream Remembered in John Steinbeck's *The Grapes of Wrath*"[24] surveys *Grapes* against its broad biblical backdrop, places it within the context of its era, and shows how today's readers can translate its version of the American Dream for their own time. After establishing the influence of the biblical story of the Exodus on both the American Dream and *Grapes*, August discusses the Great Depression of the thirties as the time that "converted the American Dream into a nightmare." August states there are three stories in particular that define "those hard times for us today. . . . First is the story told in the photographic collections like those assembled under the auspices of Roy Stryker. Second is the story told in John Steinbeck's explosive novel, *The Grapes of Wrath*, and third is director John Ford's classic film adaptation of Steinbeck's novel. Some would add Woody Guthrie's 'Ballad of Tom Joad'" (12).

Grapes, then, is in and of itself a definition of its times and a portrayal of the American Dream turned inward on the heart and soul. August's choice of the adjective "explosive" to describe the reception and impact of *Grapes* is particularly apropos both for the 1930s and for the twenty-first century, as he recognizes.

> From the moment of its publication, John Steinbeck's *The Grapes of Wrath* set off shock waves that are still reverberating. Publicly condemned and even burned, the book also became a best seller and won the Pulitzer Prize.

> Nowadays, *The Grape of Wrath* has achieved the status of an embattled classic. It has sold over four million copies and has been translated into just about every language under the sun (DeMott xxvi). It is one of the most frequently assigned texts in U. S. high schools and colleges, and also one of the most frequently banned books in America. Among literary critics, the novel still touches off lively academic skirmishes. Nor have its concerns dated: the problems of migrant workers have hardly vanished from the American scene—to say nothing of catastrophic flooding in California. *The Grapes of Wrath* may be a classic, but it is not a museum piece. (13)

August thus documents the power of *Grapes* to speak across time, to be refashioned and placed in today's context, and to take on an ever-expanding meaning so that it encompasses all humanity, most particularly those who are dispossessed and homeless in a wealthy country.

It is always gratifying when a critic writing from the vantage point of 1939 is in some way in sync with a 1990s critic. To illustrate, in Henry Thornton Moore's 1939 *The Novels of John Steinbeck*, the first book-length study of Steinbeck's work, he criticizes *Grapes* for its lack of "unity," "force," and "conflict," but he also captures some of its epic, mythic qualities, believing that in it "there are new beginnings which may lead to future developments." In accord with Moore who believes that Steinbeck is "the poet of our dispossessed" (70, 72), but expanding the concept, August specifies how the writer achieved this poetic voice.

He took the grim proletarian novel and invigorated it with all the magic of poetry. The narrative of the Joad odyssey is played off against a series of intercalary chapters that universalize the journey, provide cinematic glimpses of American life and landscape, capture the ring of American speech, crystallize the mood of Depression-era America, and place the Joads' story within the larger story of the American Dream turned nightmare. These chapters provide the novel with an equivalent of the Greek chorus that kept ancient tragedies afloat on a sea of surging poetry. In these chapters, Steinbeck's prose exults and laments, prophecies [*sic*], captures the landscape in stop-action cinematography, and provides lyric counterpoint to the prose narrative. Perhaps more than anyone else, Steinbeck made the proletarian novel sing. (13)

Although *Grapes* does not altogether fit into the category of "proletarian novel" in which he places it, August captures here the essence of what other critics have also observed: Steinbeck is a poet. And Moore captures this essence on a yet deeper level when he declares that Steinbeck is *"our poet of the dispossessed"* [emphasis added], showing that mythic level at which the text, the writer, and the reader coalesce—with all three participating together in this experience.

While August is quite correct in his acknowledgment of the "shock waves that are still reverberating" and the controversy that has accompanied *Grapes* from the beginning, at the same time we must also acknowledge that these reverberations no longer seem to matter. Sound scholarship from a variety of critical approaches and disciplines assures *Grapes'* secure stature as a classic even though some Ivy League critics are still content to damn it with faint praise. For instance, the 1997 *Steinbeck and the Environment: Interdisciplinary Approaches*, edited by a scientist, a Steinbeck scholar, and a generalist in American literature, devotes a section with four essays to *Grapes*. In the first of these essays, David N. Cassuto's "Turning Wine into Water: Water as Privileged Signifier in *The Grapes of Wrath*"[25] approaches the text from an ecological stance, suggesting that Steinbeck used water throughout the novel as "an absent signifier"— absent in the sense of drought in the Oklahoma section and absent in the sense of hidden, or not revealed, in the California section in which he does not discuss the irrigation necessary to produce such bountiful yields. At the very end of the novel, the flood serves as an opportunity to show the strength of the migrants' combined efforts in holding it back, if only for a brief time. Cassuto concludes with a focus on the present condition—not an unusual shift for *Grapes* criticism. Extended periods of drought, Cassuto maintains, have now led to the "decanonization of the myth of the garden and its accompanying myth of the frontier. These two myths, dominant since the birth of the nation, eventually ran head-long into the realities of a closed frontier and a finite hydrology" (73).

The second essay in this section, Lorelei Cederstrom's "The 'Great Mother' in The Grapes of Wrath," [26] approaches the novel from a feminist perspective. It is one with an ecological twist, however, because it is "patri-archal forces" that have brought on the disaster of the Dust Bowl. Drawing on a pagan concept of a "feminine principle" that can both nurture and destroy and a "Great Mother," who is goddess of the earth, Cederstrom traces an ascending matriarchy and descending patriarchy throughout Grapes. Ma Joad, of course, is the Great Mother, and her daughter, Rose of Sharon, follows in her lead. The final scene, according to Cederstrom, is pagan, not Christian, uniting "the naturalistic and optimistic views" and expressing "the paradoxical power of the Great Mother completely. Sword in one hand, bowl in the other, Kali, like Rose of Sharon, wears a smile" (89–90). Cederstrom fails to note, however, that Rose of Sharon carries no sword.

Third in this section is Peter Valenti's "Steinbeck's Ecological Polemic: Human Sympathy and Visual Documentary in the Intercalary Chapters of The Grapes of Wrath."[27] Valenti discusses Steinbeck's "unique ecological rhetoric" in the intercalary chapters as a documentary power that enables readers to capture a sense of urgency, a strong sympathy, and a visual immediacy. Valenti finds that "the expenditure of human life through the economic and ecological displacements pictured in The Grapes of Wrath evokes a strong response from readers" (111–12). Art, he suggests, is essential in bringing to the forefront "the moral weight of the story" and in making it possible for readers to participate in the actuality of the experience.

The fourth and final essay is Marilyn Chandler McEntyre's "Natural Wisdom: Steinbeck's Men of Nature as Prophets and Peacemakers."[28] This essay deals with Jim Casy as one who draws his vision from nature and from farmers, who are close to the earth, and it also discusses Cannery Row's Doc, whose vision is similar to Casy's. With paying attention to the natu-ral world as a starting point, both men arrive at a sense of the intercon-nectedness of all things. For both characters wisdom comes from paying attention to the "natural world," which is the source of all human virtues, including compassion and forgiveness.

Barbara A. Heavilin's 2000 The Critical Response to John Steinbeck's "The Grapes of Wrath" provides an extensive introductory overview of the criti-cal response to Grapes that includes a wide variety of approaches. Divided into two parts, "Part I: 1939–1989 Looking Back on the First Fifty Years" and "Part II: 1990–1999 Looking Forward to a New Millennium," it includes two 1939 reviews and four contemporary reviews: Viking's 1989 edition, Everyman's Library's 1993 edition, Library of America's 1996 edition, and Viking's 1997 edition.

One essay further highlights two more of the ever-expanding approaches to *Grapes*: comparative studies and postmodern. Both approaches may be observed in Chris Kocela's "A Postmodern Steinbeck, Or Rose Of Sharon Meets Oedipa Maas."[29] In this insightful essay, Kocela demonstrates that "a return to Steinbeck's best-known novel from the perspective of contemporary fiction theory vindicates aspects of its structure and characterization often criticized in the context of a strictly modernist canon." Because of the complexity of his essay, it is best to quote his description of it.

> I will argue in the first section that Steinbeck's use of the interchapters exemplifies a postmodern strategy of "frame-breaking," whereby differences between history and fiction are established within the text only to be problematized, alerting the reader to the difficulties of historical and political representation. In the second section I will use Deborah Madsen's theorization of "postmodernist allegory" to examine how the problematic divide between history and fiction is further broken down by Steinbeck's superimposing of biblical and fictional worlds on the plane of the Joads' story. . . . Finally, it will become apparent that much of the theory to which I refer has arisen specifically out of critical attempts to deal with the work of Thomas Pynchon. For this reason, and because I think not enough attention has been paid to Steinbeck's influence on, and continuity with, a later generation of American writers, I take a step toward remedying this situation in my conclusion. As my title suggests, I indulge in a brief comparison of *The Grapes of Wrath* and Pynchon's *The Crying of Lot 49*. (247–49)

Kocela concludes that Steinbeck and Pynchon share a concern for the dispossessed and that both incorporate an interest in science into their fiction—for example, Steinbeck's interest in marine biology and Pynchon's in rocket science and thermal dynamics. Further, the concluding cinematic scene of Rose of Sharon and the starving stranger in the end of *Grapes* is a point of reference for Pynchon for a postmodern "revelation" in *The Crying of Lot 49*. Kocela's essay demonstrates that a postmodernist approach and comparison with a postmodernist writer elucidate well Steinbeck's aesthetic in *Grapes*, bringing another perspective on and another appreciation for its complex artistry.

In spite of some detractors, then, representative essays demonstrate that today's critics continue to widen the scope of *Grapes* and to refashion its appeal so that it fits within the context of their own times. In summary, August shows how the novel's story defines Americans as a people, and *Steinbeck and the Environment: Interdisciplinary Approaches* provides cross-disciplinary studies of *Grapes*, in which Cassuto demonstrates how *Grapes* treats the ecology of water use in its own times and its applications for our own; Cederstrom maintains a feminist perspective of the novel's move from a patriarchy to a matriarchy, with Ma Joad as the Great Mother, who passes the role along to Rose of Sharon; Valenti takes the stance of the rhetorician and illustrates both Steinbeck's documentary method in protesting the toll on human life brought about by the "economic and ecological displacements" of his day and this method's power to evoke strong reader response; and McEntyre takes the position that Jim Casy and *Cannery Row*'s Doc draw their vision of humanity from nature, including their attention to compassion and forgiveness. Finally, Kocela's postmodern, comparative approach underscores the complex artistry of *Grapes*.

When Viking published *Grapes* in 1939, it opened something like a Pandora's box, but it was not a box of human ills. Rather, it let loose upon the world a revelation of the humanity—and often of the nobility—of those who are broken and dispossessed in America. The novel's theme is so universal that *Grapes* has been translated into languages all over the world. As August points out, its reception "set off shock waves that are still reverberating." Assertive and histrionic detractors not withstanding, John Steinbeck's people—"my people" he called them in his accompanying journal—are still living. That teenager-turned-Madonna, Rose of Sharon, with the biblical echoes in her name, still looks up and across that barn, squarely at the reader. "We still see their faces," Studs Terkel maintains in Viking's deluxe 1989 edition of *Grapes*. These Steinbeck critics have well refuted Bloom's statement that "Steinbeck is *not* one of the inescapable American novelists of our century [emphasis added]." Further, they have demonstrated skillfully that there is no doubt whatsoever now that Steinbeck *is* one of the inescapable novelists of our century.[30]

NOTES

1. Harold Bloom, *John Steinbeck: Comprehensive Research and Study Guide* (Broomall, Pa.: Chelsea House, 2000). Hereafter this work is cited parenthetically in the text.

2. Peter Lisca, ed., with Kevin Hearle, *"The Grapes of Wrath": Text and Criticism* (New York: Penguin Books, 1997), 451–52. References to this work are cited parenthetically within the text, identified as *Grapes* with pertinent page numbers.

3. Philip Rahv, "A Variety of Fiction," *Partisan Review* 6 (April 1939), 106–12. Hereafter this work is cited parenthetically in the text.

4. Louis Kronenberger, "Hungry Caravan," *The Nation* 148 (April 15, 1939), 440–41. Hereafter this work is cited parenthetically in the text.

5. James M. Vaughan, "Fiction," *The Commonweal* 30 (July 28, 1939), 341–42. Hereafter this work is cited parenthetically in the text.

6. Malcolm Cowley, "American Tragedy," *New Republic* (May 3, 1939), 382–83. Hereafter this work is cited parenthetically in the text.

7. Christopher Isherwood, "Tragedy of Eldorado," *The Kenyon Review* (Autumn 1939), 450–53. Hereafter this work is cited parenthetically in the text.

8. David Wyatt, *New Essays on "The Grapes of Wrath"* (New York: Cambridge University Press, 1990). Hereafter this work is cited parenthetically in the text.

9. John Steinbeck, "Critics—From a Writer's Viewpoint," in *Steinbeck and His Critics: A Record of Twenty-Five Years*, eds. E.W. Tedlock Jr. and C.V. Wicker (Albuquerque: The University of New Mexico Press, 1957). Hereafter this work is cited parenthetically in the text.

10. Warren French, "John Steinbeck," in Jackson R. Bryer, ed., *Sixteen Modern American Authors* (Durham and London: Duke University Press, 1990), 369–87. Hereafter this work is cited parenthetically in the text.

11. Harry Thornton Moore, *The Novels of John Steinbeck: A First Study* (Chicago: Normandie House, 1939). Hereafter references to this work are cited parenthetically in the text.

12. Peter Lisca, *The Wide World of John Steinbeck* (New Brunswick, N.J.: Rutgers University, 1958). Hereafter this work is cited parenthetically in the text.

13. Jackson J. Benson, *The True Adventures of John Steinbeck, Writer* (New York: Penguin Books, 1984).

14. Jay Parini, *John Steinbeck: A Biography* (New York: Henry Holt and Company, 1995).

15. Robert DeMott, *Steinbeck's Reading: A Catalogue of Books Owned and Borrowed*, Garland Reference Library of the Humanities, vol. 246 (New York: Garland Publishing, Inc., 1984).

16. Robert DeMott, *Steinbeck's Typewriter: Essays on His Art* (New York: Whitston Publishing Company, 1996).

17. Tetsumaro Hayashi, *A New Study Guide to Steinbeck's Major Works, with Critical Explications* (Metuchen, N.J.: Scarecrow Press, Inc., 1993).

18. Michael J. Meyer, *The Hayashi Steinbeck Bibliography, 1982–1996* (Lanham, Md.: Scarecrow Press, 1998).

19. Brian Railsback and Michael J. Meyer's encyclopedia on Steinbeck is forthcoming from Greenwood Press.

20. Tetsumaro Hayashi and Beverly K. Simpson, comps. *John Steinbeck: Dissertation Abstracts and Research Opportunities* (Metuchen, N.J.: Scarecrow Press, 1994).

21. Book-length studies of *Grapes* include Warren French's 1963 *A Companion to "The Grapes of Wrath,"* Agnes McNeill Donohue's 1968 *A Casebook on "The Grapes of Wrath,"* Robert Con Davis's 1982 *Twentieth Century Interpretations of "The Grapes of Wrath,"* John Ditsky's 1989 *Critical Essays on Steinbeck's "The Grapes of Wrath,"* Louis Owens's 1989 *"The Grapes of Wrath": Trouble in the Promised Land,* Tetsumaro Hayashi's 1990 *Steinbeck's "The Grapes of Wrath": Essays in Criticism,* Susan Shillinglaw's 1990 *"The Grapes of Wrath": A Special Issue of "San Jose Studies,"* David Wyatt's 1990 *New Essays on "The Grapes of Wrath,"* Barbara Heavilin's 2000 *The Critical Response to John Steinbeck's "The Grapes of Wrath,"* and her 2002 *John Steinbeck's* The Grapes of Wrath: *A Reference Guide.*

22. Harold Bloom, ed., *John Steinbeck's "The Grapes of Wrath,"* Modern Critical Interpretations Series (New York: Chelsea House Publishers, 1988). Hereafter this work is cited parenthetically in the text, identified by the author's last name.

23. Warren French, *John Steinbeck's Fiction Revisited* (New York: Twayne Publishers, 1994). Hereafter this work is cited parenthetically in the text.

24. Eugene R. August, "Our Stories/Our Selves: The American Dream Remembered in John Steinbeck's *The Grapes of Wrath,*" *University of Dayton Review* 23, no. 3 (Winter 1995–1996): 5–17. Hereafter this work is cited parenthetically in the text.

25. David N. Cassuto, "Turning Wine into Water: Water as Privileged Signifier in *The Grapes of Wrath,*" in *Steinbeck and the Environment: Interdisciplinary Approaches,* eds. Susan F. Beegel, Susan Shillinglaw, and Wesley N. Tiffney, Jr. (Tuscaloosa: University of Alabama Press, 1997). Hereafter this work is cited parenthetically in the text.

26. Lorelei Cederstrom, "The 'Great Mother' in *The Grapes of Wrath,*" in *Steinbeck and the Environment: Interdisciplinary Approaches,* eds. Susan F. Beegel, Susan Shillinglaw, and Wesley N. Tiffney Jr. (Tuscaloosa: University of Alabama Press, 1997). Hereafter this work is cited parenthetically in the text.

27. Peter Valenti, "Steinbeck's Ecological Polemic: Human Sympathy and Visual Documentary in the Intercalary Chapters of *The Grapes of Wrath,*" in *Steinbeck and the Environment: Interdisciplinary Approaches,* eds. Susan F. Beegel, Susan Shillinglaw, and Wesley N. Tiffney Jr. (Tuscaloosa: University of Alabama Press, 1997). Hereafter this work is cited parenthetically in the text.

28. Marilyn Chandler McEntyre, "Natural Wisdom: Steinbeck's Men of Nature as Prophets and Peacemakers," in *Steinbeck and the Environment: Interdisciplinary Approaches,* eds. Susan F. Beegel, Susan Shillinglaw, and Wesley N. Tiffney Jr. (Tuscaloosa: University of Alabama Press, 1997).

29. Chris Kocela, "A Postmodern Steinbeck, Or Rose Of Sharon Meets Oedipa Maas," in Barbara A. Heavilin, ed., *The Critical Response to John Steinbeck's "The Grapes of Wrath"* (Westport, Conn.: Greenwood Press, 2000). Hereafter this work is cited parenthetically in the text.

30. Discussions of further critical approaches to *Grapes* may be found in John Ditsky's *John Steinbeck and the Critics* (Rochester, N.Y.: Camden House, 2000) and in the introductory overview to Barbara A. Heavilin, ed., *The Critical Response to John Steinbeck's "The Grapes of Wrath"* (Westport, Conn.: Greenwood Press, 2000).

8 Bibliographical Essay

There now follow in quick succession two anthologies of criticism put forth under the name of the distinguished critic Harold Bloom, who seems to feel licensed to speak out on all writers everywhere and of whatever era. The patronizing tone . . . did not endear him to an audience . . . at one Steinbeck conference (to which he seemed to have thought he had descended, or condescended, as from clouds). . . . If Steinbeck is "not one of the inescapable American novelists of our century," Steinbeck's readership has news for him: He can run but he can't hide.

—John Ditsky, *John Steinbeck and the Critics* (2000), 89–91

DETRACTORS AND ADVOCATES

Although a critic can now maintain with a degree of confidence that, contrary to Bloom's assertion to the contrary, Steinbeck *is* one of the inescapable novelists of our century, attention must be paid to such contrary claims. Therefore, in this bibliographic essay, the voice of the Steinbeck detractor is considered in tandem with that of the Steinbeck advocate. Published on the occasion of the fiftieth anniversary of *Grapes*, two book-length studies, both part of a publisher's series and both collections of articles, are representative of Steinbeck detractors and advocates. These texts are Harold Bloom's 1988 *John Steinbeck's "The Grapes of Wrath,"* one of the Modern Critical Interpretations series,[1] and John Ditsky's 1989 *Critical Essays on Steinbeck's "The Grapes of Wrath,"*[2] one of the Critical Essays on American Literature series. (Note: although Bloom's text is published the year before the anniversary, there is no doubt that it was compiled for this occasion.) Both of these critics are not only widely acclaimed, but since the publication of these fiftieth-anniversary texts, they have published other books on Steinbeck. In 1996 as part of Chelsea House's Bloom's Notes series, Bloom published *John Steinbeck's "The Grapes of Wrath,"* and in 2000 as part of the same publisher's Bloom's Major Novelists series, he published *John Steinbeck: Comprehensive Research and Study Guide* (discussed in this text in chapter 7 on the reception of *Grapes*). And in 2000 Ditsky published *John Steinbeck and the Critics*. What these critics have to say, then, has at least the weight of longevity and bears close scrutiny. Further, observing them within the dialectic of this study makes clear where the lines have been drawn across time in the conflict between *Grapes*'s detractors and its advocates.

TWO ANTITHETICAL *GRAPES* FIFTIETH ANNIVERSARY TEXTS

In Bloom's text there are eight reprinted articles, together with an overview of the book's contents in an editor's note, a flimsy introduction, a chronology, a bibliography, and an index. In Ditsky's text there is a full introduction that includes voluminous notes and bibliographical references, followed by reprints of ten of the early reviews; illustration showing the causes of the Oklahoma Dust Bowl and depicting the westward migration, Route 66, and the topography of Arvin Camp; four new articles; and five reprinted articles.[3] While both texts fulfill the purpose of bringing together reprints of significant articles, Ditsky's is the more sharply focused, with the intent of providing a survey of the criticism of Steinbeck's *Grapes* in chronological sequence. His introduction, therefore, differs from Bloom's in that it surveys almost fifty years of reviews and criticism, placing *Grapes* criticism in a historical perspective. Ditsky's text has the additional intention of indicating "the kinds of things yet remaining to be done" (15). Bloom's introduction, however, is quite brief and makes no such historical attempt.

The Bloom text will be considered first and the Ditsky text second, followed by an assessment that draws on the 1990s and 2000 criticism.

HAROLD BLOOM'S *JOHN STEINBECK'S "THE GRAPES OF WRATH"*

> No single thread, no single echo from prior texts, no affinity or parallel with a single style, form, art, discourse, or genre will alone explain the heteroglossic design of *The Grapes of Wrath*.
> —Robert DeMott, *Steinbeck's Typewriter: Essays on His Art*, 1996 (173)

In his introduction to *John Steinbeck's "The Grapes of Wrath,"* Bloom establishes a thesis and sets an assertive, self-reflective tone. His thesis states that "*The Grapes of Wrath*, still Steinbeck's most famous and popular novel, is a very *problematical* work, and *very difficult to judge*" [emphasis added] (1). Although "problematical" is more self-reflective than objective, Bloom asserts that the novel's problems lie in its lack of "invention" and in "its characters [who] are not persuasive representations of human inwardness" (1). "The work's wavering strength," he continues, "is located elsewhere, in a curious American transformation of biblical substance and style that worked splendidly in Whitman and Hemingway, but seems to work only fitfully in Steinbeck" (1).

To establish critical criteria by which to judge this "problematical work" and to establish evidence for his thesis, Bloom asserts that "Steinbeck suffers from too close a comparison with Hemingway," that his "aesthetic problem *was* Hemingway, whose shadow always hovered too near" (1). Attempting to substantiate this assertion, Bloom chooses to compare the opening of *Grapes* and a passage from *The Sun Also Rises*, claiming unconvincingly and without substantial evidence that Steinbeck's opening "is not so much biblical style as mediated by Ernest Hemingway, as it is Hemingway assimilated to Steinbeck's sense of biblical style" (2).

The criteria by which Bloom evaluates style are left in doubt here, for even a cursory perusal of the two passages he chooses reveals more differences than similarities between Hemingway and Steinbeck. Hemingway uses periodic and balanced sentences, varied with a cumulative sentence; three "there was" or "there were" constructions; and two subject-verb inversions. He uses a form of the verb "to be" fifteen times. Steinbeck uses almost as many loose sentences as periodic, sometimes beginning them with a prepositional phrase. He uses no subject-verb inversions, no cumulative sentences, no "there was" or "there were" constructions. He uses a form of "to be" only twice, preferring strong, descriptive verbs: "flared," "crusted," "dusted," "frayed," "edged," "struck," "widened," "moved," and "paled."

The two authors use similar colors. Hemingway uses white, dusty green, brown, dark gray, and red; whereas Steinbeck uses red, gray, dark red, pale green, white, and brown. But Hemingway describes a journey leading to a peopled landscape with "red roofs," "white house," and "the gray metal-sheathed roof of the monastery of Roncevales"; whereas Steinbeck provides not just a landscape but ironic images of death: the sky and the land on which all earthly life depends are growing "pale" and "brown," seemingly dying.

Bloom praises "Hemingway's Basque landscapes" in which "the contrast between rich soil and barren ground, between wooded hills and heat-baked mountains, is a figure for the lost potency of Jake Barnes, but also for a larger sense of the lost possibilities of life." But he negates Steinbeck's achievement: "Steinbeck, following after Hemingway, cannot learn the lesson. He gives us a vision of the Oklahoma Dust Bowl, and it is effective enough, but it is merely a landscape where a process of entropy has been enacted" (3). By invoking his own theory of the literary relationships between the great writers and their predecessors, Bloom misses the point. Steinbeck's "vision of the Oklahoma Dust Bowl" is not "merely a landscape," but an ominous image of the death of the land itself, a fitting backdrop for the struggles of human beings dependent upon the land. For his further assertions that Steinbeck "lacks skill in plot, and power in the nemesis of character," Bloom offers no explanation or evidence (4).

Besides establishing the thesis that *Grapes* "is a very problematic work and difficult to judge," Bloom sets an authoritarian and negative tone, disparaging Steinbeck scholars as well as Steinbeck's work. *Grapes*, he observes, has had a "fairly constant popularity with an immense number of liberal middlebrows, both in this country and abroad." Steinbeck "aspired beyond his aesthetic means"; "he fell into bathos in everything he wrote, even in *Of Mice and Men* and *The Grapes of Wrath*" (4). Acknowledging that he remains "uneasy" about his own experience in rereading *Grapes*, Bloom searches for reasons why it cannot be excluded "from a serious reader's esteem," concluding finally that "wisdom compels one to be grateful for the novel's continuous existence" (5).

Bloom has thus provided an enlightening introduction to *John Steinbeck's "The Grapes of Wrath"*—not so much as to Steinbeck's novel as to this critic's dilemma in dealing with Steinbeck. Before judging aesthetic value with insight and validity, scholars must first establish sound criteria. Bloom's juxtaposing of passages from *Grapes* and *The Sun Also Rises* and then asserting that Steinbeck assimilates Hemingway's style into his own "sense of biblical style" is a feeble criteria by which to judge Steinbeck's art.

Arranged in chronological order, the essays in his text further highlight the search for adequate criteria by which to evaluate *Grapes*. Using as a touchstone Aristotle's argument that "poetry should be more 'philosophical' than history," Frederick I. Carpenter's "The Philosophical Joads" focuses on "the ideas of John Steinbeck and Jim Casy" and finds that the basic philosophy underlying *Grapes* is Emersonian Transcendentalism, together with Walt Whitman's religious love for humanity and democracy and William James's and John Dewey's realistic pragmatism. This combination of influences, Carpenter maintains, leads to a new definition of Christianity as actively engaged on this earth rather than passively looking forward to the afterlife (8).

The limitations of focusing primarily on the ideas in *Grapes* and of placing it against the specifically American backdrop of the transcendentalists, Whitman, and the pragmatists are revealed in Carpenter's discussion of the Joads as characters. His objections to these characters now seem quaint: the Joads talk openly and even joke about the human body, while Grampa's senile problems with buttoning his pants are not decent and should not be included in a literary work (11). Carpenter states further that the film adaptation could not tolerate such antics and omitted them, still preserving the novel's wholesome spirit. What Carpenter reveals here is not so much a problem with Steinbeck's seeming indecency as a problem with what was once a typically American prudery. In his portrayal of ordinary people, especially in scenes such as Grampa's wrestling with his pants buttons and Ma Joad's sharing her own family's meager meal with starving children, Steinbeck has more in common with Chaucer than with his American predecessors. For, like Chaucer, he has the saving grace of humor and a strong sense of true gentility.

In "The Fully Matured Art: *The Grapes of Wrath*," reprinted from his 1974 *The Novels of John Steinbeck*, Howard Levant views *Grapes* as Steinbeck's attempt to write an epic in prose, focusing on the national experience of the Oklahoma Dust Bowl. Maintaining that a novel's materials should be incorporated organically into its structure, Levant states that Steinbeck encountered an aesthetic dilemma in his attempt to elevate a particular story of his times into the universality of the epic. Steinbeck succeeds, Levant writes, in achieving organic structure in the first three-quarters of the novel. The last one-quarter he finds less effective, primarily because he believes that Steinbeck finally reduces his materials to allegory. But Levant does not consider whether the last quarter of the novel becomes artificial and allegorical, as he states, or whether the last quarter of the novel ascends into the mythic and universal, an appropriate ending for a prose epic. In his distaste for the artificiality (versus "realism" perhaps?) of the final scenes, Levant is seemingly unaware of the latter possibility.

Taking issue with the view that Steinbeck celebrated Emerson and Whitman's peculiarly American ideas and values, James D. Brasch's "*The*

Grapes of Wrath and Old Testament Skepticism" insists, rather, that Steinbeck got his major ideas from Ecclesiastes. He maintains that Steinbeck patterned Casy after the presentation of the preacher in the Old Testament and that he was influenced by Old Testament wisdom and skepticism in three ways. First, Brasch argues, his proletarian focus has parallels with the distress of exploited Israelites. Second, there are parallels between the biblical promise and the present-day warning that "the grapes of wrath" will one day be ripe for harvest. And third, both the Old Testament preacher and Steinbeck find the solution to tyranny in sympathetic and compassionate understanding. Unlike Levant, who finds the ending artificial, Brasch finds it appropriate in its depiction of Rose of Sharon's act of sympathy and compassion. He concludes that Song of Solomon and Steinbeck are in accord in depicting such acts as the means to survival in the midst of oppression (49–52).

In "Flat Wine from *The Grapes of Wrath*," Floyd C. Watkins histrionically argues from a non sequitur: that Steinbeck gets his facts wrong; therefore, his characters are not sufficiently realistic. Even if Watkins's critical assertion that fiction has to be factual were adequate, acceptable, or logical, it does not follow that the verisimilitude of characters in fiction depends on such truth to the culture or the situation. Verisimilitude of character depends on the universal, on how it might feel to be dispossessed and forced to journey in search of a home, and on how a character might act in such circumstances. To support his thesis, Watkins states that *Grapes* has almost twenty inaccuracies in language and facts, ranging from Steinbeck's use of the California word "ant lions" instead of the Oklahoma word "doodlebugs" to his portrayal of the Joads being paid by the acre rather than by the day for picking cotton.

For further evidence of cultural inaccuracy, even though there are, perhaps, two Christ figures in *Grapes*, Watkins claims that Steinbeck has a bias against Christianity and belittles all Christians. It is indeed puzzling that the creator of Ma Joad and the author who insisted (against strong objections) on keeping a mythic ending in which Rose of Sharon offers her breast to a starving man can be accused of being biased against Christianity. Watkins fails to recognize that Steinbeck has a strong dramatic sense and uses fanatics, enthusiasts, and hypocrites as foils to highlight and define the genuineness of his Christ figures.

Sylvia Jenkins Cook's "Steinbeck, the People, and the Party" explores the biological themes in *Grapes*: the phalanx, group man, nonteleological thought, and the interconnectedness of all things. Based on these biological themes, in a reductionist move, she classifies *Grapes* among proletarian novels, comparing its merits with James Agee's *Let Us Now Praise Famous*

Men. Forcing it into this proletarian mold, she concludes that Steinbeck lacks the intellectual vigor that directs Agee in creating a new kind of leftist literature and that *Grapes*, then, is the culmination of all of the tired, old proletarian models. She cites Michael Gold's praise of Steinbeck's works as among those filled with the proletarian spirit, therefore, as the appropriate epitaph for *Grapes*.

In "The Enduring Power of the Joads," Donald Pizer views *Grapes* as a tragedy in the naturalist tradition, in which none of the other elements—primitive, Christian, scientific, marxist—is dominant. He writes that Steinbeck depicts a conflict that involves the reader in primitive values centered around transcendence of self and recognition of the need of others. Pizer finds the novel flawed in its opposing the tragic to the social impulse, leading to a confusion and diffusion of theme and structure. Finally, Pizer states that it is not the *ideas* of the Joads or of the novel, but the Joads as people that give the novel its lasting power—a statement directly in conflict with Bloom's assertion.

In "Steinbeck and Nature's Self," John J. Conder states that in *Grapes* Steinbeck postulates there is another self that is not limited by determinism, thus harmonizing free will with determinism. Conder maintains that Steinbeck goes beyond the philosophy of the essential harmony and interdependence of the group self and the personal self, connecting to what he calls nonhuman nature, the suppression of which distorts human nature and creates grotesques. The realization of this connection to the whole of nature, Conder suggests, liberates human beings from the grotesque, enabling them to escape also from a deterministic economy. In *Grapes*, Conder argues, Steinbeck assumes that nature has a purpose and that human beings, as a part of nature, can find purpose and direction. Therefore, Conder concludes that Rose of Sharon's gesture in the final scene illustrates the revival of the natural self, which grows out of the nature of the biological species.

In "The Indestructible Women: Ma Joad and Rose of Sharon," Mimi Reisel Gladstein explores Steinbeck's descriptions of his enduring women in images of nature and in the typology of earth goddesses. Acknowledging that the creation of Ma Joad goes beyond the mythic and that she is a fully realized character, Gladstein nevertheless focuses on her role as a mother goddess who renews the enduring feminine principles as she passes this role on to her daughter.

Bloom's reprinted essays that are well grounded in sound critical theory provide insights on the aesthetic merits of *Grapes*. Those essays that are not well grounded, notably including Bloom's own introduction, serve to illustrate the problematic nature of criticism that begins with a shaky, ill-founded premise. Because of his lofty standing among academics in general, it is necessary to deal with his criticism directly on the grounds of sound theory and reasoning. Clearly, his own reasoning fades into the background when he is faced with the Steinbeck aesthetic, for which he has a long-standing antipathy.

JOHN DITSKY'S *CRITICAL ESSAYS ON STEINBECK'S "THE GRAPES OF WRATH"*

John Ditsky's warmth and enduring endorsement of the Steinbeck aesthetic in *Grapes* stands in stark contrast to Bloom, and his 1989 *Critical Essays on Steinbeck's "The Grapes of Wrath"* is a most valuable text. It places *Grapes* in context with four illustrations depicting geography and causes underlying the Oklahoma Dust Bowl: "The Dust Bowl 1936," "The 30s Migration West," "U.S. Route 66: The Mother Road," and "Arvin Camp: The Haven." In addition, it reprints ten of the 1939 reviews of *Grapes* and nine articles—four of them new, commissioned for this edition. Ditsky's introduction differs from Bloom's in that it surveys almost fifty years of reviews and criticism, placing *Grapes* in a historical perspective. The tone, while objective, is likewise approving of what Steinbeck called his "big book." The ethos of Ditsky's own involvement with the text and with this criticism bears the stamp of the passionately involved scholarly expert.

Ditsky's ethos as scholar and editor pervades his introduction and overview of the book's contents. He provides a history of *Grapes* criticism and appreciation (or lack thereof); he elucidates, he counters fallacious arguments, and he affirms particularly insightful and groundbreaking essays. Further, his generous notes provide minihistories of the articles, meticulously recording when and where each reprint occurred. In addition to this introductory survey's generous listing and highlighting of articles across time, the notes cite additional essays related to the topic. Moreover, he places his own text within the context of previously published book-length studies that reprint reviews and articles, recommending them and stating how his study differs. "The reader who seeks out these useful volumes will note that certain pieces have been reprinted in them at least twice; it was the intention behind this book, however, to make available materials not nearly so conveniently accessible and to commission new criticism reflecting recent changes in the way *The Grapes of Wrath* is perceived" (16). And Ditsky's authentic voice throughout his introduction and notes is that of the scholar who loves both his topic and his work.

OVERVIEW OF *GRAPES* CRITICISM

As have other critics, Ditsky observes that early reviews largely lacked any degree of objectivity and focused on the novel's documentary accuracy, tending to classify it as naturalistic. Before surveying the criticism, he considers a key article, Edmund Wilson's "The Boys in the Back Room,"[4] in which Wilson deplores what he claims to be the animalistic nature of Steinbeck's characters, whom he considers unconvincing. Here Ditsky intervenes between *Grapes* and this criticism by observing that Steinbeck "used key characters to locate magnetic poles of ideal oppositioning." Ditsky points out that Wilson fails to note that human beings share both an animal and a moral nature and to ascertain the differences among the various voices of the characters, the narrators in the interchapters, and Steinbeck himself. Such a failure leads Wilson to classify *Grapes* as propaganda—a classification that does not take into consideration its complexity of materials and form.

Ditsky begins his survey with a listing of bibliographies pertinent to Steinbeck studies: Tetsumaro Hayashi's two-volume *A New Steinbeck Bibliography*, covering the period through 1981 (now updated and expanded in *The Hayashi Steinbeck Bibliography, 1982–1996*); the *PMLA* bibliography, *American Literary Scholarship*; Warren French's section on Steinbeck in *Sixteen Modern American Authors*; and the *Steinbeck Quarterly* (3).

Louis Gannett's *John Steinbeck: Personal and Biographical Notes*, released before the publication of *Grapes*, includes a discussion of Steinbeck's journalistic essays on the migrants, first published as newspaper articles and then as a pamphlet, *Their Blood Is Strong*. Ditsky writes that this work indicates Steinbeck's public standing *before* the publication of *Grapes*. Year by year, decade by decade Ditsky cites the criticism of *Grapes*, beginning with Harry Thornton Moore's *The Novels of John Steinbeck*, the first book-length study of Steinbeck, in which Moore recognizes some of the artistic complexity of *Grapes*. Pointing next to *America in Contemporary Fiction* by Percy H. Boynton, who writes that Steinbeck has found "his true theme" in human unity and a "universal soul" and then to "The Compassion of John Steinbeck," in which Samuel Levenson maintains that love is the solution to human oppression, Ditsky notes evidence of an early understanding of the novel's complexity (4). He cites the detractors as well, among them N. Elizabeth Monroe's dismissal of Steinbeck's powers of characterization. He lists the criticism of the forties, but, most importantly, he elucidates this time span by providing a summarizing statement. Ditsky notes also that critics in the forties searched for sources underlying Steinbeck's philosophy and failed to realize that discovery of one source did not end the search.

Ditsky finds that the fifties begin with apathy toward *Grapes*, with critics such as George F. Whicher indicting Steinbeck for "cleverness" in *The Literature of the American People* and Frederick Hoffman charging that Steinbeck is sentimental in everything after *In Dubious Battle*. He cites as well the debate in the *Colorado Quarterly* between Bernard Bowron and Warren French on Bowron's classifying *Grapes* as a " 'wagons west' romance." At this point Ditsky also heralds the appearance of one of the strongest, most lucid Steinbeck advocates, Warren French, who provides one of the original essays for the text, "John Steinbeck and Modernism (A Speculation on His Contribution to the Development of the Twentieth-Century American Sensibility)."

He finds significant high points in the decade, however, one in Charles Child Walcutt's 1956 *American Literary Naturalism: A Divided Stream*, in which Walcutt discusses Steinbeck's form, noting that he does not fit well with naturalist literature. Another significant work is Tedlock and Wicker's 1957 *Steinbeck and His Critics: A Record of Twenty-Five Years*, which includes the critical history of *Grapes* to date along with brief comments on critics and criticism by Steinbeck. Ditsky finds an important milestone in Peter Lisca's "*The Grapes of Wrath* as Fiction," published in the prestigious *Publications of the Modern Language Association of America* and substantiating *Grapes* as art, not propaganda. Lisca's 1958 *The Wide World of John Steinbeck* expands on this topic. Ditsky finds noteworthy also the articles in *College English* that debate the Christian viewpoint of *Grapes*.[5] He mentions essays on the characterization of Tom Joad, the novel's ending, the economic outlook, and the theme of isolation.

Ditsky's prose continues throughout this introduction somewhat like a baseball announcer calling out plays in a strong staccato voice, with an occasional pause for a slower, fuller account of a particularly important article or the warm recognition of one of the more widely acclaimed Steinbeck critics—Warren French, Peter Lisca, Jackson J. Benson, and the like. And the chronological sequence measures out the pace: "With 1959 came," "In 1961," "In the following year, 1962," "Criticism of *The Grapes of Wrath* entered its second quarter-century," "The thirtieth anniversary," and the like.

Moreover, he keeps the reader cued by ranking, classifying, and evaluating: "In 1961 . . . the second important original volume of criticism of Steinbeck appeared: Warren French's *John Steinbeck*. . . . French's chapter on *Grapes*, 'The Education of the Heart,' indicates by its very title the theme he sees as major. French's essay is lucid" (7).[6] French's 1963 *A Companion to "The Grapes of Wrath"* is an important "first collection of original reviews and essays. . . . French's collection brought a new perspective to the study of a book that all too suddenly appeared to have turned a quarter of a century old" (8).[7] Ditsky notes that French's 1966 *The Social Novel at the End of an Era* placed *Grapes* within "the context of its times" (9).[8] The camaraderie between these scholars—and among Steinbeck scholars in general—is quite evident in Ditsky's account of the year 1971 as "busy for the workers in what Warren French calls Steinbeck's vineyard" (10).

Nor does he exclude Steinbeck detractors such as Arthur Mizener's "Does a Moral Vision of the Thirties Deserve a Nobel Prize?"[9] Published in the prestigious *New York Times Book Review*, Mizener's castigation is severe, strident, assertive—maintaining that Steinbeck was a "tenth-rate" philosopher of "limited talent." Ditsky sadly comments: "Seldom have a prize-winning author's public achievements so differed from the assessments of many of his critics than on the occasion of Steinbeck's reception of the Nobel Prize in 1962" (8).

Ditsky records, then, *Grapes's* critical ebbs and flows, its lows and highs, with 1969, thirty years after *Grapes's* first publication, as one of those highs.

The thirtieth anniversary of the novel's appearance in print led to the reconsideration piece "The Radical Humanism of John Steinbeck" by Daniel Aaron in *Saturday Review*.

> . . . Perhaps the year's biggest event, however, was the appearance of the Crowell Casebook.[10] on the novel edited by Agnes McNeill Donohue. . . . This enormously useful collection is a landmark in the specialized study of Steinbeck's most attended-to single work. . . . Also in 1969 an important critical volume was written by Lester J. Marks. . . . Entitled *Thematic Design in the Novels of John Steinbeck*, Marks's . . . book was also the first to attempt an overview of the entire career of the recently deceased novelist. (9)

Continuing his close monitoring of the reception of *Grapes* across time, Ditsky writes that the seventies brought "a second wind" and the major achievement in 1976 was British scholar Roy Simmonds's *Steinbeck's Literary Achievement*—especially valuable because it did not follow from dependence upon "standing assumptions that weaken some American criticism" (12).[11] During the two years following, however, Ditsky finds a critical low point, followed by two more years of moderate activity during which he publishes "*The Grapes of Wrath*: A Reconsideration," an overview of forty years of *Grapes* criticism, with a call for "new directions in criticism," in *Southern Humanities Review*. He duly takes note of the feminist critics—Sandra Beatty, Mimi Reisel Gladstein, Sylvia Cook, and Joan Hedrick.[12] Although 1984, Ditsky observes, showed a lack of interest in articles on *Grapes*, it also heralded the publication of Jackson J. Benson's definitive Steinbeck biography, and 1985 saw Louis Owen's book-length study, *John Steinbeck's Re-vision of America*, bringing together previous scholarship on this topic and concluding Steinbeck thoroughly evaluated and rejected America's Edenic myth. Between and among all of these works, Ditsky mentions, sometimes discusses, and always notes numerous other *Grapes* materials. Ditsky finally gives a brief overview of the book's materials, and the early reviews follow. It seems almost an understatement to maintain that this introduction has a wealth of information.

REVIEWS: A SENTIMENTAL TRACT OR POETIC TRUTH?

The ten early reviews of *Grapes* begin with Louis Kronenberger's "Hungry Caravan."[13] Possibly because of his closeness in time to the tragedy depicted in *Grapes*, Kronenberger classifies the novel as a tract—a superb, heartrending one, to be sure—but still a sentimental tract. In "But . . . Not . . . Ferdinand," Burton Rascoe flippantly claims the book puzzles him a bit, that it seems to be about vanishing frontiers and no places left for people to go. The irony here is that he is exactly right, but he has not realized the dire implications for the dispossessed. In "American Tragedy" Malcolm Cowley classifies *Grapes* with *Uncle Tom's Cabin* and denies it equal status with the works of Hemingway and Dos Passos. While both are earth-shattering books, however, *Uncle Tom's Cabin* is pure melodrama, lacking the tragic impact of *Grapes*. Earle Birney's "A Must Book" denies that *Grapes* is either a proletarian novel or a marxist novel, and although he captures its compassionate spirit, he makes no further attempt to classify it. Philip Rahv's contribution to *Partisan Review*, "A Variety of Fiction," finds *Grapes* tiresome, long, and tedious; its characters unreal; and its interchapters preachy.

In his review for *Commonweal*, James N. Vaughan, discussed earlier, takes the novel literally as a portrait of farm people that is at the same time pantheistic, anti-individualist, and antievangelical. Although some of these voices cancel out others, Vaughan takes each as the voice of the author, no matter who is speaking. Although Charles Angoff's "In the Great Tradition" does not analyze the novel's artistry in depth, it does recognize it, finding even its faults to be the "proper" ones of a "robust looseness and lack of narrative definitiveness"—faults shared with "the Bible, *Moby-Dick* [sic], *Don Quixote*, and *Jude the Obscure*," all good company (34). Angoff's appreciation for the ending is especially perceptive, for he finds Ma Joad's "final act of magnificence comes at the very end of the book, in a barn, where she has taken her shivering daughter who had just delivered . . . a dead child. Both notice a man not far away, dying of starvation." At this point Ma and Rose of Sharon exchange glances, and both acquiesce to the act that follows, in which Rose of Sharon offers him one of her breasts: "'You got to,' she said. And thus he was saved from a stable rat's grave" (35). Steinbeck would be pleased with this reader-critic, for Angoff evidently read with his heart as well as his mind, thus capturing the essence of this unforgettable tableau.[14]

Stanley Kunitz's "Wine Out of These Grapes" praises Steinbeck and *Grapes*, castigating those libraries that banned it because of its purported vulgarity and obscenity. Kunitz embraces the novel for its "truth"—a fair enough measure, for Aristotle thus praised poetry because it reveals great human truths as compared to history that records mere facts. Although Art Kuhl's "Mostly of *The Grapes of Wrath*," like Kunitz's essay, praises Steinbeck's use of language as appropriate for its subject and its style as poetic in its rhythms, he finds the characterization in the novel poor, labels it as sentimental propaganda, and maintains that Steinbeck comes very close to communism in his economic stance. Nor surprisingly, he states that Steinbeck is not a great novelist and certainly not "America's great novelist" (42). An excerpt from Wilbur L. Schramm's "Careers at Crossroads" classifies *Grapes* as proletarian, but also recognizes its poetic qualities. Finding Steinbeck like Dickens in his "fierce sympathy and in the moving quality of his writing," Schramm recognizes the forcefulness of *Grapes* but believes Steinbeck has not yet reached the height of his achievements.[15]

ESSAYS: FROM COMPOSITION BACKGROUND TO A POSTMODERN PERSPECTIVE

After these reviews come four illustrations depicting the geography and conditions of the 1936 Dust Bowl, followed by "Articles and Essays." The first article is Jackson J. Benson's "The Background to the Composition of *The Grapes of Wrath*,"[16] a synthesis of previously published materials, including his 1984 biography, *The True Adventures of John Steinbeck, Writer*. Benson places *Grapes* within the context of Steinbeck's other fiction; traces its genesis in journalistic accounts; explores his wife Carol's impact on the novel; discusses the influence of Tom Collins, who managed the Arvin Sanitary Camp; and covers his field experience with migrants. In addition, he discusses Steinbeck's intense focus on his work that made this long novel especially hard on him physically and emotionally. He concludes with a scene of great pathos: Tom Collins, to whom Steinbeck dedicated *Grapes*, along with Carol, seems to have ended his life as a derelict.

Roy Simmonds's "The Reception of *The Grapes of Wrath* in Britain: A Chronological Survey of Contemporary Reviews," an original essay written for the Ditsky book, adds early British reviews to the ten early reviews in America with which the text opens. Simmonds finds that despite—or perhaps because of—the somber backdrop of World War II, the British found something in *Grapes* that spoke to their own condition. It still sells well there, he observes, maybe because of international conditions that make its story still pertinent.

Peter Lisca's "The Dynamics of Community in *The Grapes of Wrath*" discusses the pervasive concept of community in *Grapes*—from the history of the old community now passing, to Muley's inability to change and clinging to memories of the old community, to Casy who senses the change and participates in it by taking over Ma's task of salting down the pork for their journey, to the discovery that the new community is a gathering of strangers under the aegis of "we." Lisca surveys the "forces" underlying the concept of community in *Grapes* from biological, sociological, historical, religious, and "anticommunity" perspectives (93). Mrs. Sandry, for example, and the "Jesus-lovers" at Weedpatch Camp are negative, anticommunity forces that begrudge the migrants the pleasure of a Saturday night dance. Lisca concludes that *Grapes* gathers all of the novel's perspectives on community into the final scene in which Rose of Sharon breast-feeds a starving man who is a stranger to her. For she does so in part from biological need but in part also, like Christ, as communion. Here, Lisca states, "biology, sociology, history, and religion become one expression of the community of mankind" (97).[17]

Carroll Britch and Cliff Lewis's "Growth of the Family in *The Grapes of Wrath*," another original essay, explores the question of how the Joad family can retain its own individuality and at the same time embrace the needs of humankind. In the restructured family after the grandparents, Noah, and Connie are gone, Britch and Lewis conclude that all members except Ruthie manage to "do 'more'n' themselves, and in ways that declare their individuality and their role as 'essence people,' both." They further maintain that "if ever the mettle of the American spirit and family has been tested and found strong, it has been so with the Joads" (108).

Louis Owens's "The Culpable Joads: Desentimentalizing *The Grapes of Wrath*," another original essay in the Ditsky text, should lay to rest for good the notion that this novel is sentimental. Owens cites two notable critics who have given credence to this claim: Edmund Wilson and R.W.B. Lewis, the one arguing that Steinbeck patterned his sentimentality after Hollywood and the other that his fiction is "mawkish," incapable of dealing with the dark harshness of reality (109). Owens then discusses the care Steinbeck takes to avoid sentimentality: interchapters that establish distance from the more personal Joad narrative; objectivity in establishing blame for the current natural tragedy that includes the tenant farmers because of their own misuse of the land; "a nonteleological perspective" that begins in the opening paragraph; and the shattering of the Eden myth that had sent Americans on a westward quest from the nation's beginning. "There are no innocents," Owens concludes, "a new sensibility, not sentimentality, is Steinbeck's answer" (115).

The sixth article in this section is Ditsky's own "The Ending of *The Grapes of Wrath*: A Further Commentary,"[18] in which he divides his observations into four topics: "the Bible and religion; myth and the ritual moment; the role of woman; the new community" (116). In his study of these topics, he draws on biblical echoes of Eden, the Flood, the Eucharist, and baptism—all present in the novel's final scene. Ditsky persuasively observes in part one that "the final scene completes a turning-outward into society of energies that, in Greek or Faulknerian tragedy, might have turned into unproductive incestual frustrations. In the new familial system, older terminology is replaced by simpler concepts of 'male' and 'female' roles, and only the presence of external, social demands legitimizes what might otherwise have become sexual anarchy" (118).

In part two he explores the mythic implications of the scene in the sacrifice of the stillborn child as appeasement of Nature and in the nurturing of the starving man in "the attainment of futurity in societal, or 'group' terms" (119). In part three he points out the "feminine principle" as it is portrayed in Rose of Sharon, who rises to "epic" dimensions as she is transformed in and by this final scene—her former childishness put aside. For she has now discovered, as the poetic Ditsky declares, "a timeless truth: the simplicity and goodness of cycles, the rightness of necessity, the perfectness of circles" (122). Finally, part four is almost pure poetry. Ditsky concurs with French's description of this scene as the completion of the Joad family's education, Fontenrose's declaration that this "story ends *in medias res*," and his glimpse of Rose of Sharon as "the world's center, . . . Woman picking up the pieces of the American dream and holding the man-caused shards together, the seams invisible" (123).

Mimi Reisel Gladstein's "From Heroine to Supporting Player: The Diminution of Ma Joad," another original essay, compares John Ford's treatment of Ma Joad in his film adaptation of *Grapes* with Steinbeck's careful delineation of her character in the novel. She finds that the film reduces and softens the characters of both Ma Joad and Rose of Sharon by omitting key scenes in which their characters are developed, such as Ma's hospitable sharing with strangers—a family trait, she herself declares, but one she often models. Ford's adaptation, Gladstein concludes, does not do justice to Steinbeck's strong women, who in the end "serve as both the symbols and the actors in human survival" (136).

The penultimate essay, Christopher L. Salter's "John Steinbeck's *The Grapes of Wrath* as a Primer for Cultural Geography,"[19] provides a cross-disciplinary perspective that opens the understanding of the literature specialist to new dimensions. Persuasively arguing the place for fiction, in particular *Grapes*, in the cultural geography classroom, Salter points out that

> lessons from the landscape and human movement in *The Grapes of Wrath* provide focus for instruction in migration, settlement forms, economic systems, cultural dualism, agricultural land use patterns, transportation technology, and social change. . . . To the reader of fiction who is also attempting to comprehend something of the underlying systems in this chaos of conflict and flight, the study of this novel provides a window on geographic phenomena broadly ranging from mental maps to economic infrastructures. (150–51)

Salter concludes that the class in cultural geography should draw on all available "human resources," especially fiction such as *Grapes* that is evocative, dynamic, and vital—rewarding the inquiring mind and "disciplined perspective" with illustrations of the "patterns, preferences, and problems of humankind" (151).

Although Warren French's "John Steinbeck and Modernism (A Speculation on His Contribution to the Development of the Twentieth-Century American Sensibility)"[20] covers fiction other than *Grapes*, this overview is confined to his conclusions on this novel. French defines "modernism" as that period during which a "special, exalted value . . . was placed . . . upon . . . ironic vision." And he states that *Grapes* transcends "the ironic detachment of Modernism with a new affirmative conception of individual regeneration. . . . Although the term would not have been used then, *The Grapes of Wrath* is a fiction of consciousness-raising" (155, 160). French further speculates that if postmodernism is finally defined by "conscious-raising techniques and the implications for a bankrupt industrial culture of transcendentalist philosophies," then *Grapes*, along with *Cannery Row*, may be classified as prophetic postmodernism.

GETTING UNDER THE CRITICS' SKIN

In summation, although these two fiftieth-anniversary texts are similar on the surface—both collections of essays and articles arranged in chronological order—they differ significantly. Bloom's text includes a cursory and dismissive introductory summation of the Steinbeck aesthetic and a chronologically arranged collection of essays, all reprints, mostly derogatory. Ditsky's volume includes an extensive introductory survey of *Grapes* criticism and a chronologically arranged collection of early reviews and essays, several of them originals written for his text. The difference in tone is striking. In his introduction, Bloom approaches the task before him almost reluctantly as the product of a book deal, with no passionate interest in his topic. As Ditsky has noted, he seems to condescend to take on what is for him a fairly onerous task—working with a text he does not much admire and an author for whom he holds little but contempt. On the other hand, Ditsky's tone is that of the scholar who cares passionately about his subject.

Not surprisingly, the two authors differ as well in approach. In a much belabored comparison, in which he tries to force *Grapes* to fit into his own theory of literary precedents, Bloom argues weakly that Steinbeck has somehow tried and failed to arrive at a biblical style by imitating Hemingway. The best that Bloom has to say of *Grapes* is that readers ought to be glad that it is still around, by which he must mean that it is okay with him that it is still in print. Ditsky has a scholarly mastery of his topic—tracing critical influences across time as well as providing voluminous endnotes with information in addition to documentation. In writing *Grapes* Steinbeck has every intention of getting under the reader's skin—somewhat like Socrates and his irritatingly provocative gadfly. Steinbeck certainly succeeds in getting under these two critics' skin, with very different results. For Bloom is profoundly uncomfortable with this novel while Ditsky waxes poetic in the presence of its mythic power.

NOTES

1. Harold Bloom, ed., *John Steinbeck's "The Grapes of Wrath,"* Modern Critical Interpretations Series (New York: Chelsea House Publishers, 1988). Hereafter references to this work will be cited parenthetically in the text.

2. John Ditsky, ed., *Critical Essays on Steinbeck's "The Grapes of Wrath,"* Critical Essays on American Literature Series (Boston, Mass.: G.K. Hall & Co., 1989). Hereafter references to this work will be cited parenthetically in the text.

3. Ditsky includes an endnote in which he lists texts in which selected early reviews are reprinted. These texts range from E.W. Tedlock, Jr. and C.V.

Wicker's 1957 *Steinbeck and His Critics: A Record of Twenty-Five Years*, to Warren French's 1963 *A Companion to "The Grapes of Wrath,"* to Agnes McNeill Donohue's, ed., 1968 *A Casebook on "The Grapes of Wrath,"* to Peter Lisca's 1972 *John Steinbeck, "The Grapes of Wrath": Text and Criticism,* to Robert Con Davis's 1982 *Twentieth Century Interpretations of "The Grapes of Wrath."*

4. Edmund Wilson, "The Boys in the Back Room," *New Republic* (San Francisco: Colt Press, 1941).

5. Ditsky cites Martin S. Shockley's 1956 "Christian Symbolism in *The Grapes of Wrath,"* Eric W. Carlson's January 1958 "Symbolism in *The Grapes of Wrath,"* and George De Schweinitz's May 1958 "Steinbeck and Christianity."

6. Warren French, "The Education of the Heart," in *John Steinbeck* (New York: Twayne Publishers, 1961), 95–112.

7. Warren French, ed., *A Companion to "The Grapes of Wrath"* (New York: Viking Press, 1963).

8. Warren French, ed., *The Social Novel at the End of an Era* (Carbondale and Edwardsville: Southern Illinois University Press, 1966), 42–86.

9. Arthur Mizener, "Does a Moral Vision of the Thirties Deserve a Nobel Prize?" *New York Times Book Review* (9 December 1962), 4, 43–45.

10. Agnes McNeill Donohue, ed., *A Casebook on "The Grapes of Wrath"* (New York: Thomas Y. Crowell, 1968).

11. Roy Simmonds, *Steinbeck's Literary Achievement* (Muncie, Ind.: Steinbeck Monograph Series no. 6, 1976).

12. Ditsky cites Sandra Beatty's "short but pioneering study of Steinbeck's female characters" in "A Study of Female Characterization in Steinbeck's Fiction," *Steinbeck Quarterly* 8 (Spring 1975), 50–56; Mimi Reisel Gladstein's "Ma Joad and Pilar: Significantly Similar," *Steinbeck Quarterly* 14 (Summer-Fall 1981), 93–104; Sylvia Cook's "Steinbeck, the People, and the Party," *Steinbeck Quarterly* 15 (Winter-Spring 1982), 11–23; and Joan Hedrick's "Mother Earth and Earth Mother: The Recasting of Myth in Steinbeck's *The Grapes of Wrath"* (Davis 134–43). Sandra Beatty's is also in *Steinbeck's Women: Essays in Criticism,* ed. Tetsumaro Hayashi (Muncie, Ind.: Steinbeck Monograph Series no. 9, 1979), 7–16.

13. Louis Kronenberger's "Hungry Caravan" appeared in *The Nation* 148 (15 April 1939), 440–41; Burton Rascoe's "But . . . Not . . . Ferdinand," in *Newsweek* (17 April 1939), 46; Malcolm Cowley's "American Tragedy," in *New Republic* 98 (3 May 1939), 382–83; Earle Birney's "A Must Book," in *Canadian Forum* 19 (June 1939), 94–95; and Philip Rahv's "A Variety of Fiction," in *Partisan Review* 6 (April 1939), 111–12.

14. James N. Vaughan's review appeared in *Commonweal* 30 (28 July 1939), 341–42; and Charles Angoff's "In the Great Tradition," in *North American Review* 247 (Summer 1939), 387–89.

15. Stanley Kunitz's "Wine Out of These Grapes" was published in the *Wilson Library Bulletin* 14 (October 1939), 165; Art Kuhl's "Mostly of *The Grapes of Wrath,"* in *Catholic World* 150 (November 1939), 160–65; and Wilbur L.

Schramm's excerpt from "Careers at Crossroads," in *Virginia Quarterly Review* 15 (Autumn 1939), 630–32.

16. Jackson J. Benson's "The Background to the Composition of *The Grapes of Wrath*" is a revision of the following: "John Steinbeck and Farm Labor Unionization: The Background of 'In Dubious Battle,'" originally written with Anne Loftis for *American Literature* 52 (May 1980), 194–223; "The Background of *The Grapes of Wrath*," *Journal of Modern Literature* 5 (April 1976), 151–232, copyrighted 1976 by Temple University; and chapters 19, 20, and 21 of *The True Adventures of John Steinbeck, Writer* (New York: Viking Press, 1984).

17. Ditsky reprints Peter Lisca's "The Dynamics of Community in *The Grapes of Wrath*" by permission from *From Irving to Steinbeck: Studies in American Literature in Honor of Harry R. Warfel*, Motley Deakin and Peter Lisca, eds. (Gainesville: University of Florida Press, 1972), 127–40, copyrighted by the 1972 University Presses of Florida.

18. Ditsky's essay is reprinted with permission from *Agora* 2 (Fall 1973), 41–50.

19. Christopher L. Salter's "John Steinbeck's *The Grapes of Wrath* as a Primer for Cultural Geography" was revised for Ditsky's volume by permission from *Humanistic Geography and Literature: Essays on the Experience of Place*, ed. Douglas C.D. Pocock (London: Croom Helm, 1981), 142–58.

20. Warren French's "John Steinbeck and Modernism (A Speculation on His Contribution to the Development of the Twentieth-Century American Sensibility)" is included in the Ditsky text by permission from *Steinbeck's Prophetic Vision of America*, Tetsumaro Hayashi and Kenneth D. Swan, eds. (Upland, Ind.: Taylor University for John Steinbeck Society of America, 1976), 152–62.

Index

About the Author

BARBARA A. HEAVILIN is Associate Professor of English at Taylor University. Her previous books include *The Critical Response to John Steinbeck's* The Grapes of Wrath (Greenwood, 2000).

Recent Titles in
Greenwood Guides to Fiction